The Book of Miracles

The Healing Work of Joao de Deus

By

Josie RavenWing

1stBooks - rev. 02/19/02

Table of Contents

Acknowledgments

The magnitude of my gratitude for being allowed to witness and experience first-hand the miracles described in this book, is close to Infinite, and goes first to Creator. In addition, I thank all of the staff—volunteer and administrative—of the Casa de Dom Inacio; the many people who shared their personal stories of healing for this book; those authors whose publishers gave me permission to quote them, including Deepak Chopra, Glenda Green, Bill Moyers and Caroline Myss; and Mark Thomas, who gave me permission to use some of his photographs for this book.

And finally, I thank Joao de Deus—John of God—for the dedication to his more than forty years of charity toward the many millions who have come to him for healing of body, mind and spirit. I am just one of those millions, but my gratitude is wholehearted for what I have received and for the inspiration to write this book about his work.

Author's Foreword

My prayer for this book is that God/Creator/Great Spirit guide my words in such a way as to deepen our heart's awareness of the presence of the Divine—in and around us—and in the unfathomable mystery of the journey of the human soul.

In November of 1998 I made my first journey to a healing center in Brazil called the Casa de Dom Inacio: the House of St. Ignatius. During that visit and on numerous subsequent visits, I experienced a deluge of what most people would call miracles. These occurred through the work of Joao de Deus—John of God—and the "entities" of his spiritual healing center, the Casa de Dom Inacio. A heretofore mostly invisible world—that of the spirits of the departed and their concern for the living—opened up to me. My contact with that world augmented my training as a psychotherapist and healing practitioner, and changed my perspective on the nature of health and illness, life and death, and the journey of the human soul. Through it all I found the presence of a profound and divine healing Love. It is of these matters that I now write in *The Book of Miracles*. What you will read in the following pages may stretch your beliefs or affirm your faith. If either occur, this book will have accomplished a great deal of its purpose.

Part One: The Casa de Dom Inacio

Josie RavenWing

To pass through the gates of the Casa de Dom Inacio is to pass through a portal into a parallel world. In this world is a spiritual hospital in which the medical personnel are spirits, the chief administrator is God, and daily miracles of healing are the norm. And although the portal seems to be the simple wrought iron fence that is the physical entrance to the Casa, this is not the deeper reality. The true gateway to this parallel world is the dedication of one of the most powerful trance medium healers of our time, Joao Teixeira da Faria, known most often as Joao de Deus: John of God. Here are some of his words:

"I thank all the people who have come from so far to give energy to this Casa. It is not necessary for me to say what the Casa is, because you all know what we do here. I just want to say that we are not preaching any religion here, but rather, we are preaching the Word of God and eternal life.

"We take out all the infirmities that God allows us to take out. I ask all of you who come from such distances to use all of what is offered to you here: the treatments, the herbal remedies, the medicinal soup, the blessed water. Doing so is a preparation, a discipline for the spiritual work.

"I didn't go through any kind of preparation to do this work. I've been doing it since I was nine years old. I am now working only 160 kilometers from where I grew up. It was through faith that I continued, and it is my faith that has me now at the side of God.

"Here at the Casa, we don't preach any specific religion or way. If somebody is saying, before they arrive here, that he doesn't believe in God or a Superior Being, when he steps into this Casa, he will immediately believe.

"If there are any doctors here who wish to see the surgeries, they can do so because we do not hide our work.

"Do you want to do what this power is asking you to do? I beg you, my brothers and sisters, to do what this force of God is asking of you.

"I myself am just a simple tailor from the interior of Brazil. I'm just a person with (karmic) debts just like the rest of you. And three days a week I am a prisoner of this energy from God. This work will continue as long as I do not charge for it. If the day came when I ever charged for this work, it would mean that I was not 'in entity.' You cannot charge for this spiritual work. Yes, you pay for the herbs, and you can even get a receipt of payment if you wish. But charging for the work does not exist at this Casa, nor does tithing. It is I, personally, that has the responsibility to maintain the Casa both physically and spiritually.

"Just like Christ had His apostles, I too have mine to help me fulfill my mission, to sustain the Casa and the work here. Some of those who help me give the opening speeches each morning and afternoon, because I don't have that ability—I can barely read and write.

"I know I am doing the right thing here, because I have this energy and I know we must follow God's will. Each of us should be following God, not insisting that God follow us. I now ask those of you with faith to help me receive the incorporation.* It is your work that helps me to fulfill my mission. And when someone comes to me and says, 'I am healed,' that is what gives me the strength and courage to continue in my mission.

"I have been doing this work for 44 years, since I was nine years old. I didn't go across the borders, nor did I go knocking door to door to tell people about this work. I have stayed here in Goias, within the state where I was raised. When people ask, 'oh, are you Joao the tailor, Joao the construction worker, Joao the son of Jose Nunes da Faria, Joao this, Joao that,' I say 'yes, I'm that Joao.'

"You can deceive people for one year, two years, but not for 44 years—that would be very difficult. Ze Arrigo had six years to do his work, some other mediums have had two or three years, but I have been doing this mission for 44 years. Chico Xavier has worked for 50 years, myself 44.

"There was a time in the past when I had to stay in hiding in order to attend to the people wanting my help. People were saying, 'here comes the healer'. I would say, 'I'm not a healer, I'm a tailor'. Or some would say 'here comes the Macumbairo', and I would say, 'I'm not a Macumbairo. I just come with the Word of God'. I don't even have the knowledge to do Macumba [an Afro-Brazilian trance medium way of working]. But if some day somebody comes to me and said I must do my work through Macumba in order to be at God's side, then I will do my work through Macumba."

From an opening speech by Joao de Deus at the Casa de Dom Inacio, Nov. 22, 2000

* The term "incorporation" refers to the process in which a spirit temporarily inhabits a medium's body, whether for purposes of healing or communication.

Chapter 1: The Journey Begins

"Spirits communicate through the intervention of mediums,
who serve them as instruments and interpreters"
from *The Book on Mediums*

My life has been irrevocably changed by my contact with Joao de Deus. The information and events described in this book may well challenge your beliefs. Some of the terms at first will be unfamiliar in their usage, as they were to me initially. But as we journey together through this extraordinary series of events, both terminology and the miraculous nature of what I have witnessed will become as familiar to you as they are to those that have participated in the work of the Casa de Dom Inacio. I humbly ask for your patience and an open mind.

In January of 1998 I read an article about the work of Joao de Deus. I was fascinated by what I read. The article described a Brazilian man of humble origins who had become a trance medium in his youth, taken over for the first time by a spirit—or entity, as the Brazilians say—who identified himself as King Solomon. While the young Joao's consciousness floated in a realm of light, unaware of what was happening to him, the entity worked through his body to heal a crowd of people at a Spiritist center to which Joao had been directed by a vision earlier in the day. The article described how since that time, Joao had healed millions of people over the past forty-some years, performing what most of us would call daily miracles, always in a state of trance and with an increasing number of entities working through him over the decades.

As I read on, the article listed a number of examples of healings that defied scientific and medical theory. I originally thought that the article had come my way at that time because I had been searching for help for a man who had been diagnosed with terminal stage cancer, and that perhaps he was meant to go see this unusual healer. However, the man died before I was able to discover where it was in Brazil that the Casa de Dom Inacio was located. The latter is the healing center that Joao had established over 20 years ago, named for its patron saint and one if its main entities: St. Ignatius of Loyola, founder of the Jesuit sect.

Over half a year later, in October of 1998, I read another article about Joao, and this one mentioned the name of the town in which he worked. By then, my own interest was piqued and I began to look through maps and atlases that included maps of Brazil. Nowhere could I find the name of the town. Finally, I made a trip to my local library and enlisted the help of one of the librarians. She too was unable to find the name on any of the maps she had. I was becoming rather discouraged when finally she made one more trip to the reference books and came back triumphantly waving a several-inch thick, ancient book which, by the amount of dust flying off of it, had not been touched in years. It turned out to be a book of world towns and villages not listed on any maps. The librarian opened it to the page she had marked, and there I saw the name of the town— Abadiania—with a brief description of its location in the interior of Brazil. It said the town was so many degrees south and so many degrees west of the capital city, and noted approximately how many kilometers in distance.

Although this description was not entirely what I was accustomed to for locating a place, I was grateful to have any information at all, and promptly decided to go to Brazil and find the town and the healing medium, Joao de Deus.

From the moment I made the decision to go until the day I arrived at the Casa de Dom Inacio two weeks later, I began to have a particular kind of unusual experience. Every time I would daydream and try to imagine myself there at the Casa, I would immediately feel myself pulled into what I then described as a state of deep meditation. Within this state I would feel a powerful pulse of energy going through me that was different in quality than any I had experienced prior to that time, despite all of my years of meditation and other spiritual experiences. I was intrigued by the energy but did not understand its nature or its source until I arrived at the Casa.

Finally, a friend and I embarked on the journey to Brazil together and, after a long flight, arrived in the capital city in the early afternoon and booked a hotel for the night. My friend took a nap, but I was too excited to be able to sleep. I went on a walk with the word "Abadiania" written on a piece of paper and clutched in my hand. Since I was in the center of the city, there were a number of elegant hotels nearby and I went to several. My goal was to find a hotel employee who spoke enough English or Spanish—since I did not at that time speak Portuguese—to be able to give me specific directions to Abadiania. I knew the town was within a several-hour drive and the approximate direction from Brasilia, but that was about it! So near and yet so far…

After several attempts, I finally succeeded in getting the information I needed from some women guests who were relaxing in one of the hotel's lobby, bless them! They drew me a map, and I returned contented to the hotel. The next day, God willing, I would be in Abadiania and be able to witness first hand the amazing work of Joao de Deus and the entities.

I slept restlessly that night, and awoke the next morning anxious to get on the road in order to arrive for the afternoon session at the Casa. I wasn't sure exactly when the session began, so my friend and I left in what we hoped would be plenty of time to get there shortly after noon. We had rented a car for our two-week stay in the area, and over the course of the next few hours, became intimately familiar with Brazilian-style driving and the surrounding countryside. Once we left the city, the highway took us through small towns and long stretches of lush, rolling hills dotted by strange earth-colored mounds—which we later learned were termite mounds.

Finally, after the somewhat exhausting experience of driving in a strange land with only minimal directions to our destination, we arrived at the outskirts of Abadiania. The latter appeared to be a typical third world town that included a mix of cars and horse-drawn carts, small shops and roadside food stalls, simple one-story houses and with a booming brick-making industry. We turned off the highway, and I was able to ask one of the locals for directions in my own hybrid Spanish-Portuguese. The man, who seemed accustomed to giving directions to foreigners, pointed us down the next street, upon which we drove slowly through barking dogs and curious locals till we were almost at the end of the town. Finally, we saw the blue and white painted buildings of the Casa, which I recognized from photos in the article I had read, and we turned into the large gravel parking lot at one side where hundreds of people, mostly dressed in white clothing, were milling about.

By then, I had an urgent need for a bathroom. I left my friend in the car for the moment, and found myself walking up to a pleasant-looking man who was sitting at one end of the building. I asked him if he spoke any English or Spanish, and thankfully, it turned out his native language was Spanish, which I spoke fairly well. He directed me to the restroom, after which I joined him again and began to ask him about the Casa and what time the afternoon session began and what we should do to prepare for it.

We were only a minute or two into our conversation when the crowds around us seemed to part and I saw a man walking toward me from about twenty feet away. He had slightly long black hair, piercing blue eyes behind his glasses, and looked to be a few inches short of six feet tall. My new Spanish-speaking acquaintance - who I shall call Miguel - nudged me and said, "that's Joao." Joao continued walking until he stood right in front of me. He then extended his hand with a slight smile, and said he wanted to welcome me to the Casa. I took his hand, thanked him with one of the few words I'd learned in Portuguese, "*obrigada*," and then he turned and disappeared again into the crowds. I was amazed! I also felt this was a particularly fine omen for my first visit to the Casa.

I then went to the car to get my traveling companion, told him I'd just met Joao, and then introduced him to Miguel. It turned out that Miguel had worked

7

at the Casa for years, and that part of his "job" was to greet newcomers and help orient them. Miguel was very helpful and became our personal guide and translator for the next two weeks of sessions at the Casa.

While we were waiting for the afternoon session to begin in about an hour's time, Miguel took us on a tour of the Casa grounds. He showed us the bust of Dom Inacio, which rested on a pedestal in a beautiful garden that had flowers planted from all over the country: the "Garden of All Places." Dom Inacio's bust was surrounded by little offerings, and I noticed that occasionally someone would stop before it, offer a prayer, and occasionally weep a bit.

Next to the flower garden was the soup area—a long covered verandah with rows of tables and benches. Miguel told us that after each morning session, everyone was served a hardy vegetable soup—free of charge—that was part of the treatment of the Casa. The soup was made with great love and prayers by several women, and blessed and energized by the entities to fortify everyone and add to their healing process.

Kitty-corner from the soup area was another small building painted white with a blue border at the bottom like all the other Casa buildings. Miguel did not tell us what that building was for that time. On subsequent trips to Abadiania, I discovered that it was where people received their "crystal baths." These are not baths in the ordinary sense, but rather, energy and chakra-balancing treatments using crystals, light and sound.

As Miguel continued our "guided tour" of the Casa grounds, he showed us a small room next to the main hall of the Casa. The room was piled high with crutches, canes and wheelchairs that had been left behind by those who had been healed through the work of the entities! In a second section of that room, the walls were covered with photos and other items of interest.

One of the photos was of Joao with Chico Xavier, probably Brazil's most famous Spiritist medium of written knowledge, whose many books on metaphysics are well known throughout the world. It was Chico Xavier who had told Joao over twenty years ago that it was finally time for the latter to establish his own healing center, and that he should do so in the town of Abadiania because of the powerful energy running through the earth in that location. Joao followed his direction, and I was now standing in that very place that had been suggested by Chico Xavier.

On the walls of the same room were also a number of certificates honoring Joao and his work: certificates from various spiritual centers, churches and Umbanda temples. Umbanda is an Afro-Brazilian spiritual healing path that is also mediumistic in nature.

By the time we'd finished looking into this small "room of miracles" with its pile of discarded crutches and wheelchairs and photos of miraculous healings, my mind was even more open to what I might be witnessing and experiencing that afternoon when the session began. Miguel finally took us over to one of the annex buildings where we got our free *"primeira vez"* tickets that first-time visitors were to present later when it was time to see the medium. Shortly thereafter, people began to assemble in the main hall to get ready for the afternoon session. A powerful atmosphere of excitement and expectation immediately began to permeate the area.

When I first entered the hall, I looked around at the other people already gathering there. Almost all of them were Brazilian, and looked to be from all walks of life and social status, with the varied hues of white, black and Indian racial blending typical of Brazil. Many were in wheelchairs or on crutches. Some, with their white canes, were blind. There were elderly people, young people, babies in their mothers' arms, children of all ages, most very quiet and respectful. Some people had obvious physical deformities, like large lumps on their skin or swelling of the head; some were limping. Others seemed to have neurological illnesses that resulted in them shouting out every now and then.

I sat down on the cement floor, closed my eyes, and was immediately drawn into that same deep state of meditation with its unusual pulsing that I had experienced repeatedly since deciding to make the journey to Brazil and the Casa de Don Inacio. I realized that this place and the entities that worked here were undoubtedly the source of this particular energy. I also felt that the entities must have somehow tuned in to me the moment I made the decision to come here, and perhaps had even begun working on me from that day on. Over the past few years, after talking to many others at the Casa, I have concluded that this was probably true, as others too have had experiences of the entities beginning to work on them in advance of physically arriving there.

Occasionally, as I sat in the hall, I would interrupt my meditation, open my eyes and look around to see if the session was beginning. It wasn't, but one thing I noticed was a line of people waiting to go up on the stage. One person at a time would walk to the wall at the back of the stage, upon which hung a large wooden triangle. Often they would slip a piece of paper into the bottom edge of the triangle, then, close their eyes, rest their forehead on the part of the wall surrounded by the triangle, and begin to pray. I learned later that the slips of paper were requests for healing for loved ones that were unable to be present physically at the Casa. The line moved slowly, with no one trying to speed up the prayers of their fellow human beings. Some were obviously weeping as they prayed. As each person would leave the triangle, I could see the where they had rested their forehead: an elongated, slightly oval-shaped dark mark that had been formed over the years by hundreds of thousands of foreheads resting there in prayer. The energy of faith and hope permeating the room was a tangible force and growing moment by moment as the opening of the afternoon session approached.

After about fifteen minutes of alternating between watching people and experiencing the trance-like state each time I closed my eyes, Sebastiao—or Tiao, as he is called with affection—stepped onto the small, raised stage at the front of the hall and began the orientation speech. Tiao is a small, roly-poly man who looks like an earthbound angel and who is an ex-seminary student and the official secretary of the Casa. He has worked with Joao for many years, helping in numerous ways to sustain the daily functioning of the Casa.

After telling everyone a bit about the herbs that might be prescribed by Joao "in entity" and of the accompanying diet, Tiao asked for a show of hands of all those present who had been told by the entity at an earlier time to have a spiritual operation during this afternoon's session. Those people were then asked to get in a line, after which Tiao led them through the door to the right of the stage. I learned later that they were being taken to the "operating room," a simple room with benches, where they would sit and receive their invisible operations at the skilled and guiding hands of the entities.

Once they had left the main hall, several other people stepped onstage and made speeches. I couldn't understand much of what they said, given my extremely limited knowledge of Portuguese at the time, and so I simply closed my eyes and drifted back into the trance-like meditation state that kept pulling me inward. Finally, the woman who was speaking asked us all to close our eyes and to focus on God for a few minutes. As soon as I began to focus, I heard a loud clap of thunder—the first in a growing procession of them. I immediately felt a surge of tingling energy enter under my left eye and move into my sinus. Moments later, I opened my eyes in time to see Joao walking onto the stage with two women in tow. The last speaker on the stage asked all of us to please make sure we didn't cross our arms during the time Joao was doing his work. I didn't quite understand the reasoning, but Miguel explained later that crossing one's arms or legs somehow interfered with the current of healing energy from the entities that was already flowing through all of us. Since we were all interconnected, even one person crossing his or her arms or legs could create problems once the surgeries began.

From what I'd read in the article about Joao, I knew that when he went into his trance state and incorporated one of the entities that work through him, he performed "impossible" surgeries on people. None of the patients were given any physical anesthetic prior to the operations, nor were they taken through any hypnotic suggestion of any kind. Yet, according to the article, they usually felt no pain during their operations and often, when incisions were made, they did not bleed or bled very little.

I had also read that most of the entities that work through Joao were spirits of departed doctors or other healing practitioners or great spiritual masters that wished to continue using their skills to serve humanity through the healing work they were doing at the Casa. These entities somehow had the ability to administer a form of spiritual anesthesia that allowed people to go through physical surgeries without pain, if such surgeries were deemed in their best interest rather than the invisible surgeries. These "visible surgeries" were what I was about to witness.

Once Joao was on stage, he spoke briefly to the crowd. Then, while the people in the "audience" said the "Our Father" prayer in Portuguese, Joao closed his eyes, his body shuddered slightly after a few moments, and then he opened his eyes again. As I was standing fairly close to the stage, I was able to see his face and eyes clearly. *There was a different being looking out through his eyes, one with a very intense gaze.* Even his facial features seemed to have rearranged themselves slightly. I was seeing the entity now, not Joao the man. I realized I was holding my breath and consciously relaxed, waiting to see what would happen next.

The two women Joao had led on stage were standing against the wall with their eyes closed, their faces calm and their bodies relaxed. And their purses were still slung over their shoulders. This was not a typical "pre-op" setting! Several assistants holding instrument trays were also on stage. Joao—or rather, the entity—looked briefly out at the assembled crowd as if getting his bearings, then walked slowly, a bit as if underwater, over to the first patient.

She was standing against the wall, eyes still closed. He lifted up her blouse and tucked the bottom edges inside her bra, then pulled the waistband of her slacks down several inches. He then took a scalpel out of one of the instrument trays and deftly made a several-inch incision in her lower abdomen. The scalpel—and other instruments used later and on subsequent days—was not sterilized except by the power of the entities, nor did the medium wear any surgical gloves. And yet, there had never been a case of sepsis reported as a result of any of the operations done by the medium/entity during the past 43 years of his work!

The incision didn't bleed at all as the entity stuck his bare fingers into it and moved them vigorously around for some moments. He again flicked some tissue onto the floor, took a large threaded surgical needle, and proceeded to sew and tie a single suture into the incision. There was not a flinch on the woman's face or a twitch of her body during the entire procedure. In fact, she looked as serene as if she were having a pleasant dream.

When the surgery was over, the entity had her open her eyes and tell us whether or not she had experienced any pain. She shook her head and said, "No, no pain at all."

Then the entity murmured something, and two hefty men who had been standing at the side of the stage approached, lifted the patient up bodily and carried her offstage and through a nearby doorway where they disappeared from sight. I learned later that they had gone into the infirmary—or recovery room, as it's sometimes called. Anyone receiving physical operations is taken there after their surgery, to be looked after by Casa volunteers. Usually people only spend a few hours there, and then are sent to their hotels to finish resting and recovering.

In preparation for the second surgery, the entity removed a hemostat from the instrument tray. A hemostat looks a bit like a long, slender forceps with the kind of round handles on the end that scissors have. This one was a good seven inches long and was made of stainless steel. The entity approached the second woman, who was still standing against the wall with her eyes closed. He had her tilt her head back slightly and open her mouth. Then suddenly and quickly, the entity shoved the hemostat up the woman's left nostril till all that showed of it were the round handles. I was stunned. And if that wasn't enough, the entity then began to vigorously twist the handles in circles again and again. Finally, he pulled the hemostat out of the woman's nose. This time there was a small amount of blood that trickled out the woman's nostril, but nothing like what one would expect from such a procedure.

However, as she was being operated on, twice during the procedure I heard muffled thumps in the crowd and saw the two men who had carried the first patient to the recovery room hurry through the crowd and re-emerge carrying someone to the recovery room. I found out later that it is not uncommon for people in the audience to be operated on invisibly by some of the other entities of the Casa while the physical operations on stage are taking place. In these cases, the spiritual anesthesia and trance-like state that the entities induce in the patients—who are simply people standing in the crowd—often result in those people swooning.

I have to say that the second surgery I witnessed on the stage really drove my mind into overload. One of the first things I did when I returned home several weeks later was to go immediately to my book on human anatomy and physiology. I turned to the illustration that showed the inside of the head, including the sinus cavity and location of the brain. I found that the sinus cavity extends inward—through and slightly past the nose—in a relatively straight line for only several inches. If you extended that straight line any further, you arrived at the brain.

If the hemostat that the entity used was following "natural law" as we know it, it would have forcefully penetrated at least several inches into the brain. And it was twisted vigorously in circles as well during the operation! Under normal circumstances this would probably have killed the person outright. I just couldn't figure it out. Perhaps some kind of metal-bending Uri Geller-type magic was done by the entity so that as it entered the nostril, the hemostat curved and went along the sinus cavity and down the back of the throat? Or perhaps it dematerialized somehow once it was inserted? I don't know and I may never know, although at the time of writing this book I've seen dozens of this same kind of operation. I only can say that it is miraculous by any known standards of physics, physiology and medicine.

Back to my first day at the Casa, I thought that after the second woman had been carried off, the surgeries were over for that session. But I was wrong. The entity beckoned to an older woman who had been standing in the audience to come on stage. He had her sit in a chair and proceeded to shave a two-inch circle of hair off the top of her head with a razor. He then used several instruments to poke into her scalp, and possibly into her brain, as he appeared to be using one metal instrument as a drill. He began extracting small whitish lumps of tissue. The last such lump, a major chunk, was a good half-inch in diameter. Someone next to me whispered that it was a tumor. Finally, he sutured her, again with a single stitch, and was done. Again, there was hardly any blood, and again, this woman too assured us she had felt no pain.

Once this operation was done, the entity left the stage and went through the door just to the right of it. Then those of us in the crowd were immediately told to line up in the appropriate lines. I clutched my ticket for the line for first-timers. Miguel guided my friend and I to the first-time line and stayed with us in order to help translate whatever Joao "in entity" might say to us when we met with him.

For a few minutes, the energy in the main hall was rather chaotic as hundreds of people milled about trying to find their appropriate line. There was a line for people who had already seen the entity in person for a consultation at least once in their lives. There was a "review" line for people who had had an operation a week earlier. The entity would assess their progress and see what else they might need in the way of treatment. Then there was a line for people who had gone to see the entity that morning and who had been told to come back in the afternoon instead. In those cases, I learned later, it was because the entity who was incorporated in the medium in the morning was not the entity that was to be assigned as that person's "doctor," but rather, their doctor would be incorporated in the medium that afternoon.

For those of us going to meet the entity for the first time, Miguel said that there were several things that could happen. The entity might give us a prescription for some herbs that were to help cleanse and strengthen us and would also act as a link into our bodies for the entities to continue working on us even after we left Brazil. He might tell us to return the next morning if our entity doctor would not be incorporating until the next morning. Another possibility was that he might prescribe a spiritual operation, in which case he would tell us what session to attend to receive it. It could be tomorrow, the next day or next week (as we were going to be here for two weeks) during a morning or afternoon session. The entity also might tell us to sit in his current, which would mean for us to sit down on one of the benches in the same room where he was incorporated in Joao's body, and to remain there for the rest of the session to receive healing energy. And finally, he might not say anything but simply wave us through the line. In that case, Miguel said, we would go on to the third current room, which was also the room used for the invisible operations, where we would sit for a few minutes with our eyes closed and receive an energy transmission from the entities.

Miguel also explained a bit about the first of the three current rooms, the one through which we would walk first on the way to the second one, where we would meet the entity. He said that as we passed through the first current room, we would be receiving a spiritual cleansing from the many invisible entities that worked at the Casa, and that they would also be diagnosing us. By the time we reached the incorporated medium in the second current room, the entity residing in Joao's body would already have access to all information about the state of our health—psychological, physical and spiritual. On the basis of that knowledge he would make his recommendations to us. As I had brought a few photos of friends who could not come but were requesting healing by the entities, I would probably receive herbal prescriptions for them as well once the entities had looked over their photos and attuned to their needs.

As we waited in line in the main hall, Miguel again reminded us to keep our arms and hands uncrossed as we walked through the current rooms, and to do likewise whenever we sat in the current rooms. However, while we were walking through the rooms, we were to leave our eyes open. Even if the line stopped for a while, we were not to close our eyes, as the entities already would be working on us, and due to the powerful effects of their work we might become disoriented and fall if our eyes were closed.

Finally it came time for our line to enter the first current room. My heart began beating faster and I felt a combination of nerves and excitement. We gave the man at the door our tickets, and then entered into the current, me still clutching my handful of photos. I looked around the room and saw rows of benches with dozens of people sitting with their eyes closed. I felt a powerful energy but resisted the impulse to close my eyes and sink deeper into it. As I learned later, some of the people sitting on the benches were volunteer mediums themselves who served at the Casa by helping sustain and strengthen the healing current. Others were people like myself who had come for healing and who were sitting there in order to receive more healing energy. Many of the faces of those sitting in the current had almost a translucent appearance, as if they were in a deep spiritual trance.

Some of the mediums in the first current room were more active, however, rubbing their hands vigorously together and then raising them in the air and making various gestures. Some were taking powerful breaths, others making

14

faint hissing sounds, all of which added to the electric charge running through the room.

Our line would stop from time to time, then move on again a few feet. I was, by this point, definitely feeling an energy vibration passing through me. My anticipation was building as well, and my hands were perspiring a bit. I was also praying for healing for myself and for the friends whose photos I had brought. Finally we passed from the first current room through a tiny hall and into the second room. The energy there was somewhat different. There was a palpable hush, except for the occasional voice of the entity speaking with those passing by him. Here again were rows of benches with more people sitting on them, eyes closed.

I looked to the far side of the room, and saw the medium sitting in a large armchair. As I watched, he raised his head and gave me an intense stare, then returned to focusing on the person directly in front of him. I noticed that even as he talked to that person, he was busily scribbling on one piece of paper after another and then stacking them on the wooden arm of his chair. I found out soon that these were the prescriptions for the medicinal herbs he recommended to most people, different amounts for each person according to their needs. Next to his chair was a table with a very large quartz crystal sitting on a light box, glowing from within, as well as a tray with a pitcher of water and several small glasses. I learned later that at the end of each session, everyone sitting in the current room came up and drank a bit of this *agua fluidica*—water that had been blessed and energized by the entities—as part of their healing.

Bit by bit, the line moved along until finally I was face to face with the entity, who reached out and took my hand. Miguel knelt down beside him and explained that I was from the U.S., and described to the entity my short list of physical challenges that I was seeking healing for. The entity nodded, handed me a piece of paper with a prescription for herbs, and murmured something else that I didn't understand. He quickly looked over the photos and wrote out herbal prescriptions for each of those people as well. The entire interaction took at most twenty seconds. Then Miguel had me follow him out of the second current room and into the third one where, as he had explained to me earlier, I should sit down on one of the benches, close my eyes, and receive my energy transmission. I did. And way too soon—perhaps only a few minutes later—I was told to go ahead and get up and continue out the door to the outside.

But before I left, I noticed that in this room, in addition to the benches, along two of the walls there were cots upon which people were lying with their eyes closed. There were also a number of people in wheelchairs seated along the walls. I learned later that some people who come to the Casa for treatment of serious disabilities are told by the entity to spend all of their sessions in that room.

The images - from the time I entered the first current room to the time I walked out the door of the third one into the heat of the afternoon - were a blur, a kaleidoscope of impressions that really didn't gel until I'd been through the process many more times. It seemed like everything had gone so fast—my time in front the entity, the time seated in the current with my eyes closed—and I wasn't sure what I was experiencing, although my knees were a bit wobbly and for the next twenty minutes a lot of energy was running through me. I looked down at the pieces of paper the entity had given me and each one had what looked like some kind of strange hieroglyphics.

Miguel must have sensed my bewilderment and reminded me that I was holding typical herbal prescription notations that all of the entities made. He assured me that the people at the Casa "pharmacy" would be able to decipher for me how many bottles I was to buy for myself and my friends, as the staff was familiar with the written codes of the entities.

Then Miguel smiled and said that the entity had also told me to come back the next week on Wednesday morning, the first session of the week, for a spiritual operation. I was going to get to experience an invisible surgery by the entities, and I looked forward to it with great anticipation.

Because we hadn't known what kind of hotel accommodations—if any— would be available when we arrived in Abadiania, my friend and I had kept our room in Brasilia for that night. As this was a two-hour drive, we were going to have to leave soon in order to arrive there in time to get a good night's rest and be back for the next morning's session. Miguel told us about several places— *pousadas*, as the local inns are called—where we could stay in town and said that there would be no problem simply showing up and getting a room when we returned tomorrow.

He then helped us get our herbs, which at that time were being distributed in the form of pint-sized bottles of dark brown liquid. Over the years that has changed and the herbs now come in the easier-to-transport form of capsules in small bottles. Miguel explained again that while we were taking the herbs, we must stay on the diet that the entities request: no pork, no alcohol, no hot peppers of any kind including black pepper, no bananas that had been sprayed with pesticides or other chemicals, and no fertilized eggs. For me, that diet looked like it would last some weeks, judging by the number of bottles of herbal "tea" I'd been prescribed, but I didn't mind as my normal diet usually didn't include those things anyway.

Miguel also said that sometimes people go through typical "cleansing" symptoms once they start the herbs, like mild diarrhea, occasional headaches or achy muscles, and possibly skin eruptions of various kinds. A few people will even vomit for a day. Not to worry! This would all be for the good, according to

Miguel, and what he said also rang true from what I already knew and had experienced from numerous cleansing fasts in my own past.

By then, I was feeling tired and ready to be on the way back to our hotel in Brasilia. As we drove, a beautiful and most unusual rainbow appeared in the sky. It was a partial rainbow—a straight diagonal line from the earth upward. From its apex back down to the earth on the other side was a line of light, and that line plus the rainbow plus the horizon of earth along the base formed a perfect triangle. I thought again of the triangle at the Casa and felt a sense of awe. As we approached Brasilia, a second and more fully arcing rainbow appeared, thick and saturated with vibrant colors.

By the time we arrived at our hotel and I fell into bed, I was sure I would sleep like a baby, but instead found myself tossing and turning all night. I have learned over time that this is not an unusual response to the work of the entities and the incredible energies they transmit, but at the time, I felt frustrated and longed for temporary oblivion.

By five in the morning I finally gave up on sleep and arose to prepare for my return to the Casa.

Chapter 2: The Flame That Did Not Burn

We checked out of the hotel at dawn so that my friend and I could be present for the morning session of the Casa at eight. The sky was magnificent as we drove again toward Abadiania. Flames and streaks of gold, lavender and rose illuminated a celestial portrait of Nature's glory and the renewing power of life upon the vast blue heavens above. Finally, we were once again driving down the narrow road to the Casa. Figures dressed in white were flowing quietly in the same direction as if in an angelic processional, some walking, some gliding in wheelchairs.

However, by the time I got to the main hall of the Casa, the energy seemed much more chaotic and noisy than the day before. There were about twice as many people, which may have accounted for this. I sat down and told Creator I was here again today on behalf of myself and the loved ones I was praying for. I then began to meditate, but after a bit someone startled me by touching my shoulder firmly. I opened my eyes to find one of the volunteer women of the Casa—who I had met the day before and who spoke English—leaning over me. She told me it wasn't good to meditate in the main hall before the room was "prepared" for the session, as I might absorb energies from all of the sick people there that day.

I followed her suggestion to the extent that I didn't close my eyes again, but for the next hour and a half, I had to actually *resist* meditating as the pull of the energy to go within was so strong. It was the first time I'd ever had to fight an energy that was meditating me, rather than me struggling to meditate!

Once again, just before Joao came on stage, we were asked to briefly close our eyes and turn our thoughts toward God, and once again, just as we did so, there was a huge crash of thunder followed by the beginning of a heavy tropical downpour! Just moments later Joao appeared.

He again incorporated an entity, one who seemed warmer and friendlier than yesterday afternoon's business-like entity. He then performed a single but amazing operation. I noticed that my mind seemed to be stunned into silence by the staggering nature of what was going on just feet away, the truly paranormal aspect of what I was witnessing. In fact, due to the fact that my mind was, for a change, silent and overwhelmed, another part of me began to feel that what Joao was doing was in fact completely normal. I had entered into a different realm in which the miraculous was becoming home.

To begin the surgery, the entity pulled open the patient's left eyelid with one hand. With a kitchen paring knife in his other hand, he began to vigorously scrape on the patient's eyeball!

Even though I'd read in the article about these eye surgeries, I half expected the patient to begin screaming and running off the stage. But the man remained silent, and judging from his body language, totally relaxed. This was truly mind-boggling. I kept thinking about different times I'd gotten a bit of dirt in my eyes, and how just one tiny speck could make me miserable till I removed it. And here was this man, totally unfazed, while a kitchen knife was being almost brutally scraped over his eye to the extent that I could see the eye moving under the pressure being exerted on it. The entity would occasionally flick something off the tip of the knife and then return to the scraping. After he finished with the first eye, he repeated the entire process on the man's other eye. The man was then taken to the recovery room, and most of the rest of the people got in their respective lines to prepare to see the entity.

After the surgery, I went directly to the first current room. I had already passed by the entity yesterday and did not need to do so again today. I sat down and began to meditate. It was a great relief to finally be able to let go to the force that had been pulling me inward toward deep trance or meditation since I'd arrive hours earlier in the main hall. The benches were not terribly comfortable and I was squished between a number of others occupying the same bench as me. Nonetheless, as my body settled down for the duration of the session, I could feel once again the unusual energy pulse that had begun before I left for Brazil and that had its source here at the Casa. It drew me deeper and deeper into silent meditation, where I remained suspended until the end of the session several hours later.

Then, like the others, I went to receive the small glass of blessed and energized water that all of us are given at the end of sessions in the current.

I followed the crowds to the soup line, where I waited, along with hundreds of others now pouring out of the main building of the Casa, for my turn to receive a bowl of soup. When I arrived eventually at the front of the line, the women tirelessly distributing these bowls through the little windows that opened into the kitchen looked like selfless angels to me. I received my bowl and thanked them. Then I sat down at one of the tables and ate the soup that had been prepared with so much love. It was delicious and provided grounding for the semi-floating state I was in as a result of the effects of the morning session.

As I ate, I looked out over the crowds of people having their soup, waiting in line, or strolling around the gardens of the Casa. I felt touched and humbled today, just as I had yesterday. There were people there with such obviously serious illnesses and problems, many with a friend or family member attending to their needs. There was no pushing going on in the soup line, even though it was long and the day was hot. Everyone simply waited patiently for their turn, sometimes silently, sometimes conversing with those near them in line. I witnessed many small gestures, smiles and other acts of care that began to add up to an overall aura of gentle loving-kindness and faith that touched my heart and soul. And my faith in the basic goodness residing in human beings took another leap.

I believe that this energy of goodness and kindness exhibited by so many people at the Casa—as well as by those who run the many *pousadas* where visitors stay, eat and sleep during their time in Abadiania—has contributed a great deal to my own personal healing. Yes, the entities have done their share—and it's been massive—but the overflowing abundance of human love at and around the Casa has also done its work.

One woman commented to me, "Part of what touches me here is all of these desperate people—people who have not been able to be helped by any other means—rejoicing in the energy here. Even people who have never thought about what God really means, what love truly is, come here and meet Love face to face, heart to heart. And they see that here is hope with a capital 'H,' and a new chance at life."

I, like all of you, have been subject to the great tumbler of life. We have all been polished again and again by the impact of other people's rough edges colliding with our own, wearing down the irregularities of our emotional and mental surfaces, our egos, hitting our weak points and causing the occasional fracture. Through this process, humanity collectively moves blow by blow, back toward our awareness of the deeper and gem-like perfection within each of us.

Prior to going to the Casa for the first time, I'd had my share of heartbreak and suffering as well as the joy of spiritual gifts of love and illumination. I'd gone through a particularly trying period a few years before going to the Casa, one that had left me questioning all the spiritual knowledge and experience I'd ever experienced to that point as well as the existence of true human goodness: a typical dark night of the soul. This crisis had also left me feeling empty, bereft, disappointed with myself and others, and questioning God's true nature.

Before leaving for Brazil I had prayed that when I arrived at the Casa, I might not only experience healing for some of my physical complaints, but also that my faith in Spirit might be rekindled by some undeniable event or events. By the end of the morning, having only experienced two sessions at the Casa, these prayers were already beginning to be answered by what I was seeing and feeling there.

My friend and I were able to find accommodations at a nearby *pousada*. Once we'd unpacked, eaten a delicious buffet-style lunch and rested a bit, it was time to go back to the Casa for the afternoon session.

The rest of the afternoon passed in a blur of powerful energies—more surgeries performed by the entity followed by a long and satisfying session of meditation in the current room. Then back to the *pousada* for dinner and chats with other English-speaking foreigners staying there, followed by a leisurely stroll around the town. By ten o'clock everyone else had gone to bed, but I was still wide-awake and "wired" from the experiences of the day.

I went to the *pousada*'s dining hall, which was now empty except for the owner who was tallying up the day's receipts. I'd brought a book with me, hoping that reading would relax me enough to eventually be able to go to sleep. Since no one else was in the hall, I asked the owner if it would be okay for me to smoke for a few minutes, hoping that doing so would help me further unwind. She said that was fine, and then left the room to go get something.

I reached in my pocket to search for a lighter, with no success. I was about to abandon the idea of a smoke when I noticed several candles burning on a little ledge across the room. So I walked over, lit the tip of my cigarette from the shorter one, and then sat back down at my table.

I had only had a few—but immensely satisfying—puffs of smoke, when the door to the *pousada* burst open and in walked Joao with a few of his assistants from the Casa! He greeted me with a nod, but the one female assistant with him seemed to be giving me a rather disapproving look. I was taken by surprise at Joao's arrival, to say the least, and simultaneously embarrassed to be caught smoking by the great healer himself and his assistant. I immediately stubbed out my cigarette and looked in dismay at the hotel owner, who by then had returned to the dining room. "Should I leave?" I asked her. "Would they like the room to themselves?"

"No, stay here, *querida,* it's fine. They just came for a bit of dinner."

So I stayed put, but felt awkward. I felt it would somehow be rude to start reading my book with Joao in the room, but I also felt ridiculous just sitting there staring into space. My dilemma was soon resolved, but not my discomfort.

Joao walked past me, giving me an intense look, and went over to the little ledge where the candles were, about ten feet away from me on the opposite wall of the room. He then passed his hands over the candle where I'd recently lit my cigarette, and began to pray out loud. If I could have disappeared into the earth at that moment, I would have done so gladly. For it was in that moment that I realized that the candle was a votive candle, that the little ledge holding it and the long slender candle was a small altar, and that I had lit my cigarette off Jesus' or Mary's or some saint's prayer candle. Not only was I mortified, but I felt a growing certainty that I was now in serious spiritual trouble. How could I have been so blind not to have even seen the little religious statues that now seemed to glare at me from the altar?

I slumped into my chair, but straightened quickly as Joao turned around to face me, standing just to the side of the little ledge altar where the candles continued to glow. *This is it,* I thought to myself. *I am now going to be royally chewed out, then cast out of the Casa and Abadiania for good, the gates of Heaven will be barred to me permanently, I'm doomed.*

As Joao stared at me, he reached his right arm out to the side and lowered the palm of his hand toward the longer candle until its flame was touching his palm. Then he curled his fingers downward and, leaving his palm in the flame, grabbed the candle itself with his fingertips and lifted it up. He then stood there holding it, gazing at me from time to time. The glow of the flame burning within the small cage of his hand was lighting my way down yet another path of the paranormal. As it continued to burn, Joao began to speak about the power of transmutation of energy. He was speaking in Portuguese, yet it seemed as if I could understand the essence of what he was saying.

I kept looking at the candle burning within his hand, and as the seconds ticked by, the glow began to expand until it appeared that a huge ball of white light surrounded his hand. I'm sure that my jaw must have been dropped wide open by then. Joao finally turned, placed the candle back on the ledge, and beckoned me over. I got up in a daze, walked over to him, and he showed me the palm of his hand. It was completely unmarked by the flame—not a sign of burning, blistering or even redness anywhere—even thought the flame had been touching it for several minutes. The only mark was a dark wavy line left by the smoke from the candle.

Joao then left the room and I went back to my table and sat down. I was in a very strange state by this time. I glanced at the owner and she nodded and smiled at me. I automatically smiled back, then returned to staring into space, trying to absorb what had just happened. After about 15 minutes of sitting in this semi-trance, Joao came back into the dining hall. He sat down with his assistants and joined them in their meal. Before leaving, he came over to me and told me I should come back to the sessions at the Casa the following week and to be sure to stand near the stage so I could watch him operate. I nodded my head and told him I would be there. Then he and his group left.

I found out later that when Joao had left the dining hall and walked down one of the corridors of the *pousada* right after the candle demonstration, he had gone to the room of someone who was seriously ill and done some healing work. Apparently, from the time he had first passed his hands over the candle and prayed, he had gone into trance and incorporated one of the entities. This was why he wasn't burned while holding the candle for several minutes. When Joao is incorporated, the entities protect his body and give it "super-human"

22

properties, including protection from infection from his patients' blood when he does the surgeries without gloves. The entities are masters of transmutation of energy.

After Joao and his group left the room, I closed my eyes and sat in silence, overwhelmed by all that had occurred. As I sat there, a voice began to speak inside my mind. I believe it was the voice of the entity who had been incorporated in Joao while he was at the *pousada*. The voice said, "We know that you have smoked cigarettes off and on for years, and that there have been times when you've wondered if you should quit for good as you've been worried about possible health risks even though you smoke very moderately. We want you to know that if you choose to continue smoking, you can stop worrying about negative effects. We have given you a gift of transmutation of energy tonight, and the cigarettes will not harm you."

I listened to these words, gave silent thanks for the blessing and for all I'd been allowed to witness and experience that night, and finally floated off to my room in a daze. Once in bed, I drifted smoothly but quickly into dreaming. But this was not an ordinary dreaming state. Rather, I was in a state of what is called "lucid dreaming," in which the dreamer is aware that he or she is dreaming.

In the dream, I was taken through a rapid "travelogue" of Brazil, shown old houses, tenements, village streets, big cities, etc., and Joao's presence was there in the background as if he was showing me his native land and where he "comes from" on various levels. His voice was saying that there were both riches and poverty in the material and technological world, but that none of that meant much to him any more. Then suddenly I was sliding down this dark slanting space and became a bit frightened. I had the sense that Joao was both showing me and acknowledging the various dark spirits and forces that I'd dealt with at various times in my life through my shamanic work as well as within the terrain of my own psyche. Perhaps they were forces that he too had had to deal with. Then the fear lifted as suddenly as it began, and I was immediately out of the dark space.

I then surfaced from the dream, thoroughly reviewed its details in my mind so I wouldn't forget them by morning, and finally drifted into normal and untroubled sleep.

I did remember the lucid dream the next morning and made notes in my journal. As I reflected on the events of the prior night, I realized that yet another prayer had been answered—one that I had made before leaving for Brazil. What had motivated my prayer had been a succession of disillusioning experiences with past spiritual "teachers," a loss of confidence in myself and the many spiritual experiences I'd had over my lifetime, and an urgent need—arising from this dark night of the soul phase—for some kind of "proof" of the miraculous or paranormal. I needed to see this proof with my own eyes, experience it for myself and not simply have to take someone else's word that "miracles" of various sorts did indeed occur.

That prayer had been answered and then some. Not only had I witnessed the miraculous surgeries performed by the entity, but I'd had my own "close encounter" with the entity and the paranormal.

As the day was Saturday and there would be no more sessions at the Casa until the following Wednesday, my friend and I got in the rental car and proceeded to explore more of Brazil. The places we visited were primarily other spiritual centers and beautiful parks. All in all, I was falling in love with this wonderful land and its spiritual treasures.

Chapter 3: Week Two at the Casa

I returned to Abadiania energized from my weekend travels and looking forward to the first session of the week, the session in which I was to receive my invisible operation at the "hands" of the entities. I awoke early Wednesday morning to the now-familiar clamor of roosters, parrots, and hymns being sung at dawn at a nearby church. Filled with a sense of anticipation and excitement, I showered and put on a white dress, ate a bit of fresh papaya in the *pousada*'s dining hall, and walked to the Casa.

The street was lined with large tour buses that had brought people from all over Brazil, some of whom had been riding for 48 hours to this little town not found on maps, in order to be healed from maladies of the body, mind and spirit. We arrived at the Casa with prayers in our hearts for ourselves and for our fellow human beings.

At the opening of the morning session, we all assembled in the main hall and Tiao gave the orientation speech. He, as always, then called for a show of hands of those who had been scheduled for operations that morning. Dozens of us raised our hands, and at Tiao's instruction, lined up outside the door to the first current room. We then stepped through the door after him, walked through the first and second current rooms where people were already sitting in prayer and meditation, and on to the third room in which our operations would take place. All of us would be worked on simultaneously by the many "spirit doctors," or entities, of the Casa de Dom Inacio.

Once we were all seated on the benches (and Miguel had told me in advance what to expect so that I wouldn't have to worry about translation), one of the volunteer staff of the Casa reminded us to close our eyes and keep our hands and feet uncrossed. We were then told to put one hand over the area that we were wanting healed if it was a physical area. If it was not physical, but rather emotional or spiritual, or if there was more than one physical area needing healing, we were to put our right hand over our heart. Either way, we were then to concentrate in our mind and prayers on those areas we wanted healed.

As I had several physical areas in addition to psychological and spiritual ones that I felt needed healing, I placed my right hand over my heart. Within seconds

25

I felt an overwhelming wave of energy pass through me that was of such a pure quality of Love that I dissolved into tears. The wave was warm, almost hot, like a flame passing through me and burning away all that was not love. I tried to keep from sobbing out loud so as not to disturb the others, but I felt like I was being absolutely melted by this Love. As I continued to weep quietly, I heard Joao come in and ask if anyone there wanted a physical operation. I could hear a few people get up and follow him out of the room—and probably to the stage—for their surgeries. Then all was quiet again except for the soothing voice of the volunteer urging us to relax and to stay focused in our prayers.

I do not know how long I sat there being washed through and through by the power of that Love. It might have been minutes or it might have been an hour. But finally, I heard Joao—or probably the entity, as Joao was incorporated by the entity by then—come into the room and say, "By the power of Jesus Christ and God's will, you are healed." He left the room once again and then someone came over and touched my arm. As I opened my eyes I could see that the session was over. But the healing had really just begun and has continued ever since.

I floated out of the current room, my legs a bit unsteady. Miguel was waiting outside and escorted me over to a bench in the garden, where I sat and rested quietly for a while. I was still shaken by the power of my experience and could not even talk for some time. Finally, Miguel told me it would be best if I returned to my room at the *pousada* to rest for the remainder of the day. He reminded me that I had been operated on, albeit invisibly, and that just like with a normal surgery, rest was critical. He also said that the entities often continued various stages of the operation for a period of 24 hours or more after the initial session, and that when people over-exerted during that time, they could even undo some of the internal stitches made by the entities during the surgeries.

Once again, I found myself considering yet another mind-boggling concept. Amazed, I asked Miguel if the entities really leave internal stitches. Miguel assured me that people who had been operated on invisibly often had x-rays taken later by their own medical doctors to assess the results of their surgeries, and sometimes the x-rays showed these internal stitches.

I myself had the opportunity to interview one such man—a Brazilian—at a later date. The man previously had been diagnosed with a serious heart condition and told by his doctors that he should have a triple-bypass operation soon; and that even with the surgery there were no guarantees that he wouldn't have ongoing problems for the rest of his life.

The man had thanked his doctor for the advice, but told him he first wanted to make a trip to the Casa de Dom Inacio to seek treatment from Joao de Deus. His doctor was very skeptical and insisted that the man return to his office immediately after the trip to Abadiania. His patient agreed, and set off for the Casa.

While he was there, he underwent an invisible operation, and within days his energy—which had been quite low due to the heart problem - was returning rapidly. The pain in his chest was subsiding as well. After a week of sessions at the Casa, including time in the current, he returned home and went to see his doctor as promised. He told his doctor that he really didn't want the triple-bypass, as he had been operated on at the Casa.

Again, the doctor gave him a skeptical look and asked if he could take another x-ray of his patient's heart to assess his condition. This was done, and when he came back, he exclaimed to his patient, "You were operated on in two places, not just one! I can see the stitches in the x-ray. Why didn't you tell me you were going to have your surgery someplace else?"

The man looked at this doctor and said that he *had* told him. He said he had been operated on by the entities of the Casa and that he felt so much better that he wanted no further surgeries. With that, he left, leaving his doctor to sort out a major paradigm shift!

And Miguel told me that not all of the invisible operations at the hands of the entities took place in the operating room. Sometimes they happened "spontaneously" in other areas of the Casa, and even in the *pousadas* while people were sleeping or just resting in their rooms. He recounted a story of one such spontaneous operation that had just happened that day after the morning session.

One of the men who had come to the Casa that day was eating the medicinal soup when suddenly he noticed that his white T-shirt felt wet. Probably thinking he had spilled some soup on himself, he looked down, and found to his surprise a horizontal line of blood seeping through the fabric. He pulled up his shirt and found a thin, several-inch long incision on his chest. He had just received an invisible operation that had manifested a physical incision!

These stories and many others that I heard during my first—and proceeding—stays in Abadiania served to deepen my belief in the reality of the invisible surgeries, as did my own experiences. But it was now time for me to go and rest, to allow the entities to continue their work. Miguel relayed the "doctors' orders" given by the entities to those who receive operations at the Casa, whether visible or invisible. He said that we were not to return to the current rooms for about 24 hours after surgery, and it was best really to stay away from the Casa entirely during that period. The reason for this was the following. Apparently when the entities operate, they open up each patient's energy field to quite an extent. This enables the patients to access more high-level vibrations for their healing, plus the entities can thus continue to access the patients' energy body more easily for the post-operative work. The "downside" of this opening is that it also leaves the patients much more vulnerable to external energies that might *not* be so beneficial for them. And so if I were to go sit in the current room too soon after my operation, I could inadvertently pick up some of the negative energies being discharged by others on whom the entities were working.

This made sense. I would go rest, and I would stay away from the Casa till the next morning as I didn't want to take any chances. I went back to the *pousada*, and soon I was resting quietly on my bed.

I frankly do not remember much of the rest of that afternoon. Often people are in somewhat of a twilight state after their operations. Some even sleep for the next 24 hours, more or less. I was in that twilight state for the afternoon and stayed in bed. I could feel work being done in the region of my stomach. The pain that had been ongoing in my right hip and lower back for months had disappeared. Off and on an inner voice would direct me to do one thing or another, such as massage the heels of my feet, rest, concentrate here or there, etc.

But by evening, I was becoming increasingly restless. I finally got up and ended up talking to several people about their experiences at the Casa, then eventually went back to bed and slept through the night.

The next morning I stayed at the *pousada*, feeling a bit left out as I wasn't able to go to the current room of the Casa. Around 9:30, however, I suddenly got the "message" to go over to the Casa, so I walked over there, trying to go slowly and not exert my body too much. I arrived there and sat out in the garden, figuring it would be safe—energetically speaking—since not too many people were around, most being in the main hall. After a few minutes I saw Joao come outside, still clearly "in entity" judging by the way he moved and by the trance-like look in his eyes. I kept wondering why I had been "called" to the Casa.

Then Miguel came over and we began to chat. He told me a story about an experience he'd had in the current room one day when there were just him and 8 other mediums present. Joao entered the room in his healing trance. Three entities in a row incorporated through him in rapid succession. The first was King Solomon, who told the mediums he had just two things to say to them: "peace" and "love." Then an unusual entity came through—the spirit of King Arthur, holding a sword in his hand. He drew the sign of the cross in the air with his sword and said, "You are all healed." And finally, Dom Inacio incorporated and Jesus manifested and showered all nine mediums with yellow rose petals that all of the mediums saw and felt. By this time the mediums were weeping and overwhelmed by this divine visitation.

I too was weeping by the time Miguel finished his emotionally charged recounting of his experience, and I concluded that hearing it must have been the reason that I was "called" to the Casa. I thanked Miguel for sharing such a powerful personal story with me, and then went back to the *pousada* to rest and have lunch before the afternoon's session.

When I got back to the *pousada,* I happened to look in the mirror to see if I'd gotten a sun burn, as I'd forgotten to put any sun block on my chest that morning and had been wearing a tank top. Thankfully I wasn't burned, but I did notice something that made an even bigger impact on me.

Several years ago, a fairly large lump had formed on my chest, just slightly to the left of center. My doctor had told me she wasn't too concerned, but that I should keep an eye on it and notify her if anything changed.

During my invisible surgery the day before, I had focused on several physical issues but had not even thought to ask for work on the cyst. To my surprise, when I looked in the mirror just one day after my invisible surgery, I discovered that the cyst was completely gone! I ran my finger over the area where it had been, and there was not a trace of it even below the surface. It never did come back.

For whatever reasons, the entities had decided to operate on it and remove it. Perhaps it was a harmless cyst but they wanted me to have tangible, visible proof that they had indeed worked on me. Or perhaps there was a potential for problems developing with the cyst in the future, and they caught something before it could worsen. Miguel had told me that some of the work the entities do during the operations is preventative. They can catch a cancer developing when it is still minute in size and remove it before it can spread. One American woman had been told by the entity that she needed to sit in the current every day during her stay in order to prevent the development of osteoporosis, which she was told would have developed within the following three years had she not done so.

And I can attest to the psychological benefits of the current and invisible operations. After my stay in Abadiania, it was as if some kind of weight had been lifted from my mind, and I felt a good deal lighter than I had in a long time—perhaps ever! Many people who go to the Casa are told upon returning home by those who know them that they seem more at peace, more loving, more self-confident. So the entities are spiritual psychotherapists as well as surgeons.

In addition, as I learned during my stay and understood increasingly during subsequent trips to Abadiania, the entities also do a lot of work on people with "obsessive" or attached, earthbound spirits. Miguel and other mediums of the Casa have told me that these obsessive spirits are the cause of serious illnesses physical and psychological—in 80 to 90 percent of all the people who come to the Casa. The mediums of the Casa are not alone in this perspective on the cause of many illnesses. I have since had the opportunity to speak with people from other spiritual centers in Brazil, including Spiritist and Umbanda centers. All of them take the interference of obsessive spirits into account in their perspective on illness and spiritual healing. I have even attended several kinds of ceremonies—at the Valley of the Dawn and at Umbanda centers—in which the work has concentrated on the removal of these spirits.

An obsessive spirit is, according to the definitions I've heard, the spirit of a human being who has "died"—or "disincarnated"—but who has not moved on from the earth plane. Often the human being died suddenly and/or violently and had no time to prepare for his or her death. The spirit was then confused and did not understand that it was no longer in a body. So it continued to hang around the earth plane trying to interact here. Eventually, it would find someone with a weakened energy field and increasingly attach itself to this person, thus causing for its unaware host a variety of problems—spiritual, psychological and physical—over time. These attached spirits *can* be reconciled to their true situation by spiritual practitioners who know what they're doing, in order to then be released and directed home to the Light and to the next phase of their soul's journey.

This concept was not unfamiliar to me before arriving at the Casa. Through my shamanic work I had received some understanding of this type of situation and had worked with several spirits of the recently departed to assist them in their journey home so that they would not get stuck on this plane. One even paid me a visit—the spirit of my grandmother—on the day of her "death." A rather reserved and unhappy woman in life, in spirit she was much more liberated, and we danced together to some wild rock and roll music before she finally said good-bye and left for the Light!

I do not know exactly how the entities of the Casa deal with the unhappy obsessive spirits, but I know that they do. I have witnessed "exorcistic" type work going on at the Casa. Often the obsessive spirit will first object to leaving its host and this earth plane, and moan or even yell, using its host's voice to do so. Once, an obsessive spirit sang a mournful gypsy song through its female host before it was finally able to let go and move on. Apparently it had been a gypsy when it was still in human form. There are so many layers and levels to the work of the entities, and each day at the Casa is like attending a spiritual university.

When I returned to the Casa for the afternoon session on the day following my surgery, I decided to go through the "*segunda vez*" line so I could ask some questions of the entity. What was foremost in my mind was to get clarity on what my "mission" was for this next cycle of my life. Before coming to the Casa, I felt as though I'd been in a state of "suspended animation" for a few years—that dark night of the soul period that I mentioned earlier. So I felt an urgent need to focus on the future in the proper direction for my soul's purpose here.

When I posed my question to the entity, he seemed to look deeply into my being and then said, "Your mission is to bring people here to the Casa from your country or from wherever else they find you. You will have the support of Dom Inacio, of the medium Joao, and of the workers here." I was more than happy at this statement, and my mind had already begun running around that very possibility over the past few days.

The entity then told me, "You carry a great deal of light and have a strong connection to God. You have no more need of earthly (human) spiritual teachers, but need only to seek guidance directly from Spirit."

I left the Casa that afternoon filled with joy and gratitude. The entity's last comment brought a profound sense of peace and resolution to my soul. As I mentioned toward the end of the last chapter, throughout my adult life I had sought out spiritual teachers and teachings from many different cultures and approaches. I had learned a great deal in the process, sometimes by default, and had also had many disappointments when my "teachers" turned out not to be the shining examples I'd originally hoped for.

My judgment of them, however, was decreasing over time as I became more honest about myself. I too had had many students and had taught spirituality and healing workshops for years. And yet I knew that I too had a long, long way to go before I reached the level that I had sought for and expected in my teachers. Increasingly I was seeing that we are *all* on a journey and all have much to learn as well as to share.

Nonetheless, hearing the entity tell me I had no further need of formal teachers was both a relief and a challenge. The challenge was to continue to deepen my personal link with Spirit and to rely on that for guidance, rather than turning so often to my fellow human beings. This brought up a major issue for me: trust. To rely on a personal link to Spirit, I was going to have to trust more in what my inner "voice" and vision revealed to me. Of course, this was basically what I'd been encouraging my students to do for years and thought that I was doing it to a large extent as well, but I realized now that I had a ways to go in this process myself.

A very few individuals whom I have met over my life seem to have never lost the link to Spirit, to God, that they had when they first came into this world. No matter how much other people thought that they were crazy or misguided, they held true to their inner knowing. However, most of the rest of us, myself included, had been deeply effected by the authority figures around us since childhood, including parents, teachers, doctors, priests, and other "officials" who purported to know better what was good for us than we did ourselves.

Therefore, for most of us to learn to trust the quiet—or booming, as the case might be—inner voice, vision or intuition, is to make a 180-degree turnabout. It requires the willingness to sometimes go against the powerful momentum of social conditioning and the opinion of others in order to follow the guidance of Spirit.

So in a way, the entity had clarified two aspects of my mission for this next cycle of my life: to bring groups to the Casa and to deepen my internal link with Spirit.

The next day was Friday, my last day at the Casa for this first stay in Abadiania. I spent time in the current room during the morning session. While doing so, I focused on helping those people of whom I'd brought photos, friends in need of healing. As I sank deeper into the current and tried to send healing energy to my friends, I saw two pure white eagles appear in my inner vision, accompanied by Jesus. Suddenly I was lifted, transported out of myself and was with hundreds of winged, angelic presences. It was literally heavenly! Simultaneously, I could sense the energy in the current room becoming even more powerful. I could hear some of the mediums directing energy through sound as they worked with the current. By the end of the session I felt drenched in some kind of divine nectar.

When I went back to the Casa in the afternoon, I watched Joao/entity perform five physical surgeries in a row. He worked on several people's eyes, including that of a famous young Brazilian soccer player, and then did another of the "nose job" operations. This time, he stunned me even more by putting *two* hemostats up one man's nostril, and the entity left them there for a long time while he did a surgery on a woman.

When he finished the operations, instead of leaving immediately for the second current room, he stepped off the stage and wandered through the crowd for a while, letting people take photos of him, talking with individuals and receiving a bouquet of flowers from some grateful attendees. He immediately distributed the flowers among the crowd. It was a very "family" kind of atmosphere.

Finally he left the room and I got in line to say good-bye to the entity and to try to ask a few more questions. The answers I was given were somewhat vague, and I felt part of them were not translated completely by my interpreter. But I also had faith that I would find the answers I needed as my life progressed and I listened more deeply to Spirit within. Perhaps this was the deeper answer given to me by the entity.

My two weeks at the Casa had come to an end, but the inner results of my stay were only beginning. I had received more than I could have imagined prior to the trip, and was filled with gratitude and renewed hope and faith. I knew I would be returning in the future for more healing and experience. And I had already decided to take a Portuguese intensive language course the next time I came, so that I could be a good guide and able to do some of the translation when I started my mission of bringing groups to this house of miracles.

So as I left the Casa, I was already looking forward to returning once again.

Chapter 4: The Spiritual Surgeries of the Entities

Between returning home from my first stay in Abadiania and leaving for my second trip to Brazil, I had several powerful dreams that related to the spiritual workings of the Casa. The first was on Christmas Eve. In the dream a voice told me, "When you go back to Abadiania, you will all dance in the Christ energy and light of absolution." The voice was so loud that it woke me from the dream and I lay there in bed feeling surrounded by light and divine presences. Perhaps they were the entities of the Casa.

Following my first trip to Abadiania in November of 1998, I did indeed return there again and again. The first time was several months later, during which I spent two weeks in the lively beach city of Salvador do Bahia, participating in an intensive Portuguese language course and exploring what the city had to offer—especially in the spiritual realms. I was able to attend a Candomble ceremony and had a session with a wonderful trance medium painter.

By the time I left Salvador, I felt that I had an expanded perspective on Brazilian culture and at least a basic ability to communicate in Portuguese which I intended to continue polishing and expanding during the following four weeks that I was going to stay in Abadiania. I hoped that by the end of a month of sessions at the Casa, I would feel grounded and knowledgeable enough in the various processes and aspects of what was offered there that I would be confident in beginning my mission of bringing groups.

As I arrived in Abadiania for my second stay, I was already beginning to sense that it was my home away from home, and felt a great deal of joy to be there again. I quickly entered into the rhythm of daily sessions at the Casa each Wednesday through Friday, regular walks in the lush countryside, and an ongoing process of interviewing people (with the idea in mind of possibly writing a book or some articles about the Casa). The stories of personal healing and other spiritual experiences were endlessly fascinating to me. I also began doing a lot of translation for the English-speaking foreigners who were seeking treatment at the Casa. My language studies in Salvador had truly benefited me and now were also benefiting others!

Initially, watching the visible surgeries of the Casa was one of the most important things to me, as I felt I needed this regular confirmation of the astounding and miraculous nature of the work of the entities. And several years later, I am still impacted when I see them.

On the level of the purely physical, the entities demonstrate medical skill that is impressive, especially given the fact that Joao the man only spent two years in school as a child. I have seen several cases in which the entities have performed tonsillectomies—with the patient standing on the stage—and as always, without physical anesthesia. Both times there were medical doctors on the stage observing, and who confirmed to the rest of us that the entity had indeed snipped off the offending and infected organs.

The entities have also performed many surgeries on lipomas—large fatty tumors that are not initially cancerous but can become so or can interfere—by their sheer size—with the normal functioning of surrounding tissue or organs. I watched one such surgery done on an English woman. She had a lipoma that was a good 5 inches in length, 3 inches in width, and protruding close to an inch. This tumor was directly over her spine in the middle of her back.

The entity made a small incision—perhaps an inch at the most—over the tumor. Using a forceps, he began to pull out pieces of the tumor and stack them in a metal bowl. The entire operation took about 15 minutes, after which he stitched up the incision with a few sutures and sent the woman to rest in the infirmary.

I was standing next to an American emergency room doctor during the operation. Afterwards, she said that a medical doctor could not have done a better job of either operating or suturing, and in fact would have probably used a larger incision and left more scarring.

When the English woman passed by the entity the following week for a review of her progress, she was pronounced doing well. The entity also told her that if a regular doctor had performed her operation, she would likely have ended up paralyzed afterwards, as the tumor had already wrapped itself around her spine and the danger of injuring the spinal cord during such an operation had been great.

I have also seen the entity insert a needle into large areas of swelling on patients' bodies and extract a great deal of liquid out of the infected areas.

Frequently the entity will put into bottles tumors he has extracted so the patients can have them taken to their doctors to be tested. Always the results show that indeed the tissue is human cancer tissue, not chicken guts or something else substituted by sleight of hand. Many medical doctors have witnessed these and other surgeries from a distance of several inches, and have confirmed that there is no sleight of hand going on.

34

Recently, I was standing in the line to go before the entity, who, on that particular day, was Francisco Xavier, a very active entity who enjoys performing a lot of physical surgeries. Standing directly in front of me was an elderly Brazilian man. When it was his turn to speak to the entity, he said that he had a lot of dental problems, rotting teeth, and constant pain in his jaw.

The entity told him he would remove the old man's pain permanently. He then asked the man if he wanted to be operated on and the latter said he would. The entity called for an assistant to bring over the instrument tray that had the dental tools. As I watched, fascinated, the entity took a metal hammer-like instrument, had the patient open his mouth, and began pounding on different teeth with great vigor. Occasionally he would stop and ask the patient if he was experiencing pain, to which the patient always responded, "Thanks to God, no!"

The entity then took what appeared to be a rounded pliers-like instrument and began grabbing various teeth and manipulating them in ways that produced loud crunching sounds. I am not generally squeamish, but I have to say the sounds were quite evocative!

Next, the entity took a different instrument, again with pliers-like function, grabbed a front tooth, and suddenly pulled it out by the roots. The patient felt no pain whatsoever. Over several minutes this process was repeated until there were 5 teeth in the little bowl held by the assistant. Those that remained in the front of the patient's mouth, which had been crooked at the beginning, were now straight, and there was no space in the middle from where the initial front tooth had been pulled!

The entity paused in his work and said that when he was last in a human body (at the time of St. Ignatius of Loyala), he used to cut hair and pull teeth. He said at that time he had to give people alcohol as the only available form of anesthesia when he pulled teeth, but that now, as a spirit entity, he could simply give them spiritual anesthesia and it worked even better! He also asked the patient if he wanted to keep the rest of his teeth or have them all removed. At that point the man had very few teeth, spaced irregularly throughout the lower and upper gums. The patient said the entity may as well pull the rest of them.

The entity responded by saying that it been a long time since he had last been in a body, so he didn't know the correct name for what he was about to describe. He went on to say that if he left a few teeth in the man's mouth, the patient could have something created that would be like a new set of teeth held in place by the few old ones. What he was referring to, or course, was a dental bridge of artificial teeth. He encouraged the man to get a bridge, and said if it was a matter of money, the Casa would pay for half of the dental costs. The man said he could afford it and decided to have his remaining teeth left in place.

The whole process was quite amazing to me, and part of the amazement was the fact that shortly before arriving in Brazil on that particular journey, I'd had the thought that I wanted the opportunity to see one of the entities do dental work some day! The afternoon that I had that opportunity, when we were getting in line to see the entity, I noticed the elderly man getting behind me. I was holding a large pile of photos that I'd brought of people wanting long-distance healing and herbal prescriptions. I told the elderly man that if he wanted, he could get in front of me as he'd have a long wait if he remained behind me. And from that small action I received the chance to watch the amazing dental surgery!

In the case of the dental patient and with some other kinds of operations, what we can see with our eyes is pretty much the majority of the physical work being done by the entity. But the more I watch the visible surgeries, the more I realize that more often what we are seeing with our eyes—what is being done with the various surgical instruments—is frequently only a fraction of what is really going on in those operations.

I'll give you one example. I witnessed one operation early in my second stay in which the entity pushed the hemostat up a man's nostril. In one of the few opportunities I had to find out immediately after the surgery what the entity had been operating on, I was told that it was for the man's hernia. The hemostat operation is always mind-bending in and of itself, as I mentioned in an earlier chapter. But to find out that the physical location of the surgery was the nose, and the hernia was in the man's abdomen, forced me into yet another paradigm shift. I had wrongly assumed up to that point that the physical location of the surgery was where the corresponding problem was.

And sometimes the latter is true. I've seen the entity operate on tumors and remove them. And I think that most of the eye operations are for eye problems, although I think that sometimes they are to correct problems with a person's spiritual vision as well. But I have seen many operations in which what seemed to be the location of the problem was different than the site of the surgery—the hernia operation I mentioned above being just one example.

What to make of this? One conclusion that I have arrived at is that all of the visible operations are actually invisible operations. What I mean is that even though an incision, for example, is being performed in a way and location that we can see, the real surgery is still taking place invisibly within the body and energy system of the patient through the work of the various entities of the Casa. In fact, there have been several times when Joao has been "in entity" that the entity has told people that the physical operations are really not necessary and may some day soon be a thing of the past.

This by no means is to say that the physical operations don't work. But from what I gather, they are done primarily to raise the level of people's faith by demonstrating the paranormal qualities of such surgeries, and perhaps to convince the patient's mind that he or she is indeed being worked on. Out of the many people receiving spiritual operations during each session at the Casa, only a few—if any—receive visible operations on a given day. The majority of the work is done invisibly by the entities.

From all that I have heard and experienced at the Casa, the entities always work on the source of the problem. That source could be mental, emotional, physical or spiritual, or a combination of any of these elements, although I have been told by the volunteer staff of the Casa that the entities say that from their perspective, the source is almost always spiritual. And because the entities work on the source, true healing takes place, not just the curing of symptoms.

One of the most unusual examples of healing from a series of invisible operations was the case of a young Brazilian woman. Several years before I saw her at the Casa, she had had rheumatic fever, an illness that left her in physical pain and unable to see. After a series of treatments at the Casa, all of her maladies were gone and she could see once again. The odd thing about her vision was that, according to the tests made by her ophthalmologist, there was absolutely no functioning of her optic nerves and she should still have been blind!

When I first heard her story, the young woman was on stage and telling it to those of us in the main hall. She confirmed that she had been healed by the entities and could indeed see. A skeptic in the crowd hastily wrote a note on a piece of paper and passed it up to her as a test of her ability to see. She read it to us, and the skeptic's doubts vanished. What did the entities do to allow her to be able to see despite the lack of optic nerve function? Did they somehow rewire her brain? Or did they create an entirely new way for her to be able to perceive this world? This is one of the many mysteries of their work.

I interviewed another young woman who was 19 at the time. She told me that when she was 16, she had been diagnosed with terminal lymphatic cancer, and her doctors had told her they could do nothing more for her. A friend of the family found out about her illness and suggested to her parents that they take her to the Casa. They refused, saying that they didn't believe in that kind of thing.

So the man who was the family friend went to the Casa himself without telling the girl or her parents, passed by the entity, and begged for healing for the girl. The entity agreed to help her. That night, she went to sleep and had a dream that several glowing, luminous forms came and operated on her. When she awoke the next morning, she discovered a large mark on her back. During our interview, I asked if I could see it and she showed it to me. It looked like the kind of indentation formed when a person lies on a wrinkled sheet for a long time, but it had a specific shape. It was the outline of a large letter J with a T-cross at the top and another crossbar halfway down like in the letter F. The three initials combined in this symbol—J, T and F—are Joao's initials: Joao Teixeira da Faria. The entities had operated on the young woman and then left this mark so as to leave no doubt who was behind it. Within three months all traces of her cancer were gone, to the bafflement of her doctors.

This issue of the entities leaving marks is not unique to her case. I interviewed one Brazilian man who was a skeptic when he originally came to the Casa. When he first saw Joao "in entity," the latter touched him briefly on the forehead. After passing by the entity and going outside to meet the friend who had brought him to the Casa, his friend asked him what that was on his forehead. The man said he didn't know but that the entity had touched him there. When he went to examine himself in the mirror, he found a wine-colored mark in the shape of a star.

I once brought a photo of a friend, at his request, to the entity on one of my trips to Abadiania. The man was asking for a long-distance healing. When I returned home from that trip, I called the man to find out how he was doing. He was very excited and told me he had felt the presence of the entities very strongly on the day I took his photo to them. The next morning he was getting dressed and he noticed several wine-colored marks on his thigh that hadn't been there before. The largest of the three was in the form of a little "star man," as he called it, with several arrow-like marks next to it.

These marks and the incision scars sometimes left after *invisible* surgeries are yet more ways in which the entities show that their spirit presence and work is indeed impacting our physical bodies.

Although at its purest essence I believe that the invisible operations of the entities consist of a major transfusion of spiritual energy, light and love, they do effect the physical in a variety of tangible ways, sometimes immediately. Many people have felt invisible hands moving within their bodies rearranging things here and there during the operations. I almost vomited once during an invisible operation on my stomach, and I could feel my stomach actually being moved around as the entities worked on it.

A friend of mine received several long-distance healings from the entities before she was able to go in person to the Casa. At the time of her first long-distance invisible operation, she felt a powerful wave of love go through her that made her a bit weak in the knees, so she went to lie down. The love energy continued on for around an hour before dissipating. Within a few days of the operation, she noticed that her energy was higher, her bladder infection was gone, and her fistula had healed. A fistula is like a tunnel of scar tissue. In her case it went from the bladder into the wall of the uterus, and the seepage of urine had caused her numerous infections. Her doctor had told her the only cure was surgery. Well, she had surgery, but by invisible hands. When she was finally able to go to the Casa in person, she had an invisible operation there, which cured her problem with breakthrough bleeding—intermittent, off-cycle menstrual bleeding.

Another woman who came with one of my groups had had extremely low energy for years due to severe environmental allergies. As a result, she had undergone a tubal ligation long ago as she felt she couldn't risk another pregnancy. She came to the Casa hoping to be healed of her allergies, and was praying that if they were healed, she could have another child somehow.

Shortly before her invisible operation, she was meditating in the Casa garden when she heard within herself the voice of the entity telling her that she needed to have her tubes untied for her healing to be complete. From what she gathered from the entity's words, the tubal ligation was interfering, in her case, with the free flow of vital energy through her system. After her invisible operation, her abdominal region began to feel very tender in exactly the same area and in the same way it had felt after her tubal ligation. She was very uncomfortable throughout the night. The next day she passed by the medium and asked him if her tubes had been untied during her invisible operation. He said yes.

When she went home, she had her doctor take an x-ray and sure enough, it showed that the tubal ligation had been undone and her fallopian tubes were now connected again. By then she was also noticing that her overall energy had improved immensely. Several months later she was pregnant. Although she miscarried and during a subsequent trip to Abadiania the entities told her she needed a little bit more work to carry a pregnancy to term, this was proof that the invisible surgery had indeed accomplished what the entities had told her.

The soreness she experienced after her invisible operation is not uncommon. One participant in my group was tender all over for a good week after her operation, and she was certain that the entities were doing major work on her entire lymph system.

A man in one of my groups went into an altered state that lasted for days after his operation. He had asked for the entities to heal a chronic wrist problem, but the entities were obviously doing intense spiritual work with him as well. When he returned home, without talking first about his trip, a gifted psychic/seer friend of his asked him what had happened. He said, "What do you mean?" She told him that it looked like his wrist (from the inside) had been completely re-wired and reattached to his arm in a new way.

I have spoken to people that have been healed of pretty much every kind of cancer through the work of the entities of the Casa. There are a number of medically documented cures of AIDS as well, of HIV disappearing, and of AIDS patients who still have the HIV virus but whose level of health and quality of life improved significantly after treatment at the Casa.

As I mentioned earlier, not all of the invisible operations take place at the Casa itself. Some are performed "long distance" on people who have sent their photos to the Casa. Others are done in people's rooms at the various *pousadas* in which they stay in Abadiania. These are spontaneous operations done by these entities for whom space and time are not limitations.

I had one such operation myself. During a stay in Abadiania, I had slipped and injured my back somewhat. I was feeling irritated with myself about the whole situation, and concerned that the fall had undone whatever work the entities had already performed on my back—which had originally been injured decades earlier in a car crash. I was in some pain when I went to bed the night that I fell.

Toward morning, I dreamed that the entities were operating on my back. The intensity of the discomfort from their work finally woke me up, and indeed, my back was hurting even more than it had the night before. My first reaction was to become upset. But then, as the pain continued, I noticed I could feel various kinds of subtle movements going on inside my back. The light finally dawned, and I realized that my dream had been a reality—one that was still going on! The entities were performing another invisible operation on me, this time in my own bed. After about half an hour, the pain subsided, I fell back asleep with prayers of gratitude, and when I got up later, I felt significant improvement in my back.

Other people I have spoken with, including people I have brought to the Casa, have also experienced these invisible operations in their rooms while resting or sleeping. Some have even seen the glowing forms of the spirit doctors there in the room with them during the procedures.

In cases of cancer, the work of the entities has shown up in various ways. Sometimes after one or a succession of spiritual operations over a series of return trips to the Casa, the cancer completely disappears. Other times, a tumor may remain in the body but stops growing and is encapsulated by the entities in such a way that it does no further harm. I heard the story of one man who had come to the Casa almost at death's doorstep. He had a massive cancerous tumor growing around his spine, and the doctors had given him no hope of surviving. The entities performed their invisible surgery on the man. Within several days, people noticed a dramatic improvement in his appearance and energy. A year or more later, the doctors' x-rays show that the tumor is still there, but it is not interfering with the patient's now-excellent health.

Another cancer patient told me that the entity had informed her he would shrink her tumor over time until it was small enough that she could have a medical surgery to remove what was left of it without danger to her system. The tumor was, by the time of our conversation, already shrinking and she was awaiting the words of the entity to know when the time was right for her to have the rest of it surgically removed in a hospital.

Occasionally, people come to the Casa for the first time at the end stages of such serious illnesses that the entities cannot reverse the physical problem. When that is the case, they will often tell such patients that they are preparing to disincarnate and that they should return home to their loved ones to spend their final days on earth. In such cases, the entities are usually able to help the patients in such a way that their final days are free of pain and their transition is peaceful. Often, the entities will send these patients home with a bottle of the blessed water to be used to help facilitate whatever further spiritual healing they need in order to make a peaceful transition out of their body and into the next world.

The fact that the entities do not tell a person that they can heal them physically when they can't is a positive reflection of the integrity of these spirit doctors. And sometimes the reason they cannot intervene has to do with the person's karma—in the sense that on the soul level the patient has chosen a particular illness or injury for their growth in this lifetime.

Some people who come to the Casa do not receive operations. Instead, they are told that their healing will take place in the current, where they should spend as much of their time as possible. Should you ever go to the Casa and not receive a spiritual operation, this does not mean that your condition is hopeless or that the entities aren't helping you just as much as if you were to have an operation. It simply means that they feel you will receive the most benefit from their work with you in the current rooms.

For me, one of the many mysteries of the entities is the issue of spiritual anesthesia and the lack of blood—or the relatively small amount of it—during the physical surgeries. Spiritual anesthesia is provided by the entities for both the visible and invisible surgeries, although sometimes patients still feel some sensation during the process. Having experienced several invisible operations myself and been there first-hand for people being prepared for physical operations, I can attest to the fact that there are no trance inductions or hypnotic suggestions performed on those about to receive surgeries. In fact, many times I have seen Joao in entity pluck someone out of the crowds in the main hall, or out of the line filing by him, and suddenly begin doing a physical operation on that person. In those cases it is obvious that there is simply no time for any kind of hypnotic preparation.

After the surgeries—usually several hours later—the anesthesia wears off. Sometimes there is discomfort then, and sometimes there is none. Usually the discomfort is gone within a few days or less, although if the entities are doing ongoing work on the person, it may remain for longer than that.

One day when I was sitting in the current room in which the entity receives people and prescribes their treatment, the entity decided to do an operation on one of the men who was in line at the time. The entity asked that a cot be brought in, and had the man lie down on it on his back. Those of us sitting in the current were told that we could open our eyes and watch the process. The entity then gave a dramatic demonstration of his control of spiritual anesthesia.

He told the man to close his eyes and said that he was going to anesthetize him. Then he had a woman push firmly on different parts of the man's body and the entity asked the man to tell us where the woman was touching him. He said that he didn't know, as he couldn't feel anything. Then the entity would have the man open his eyes and the entity would somehow lift the anesthesia. The man could then move, sit up, and feel his body normally. The entity would have him lie down once again, close his eyes, would induce the spiritual anesthesia and then have the woman test the patient once more. This was repeated several times. Finally, the entity took a scalpel and made an incision on the man's chest—which the man didn't feel either—then reached into the opening with his fingers, did something invisibly, and then proceeded to suture the incision with a few stitches. Afterwards, the man assured us once again that he had felt no pain during the process.

On occasion, the entity has asked for volunteers to come up on stage and poke a needle into the medium Joao's body to prove that the medium too is invulnerable to pain while incorporated. No one has taken him up on that offer while I've been present, but it has been made several times. The entity has also said that the medium's body does not take on any illnesses from the people being worked on.

There have been several dramatic examples of this spiritual protection beyond the typical "no gloves" operations that Joao in entity performs. In one case, a patient was led onto the stage for an operation. His leg was completely covered with open ulcers, some seeming to extend a good 1/8" or more inward, and the skin was dark and discolored. I don't know if this was due to some kind of infection, leprosy, or what, but under most circumstances doctors would have amputated such a limb.

The medium incorporated the entity King Solomon—which happens rarely anymore due to the fact that that entity's energy is so powerful, it puts the medium's body under a great deal of stress. The entity first splashed some of the blessed water over the man's bare leg and began to rub it vigorously. He stated to the audience that the medium's body does not take on any infections from his patients. Then, to everyone's shock, he bent down and put his mouth directly on the man's leg and for some seconds, seemed to be actually sucking the poisons out. Afterwards, he did not spit anything out, although a bit later he did wipe his mouth with some of the blessed water and dried it with a towel.

This kind of technique in the shamanic world is known as "sucking medicine," and is considered one of the most dangerous forms of healing that shamans can undertake, due to the risk to the shamans of absorbing into their own body that which has been extracted from the patient. Most shamans I know who do this kind of work will spit and/or cough vigorously after the work, sometimes even vomiting. Joao in entity did none of the above, and, as this operation took place several years ago, the medium's body has obviously suffered no adverse effects as a result.

I was told of another equally dramatic demonstration of the healing abilities of the entities. During my first year of going to the Casa, one of the people staying at my *pousada* recounted the following event that he had witnessed.

There had been a German man with AIDS who had come to the Casa seeking healing, and he had been told by the entity to stay there for several weeks for treatment and spiritual operations. Finally, the entity told him he was healed and that he could go home. The man began to argue with the entity, telling him he felt like the AIDS was still in his body. The entity assured him that he was healed. They went back and forth over this several more times until finally the entity asked one of his assistants to bring him a surgical needle. Once he had the needle, he took the German man's arm and poked the needle into a vein until there was a drop of blood on the tip of the needle. Then the entity took the needle and plunged it into a vein of the medium's arm. He then said, "Son, if you still have AIDS, now Joao has AIDS. But you don't have AIDS. You are healed. Go home!" At that point the man finally accepted his healing.

Back to the subject of spiritual anesthesia, occasionally the entity does not use it. Once I heard him tell a woman on whom he was about to do a physical operation that she was going to feel it. It was obvious that she did. I do not know why this was done, but for some reason the entity felt that the woman needed to experience the work fully on the physical level.

I can offer you no conclusions as to the nature of the spiritual anesthesia or how the entities induce it. I can tell you it is real, as can tens of thousands of others.

Another element I continued to wonder about was why the incisions performed by the entities rarely bleed, or bleed very little compared to what would occur under "normal" circumstances. I was given my answer in a unique fashion.

One day, I was standing near the stage in the main hall when Joao in entity was performing the physical surgeries. A thought went through my mind: I wished that some time I could be on stage during the surgeries in order to witness them up close.

As I made that wish, the entity had already made an incision on a woman's belly, reached in, pulled something out, and began to suture the incision with a large surgical needle. Oddly, as he began pressing the needle into her skin to begin the suturing, the needle snapped in two and he had to wait for an assistant to run to the back room and bring him another needle. During this time, the woman's incision was being held open by a kind of clamp left by the entity on the bottom half of the incision and just dangling there. There was no blood at all. After a few minutes, the entity was given another needle and he began to poke at the incision once again after finally removing the clamp. He again seemed to be having trouble being able to puncture the skin with it. Finally, he looked out at the crowd and said, "Is there anyone here who knows how to sew?" I found my right arm shooting upward of its own volition. The entity looked at me and beckoned me on stage! My prayer of just a few minutes earlier was being answered in a most unusual way.

My heart pounding, I stepped onto the stage and approached the patient. The entity put the threaded needle in my right hand, and then guided my left hand to the woman's belly to hold the skin on either side of the incision. I felt a moment of shock. Her skin felt like cold rubber or leather, quite unlike skin normally feels. But I didn't have time to consider the reasons for this. I was now trying to push the needle through her skin in order to suture the incision. I pushed so hard that the needle began to buckle and I was afraid that yet another needle was going to break. I eased off, said a silent prayer for help, and tried again. And again. The needle would simply not puncture the skin.

During my lifetime I have removed numerous splinters, etc. from my own body and that of siblings and friends, and never had I had such a problem. Finally the entity took the needle from me and smiled, then gave it to a man who was also onstage, and asked him to try. Like myself, he too was unable to puncture the woman's skin with the needle. Finally the entity had someone carry the woman to the recovery room with no sutures at all. And her incision was still not bleeding.

As this was the last of the operations for that session, the entity left the stage and I went immediately to the current room, sat down and closed my eyes. I silently asked the entities of the Casa why none of us had been able to stitch that woman up. A voice answered within me quite clearly and said, "She didn't need any stitches. We were already healing the incision."

After the session in the current, I approached one of the assistants who had been on stage holding the instrument tray during the operations. I asked her aloud the question I'd asked silently in the current room. She smiled and answered me with the exact words I'd heard internally in response to my question in the current. In addition, she said that the man who had tried to suture the patient right after me was a surgeon and had probably performed thousands of sutures in his life. She commented that the entities probably had been demonstrating to him that there was something going on that he truly could not explain in normal medical terms.

Later, I reflected some more on the temperature and texture of the woman's skin when I touched it. Why had it felt so cold and strange? Finally, an answer came to me that I believe explained the situation. The reason that the incisions don't bleed, or bleed very little, is that the entities are somehow able to pull the circulation temporarily away from the area being worked on just before the

44

incision is made and during the work itself. This would also explain why the woman's skin was so cold to the touch.

I was invited onstage by the entity yet another time to observe a surgery. This was on the anniversary of Dom Inacio's birthday in July of 2000. Often Dom Inacio incorporates on his birthday and is very powerful. On this occasion, as I arrived on the stage after having been asked to do so by the entity Dom Inacio, the latter was preparing to perform an eye surgery. Just prior to doing so, Dom Inacio asked one of the assistants to hand him a towel which he then wrapped several times around his own head so that his eyes were completely covered. He then proceeded to do the eye operation blindfolded, to the excitement of all present! This was yet another demonstration of the power and true vision of the entities that use the medium Joao's body as an instrument of healing. They have "x-ray" vision, in the sense that they can look into a person's body/mind/spirit to diagnose his health and progress in treatment. So why shouldn't the entity be able to see what he was doing during the operation, whether the medium's eyes were covered or not?! I watched the surgery performed and it went as smoothly as always.

I want to tell you about another type of "visible" operation I have seen at the Casa. This type falls in the category of a purely spiritual operation.

The first one I saw was performed on an American man. He had been involved in shamanism for many years prior to coming to the Casa, and had been healed of a painful hernia through an invisible surgery during his first trip there. It was during his second trip to the Casa that he received a different kind of "operation."

The entity brought the man up on the stage in the main hall and had him kneel down. He then took an inch-long steel pin, and slowly pushed it through the top of the man's hand until we could see the tip causing the skin to bulge on the palm. The entity said he was doing a specific kind of work to help the man in his own spiritual life and growth. After leaving the pin in place for a minute or so, he pulled it back out. I spoke with the man afterwards and he said he had not experienced any pain during this procedure.

Then the entity asked the man to stand up on the stage. He told the man to soften his eyes and to look out over the assembled crowd to see if he could see anyone there with a yellowish cast to their aura. The man looked for a while, then pointed to a Brazilian man in the crowd and, at the entity's request, beckoned him to the stage as well.

The entity then told the American man to place his hands over the Brazilian's aura and to begin transmitting energy. He did so and after a few moments his body began to vibrate with energy. This went on for a few minutes till the entity told him he could stop.

45

Then the entity asked the Brazilian patient what kind of problem he had had and what he felt. The patient said he had injured his back in a car crash a week earlier, and that he had been in a lot of pain since that time. He said that after the American finished working on him, the pain was gone.

The second purely spiritual/physical operation I know of was one that took place while I was at the Casa, but I didn't see it in person. The details were related to me in an interview with one of the recipients afterwards, and I then was able to see it on a video that had been filmed during the procedure.

This operation was done on two American doctors who were friends, and was performed by the entity in the second current room rather than on the stage. The entity had the two doctors lie down side by side on the floor on their backs. He then took a threaded surgical needle and pushed it through the top of the hand of one of the doctors, pulling the needle and part of the thread as well through the palm, so that the end of the thread was still hanging off the back of her hand. He then pushed the needle through the hand of the other doctor, so that they were in fact sewn together, hand to hand, with a six-inch length of thread linking their palms.

The entity let them lie there for a while, and then told them that he had helped create a link between them through which he would send energy in the future for their work. He also said he "saw" that they would be working together some day, bringing spiritual energy work into the medical world.

He then cut the thread between them, sent them to the infirmary to lie down for a while, and eventually told the nurse there that she could pull the thread out of each of their hands. The doctor—one of the two women that I interviewed the next day—said that the energy during the "operation" was very powerful, and she and her friend were looking forward to seeing what the results would be in their future work.

One of the most dramatic physical operations took place over ten years ago, when Joao was 45. Prior to that event, the medium Joao had traveled to the city of Belo Horizonte one weekend, and as always when he travels, thousands of people had gathered to receive his help. While he was there, he suddenly began to feel quite ill, and was immediately taken to a nearby hospital where it was discovered that he'd had a massive stroke.

When the physicians were about to perform the usual series of tests such as brain scans, etc. with their equipment, all of their equipment mysteriously fused and burnt out. As the doctors rushed to try to repair the equipment and were preparing to take Joao for surgery, he quietly left the hospital and was taken home by his family.

The after-effects of the stroke left Joao paralyzed on one side of his body. After a while, with his typical dedication, he resumed his work at the Casa despite his condition. While he was incorporated, his body would show no signs

46

of the paralysis, but in his normal state the effects of the stroke remained. Finally, after several months, the entities intervened. When Joao went into trance one day, the entities guided his own hand to make an incision on his chest, which, as is often the case, bled very little. Then they guided his fingers into the incision, performed some invisible work, pulled out a blood clot and sutured the incision. After the surgery when Joao returned to his normal state, all signs of the paralysis were gone and have never returned.

These, then, are some of the miracles of the entities performed through the visible and invisible surgeries of the Casa de Dom Inacio.

Before ending this chapter, I want to share a few thoughts about healing in addition to those that are in Part III of this book.

The more I learn about healing, the more I see that the physical locale of a symptom is not always the same as the underlying problem or origin. The latter is often emotional or spiritual trauma that has eventually built up in the body enough that it manifests in the latter one way or another.

The entities always work on the source of the problem. The volunteer mediums of the Casa have told me this on numerous occasions. This is true of the surgeries as well as during the sessions in the current rooms. And this is the nature of true healing—as contrasted to our more Western approach of alleviating symptoms, an approach that is sometimes urgently called for but that does not always complete the process of healing. The work of healing is to find the source and deal with it—whether by removing it, resolving it, or in some ways, by loving it. Many of our problems have their root in emotional pain or trauma that has left us feeling unloved and unlovable. Therefore, at the most basic level, finding love and compassion for ourselves, for those who have hurt us, and for life with all of its challenges, is the source of healing.

But there are often many stages to this healing work. Frequently the first step is awareness, and it is often pain—spiritual, psychological and/or physical— that brings our awareness to the fact that there is a need for healing and motivates us to begin seeking it. The entities of the Casa have said that people come to the Casa *"pelo dor ou pelo amor"*: out of pain or out of love. Our pain is a messenger that tells us something is out of balance, and so in a sense, we can be grateful to this messenger. Once the messenger has arrived, there are numerous ways of going about finding the help and methodologies that will best assist us, including psychotherapies, body therapies, energy healing, etc.

The most profound form of healing, I believe, is spiritual. As many wise beings throughout the ages have found, what we really are is quite different than what we think we are. We are, at the core, spirits or beings of light that are part of the Great Spirit, and we are only temporarily in a human body, suffering from a form of temporary amnesia. We can awaken from this state and rediscover our true nature, primarily by practicing the age-old "technique" of becoming the observer of the false self and thus beginning the process of spiritual healing.

The balm of self-love and knowing the self's connection to the Source of love is the essence of spiritual healing. The negative energy-body that has been created over the years—due to forgetting who we are and thus causing all kinds of health issues—is dissipated through this love. We then can move forward, breath by breath, facing life with faith and peace in our hearts, and with bodies that reflect this peace through radiant health and vitality.

You may ask what this has to do with the work of the entities of the Casa de Dom Inacio, who perform miraculous and sometimes instantaneous healings day in and day out.

Again, they work on the source of the problems, which is spiritual. Increasingly, I sense that what the entities do in the surgeries is to infuse the patient with so much light energy that the cellular patterning is rearranged and moves toward a new and healthier equilibrium. Tumors then begin to shrink, viruses—even HIV—are overcome and transmuted, and the blind see. Love is the predominant healing energy of the Casa, and it is this energy, I believe, that is behind all of the work that is done there.

***

This chapter included many stories of miraculous healing through the visible and invisible surgeries of the entities. There are surely tens of thousands of other stories from over the past 40-plus years of Joao's work, and others will be told in the interviews later in this book. And still others occur through the power of the current at the Casa de Dom Inacio.

Chapter 5: The Healing Gifts of the Current

In my dream a current of electricity is running through me. I like it. I awaken from my dream at home, thinking about the current rooms of the Casa.

Everyone has his or her own unique experiences in the current of the Casa de Dom Inacio. I offer you my experiences and those of others simply to introduce you to its potentials in the best way I know.

Over the past few years I have spent hundreds of hours in the current rooms of the Casa. During my first few visits, I was not really aware of what a gift the current rooms are. As I mentioned in the prior chapter, I was fascinated by the visible surgeries and usually spent the first part of each session in the main hall hoping to be able to see some.

However, one day—during my second trip to Abadiania—when the entity was right in the middle of a visible operation and had already made the incision, he turned to me, gave me a powerful look, and told me to go to the current room. I did so, and while I was there I had the impression that I was to generate energy and send it to be used by the entities for the healing work they were doing onstage.

Since that time, the entity always tells me to sit in the current each time I go to Abadiania. During the following trips after the event described above, if I am lingering a lot in the main hall to watch the physical operations at the beginning of the sessions, the entity usually gives me a look as if to say, "What are you doing out here? You should be in the current!" When I take groups there, the entity usually gives me the first few days with the participants to help them get oriented, to go through the line with them their first time or two, to prepare them for any operations they might have, and to take the photos of loved ones that they have brought to the entity. But once I've accomplished all of this, the entity always tells me that now I should start spending the sessions in the current.

One of my requests to the entities early on was to ask for their help in becoming a more effective healer—and possibly medium—myself, as well as to open my other spiritual abilities further. They said that they would help me in

49

both areas, and that this would take place in the current. They also said that the majority of my own healing would occur in the current.

During the first six or seven trips to Abadiania, I found sitting in the current to be a physical challenge as well as a blessing. Part of the healing I was seeking from the entities was for my back, which had been injured in a serious car crash decades earlier and the condition exacerbated by several less serious car crashes over a ten-year period after the first one. My spine had been whiplashed during each of these crashes, and the soft tissue in my back had developed a lot of scarring as well. I had been in pain to some degree almost every day of my adult life as a result. And sitting for long periods of time was usually one of the most uncomfortable things for me to do.

At the Casa, frequently I would sit down in the current room for the morning and afternoon sessions, and within ten minutes the muscles of my back and neck would begin to complain loudly. I would pray, I would shift my body now and then, but the discomfort was a nagging thing that seemed to get worse minute by minute.

I had been told several times by the Casa staff that the kind of discomfort I was experiencing in the current was most likely due to the fact that the entities were working intensely on my back. I should try to turn my attention elsewhere while I sat in the current. Easy for them to say, I thought. When you feel like knives are plunging into your back and neck and going deeper moment by moment, hour after hour, it's not so easy to focus your attention elsewhere!

However, I noticed that by the seventh or eighth trip to Abadiania, this intensified pain in the current was no longer taking place. Instead, within ten minutes or so of sitting down, my body would enter a state of deep relaxation and I would begin to drift somewhere else for the rest of the session, a place where there was only silence and peace. This was much more pleasant than being in pain!

But this "enforced trance state" was also disconcerting in its own way. After coming to the Casa so many times, I had begun to feel I should be taking a more active role in my healing process while I was in the current. I would therefore enter the current room armed with goals: I was going to use the time to look into my past—or present—to see what I had done or was still doing that was getting in the way of my total healing. I was going to take full responsibility for my condition and get to the root of it, examine it, release it, and move forward!

With this agenda in mind, I would sit down and begin focusing on my goals. Actually, during the initial minutes of meditation, I would often receive some insights about the issues I was there to resolve, or sometimes an emotional release of one kind or another. But within a short time, I would then begin to feel like some sort of vise had clamped down on my mind that prevented it from thinking any more—about anything, even my own healing process. Then I would go into this groggy, super-relaxed state I described earlier, and would remain there for the duration.

When this started happening regularly, I became discouraged and thought I was literally falling asleep on the job. However, it was not like normal sleep, even though my head would bob up and down occasionally. It was more like I was actually being put in some kind of deep trance by the entities. They seemed to want to get my thinking processes, no matter how well-intended, out of the way entirely so that they could go about their business with me unhindered.

This is not the case for everyone. Some people will sit in the current room and receive all kinds of messages about their condition and what they need to do about it for hours on end. They'll get information about their past lives, this life, details about the source of their problems, etc. Each person is dealt with very individually by the entities.

Some of the participants in the groups I have taken to the Casa have smelled the perfume of roses in the current rooms—and sometimes in their own rooms at the nearby *pousadas*—when there were no physical flowers present or nearby. It is some kind of spiritual essence that these individuals are being allowed to perceive. One woman had a visual experience of roses in the current room. Each day she would go there and be amazed by the beauty of the pink roses that sat in numerous vases on shelves along the back wall of the second current room. On her last day at the Casa, as she passed through the current room to say good-bye to Joao "in entity," she noticed that the flowers were gone. She asked me about that afterwards, and I looked at her in astonishment. I had been in the same room every day for those two weeks and had not seen any such thing, nor were there shelves along that wall. The woman spoke to other people in our group and none of them had seen any multitude of flower vases with pink roses in them either. Those flowers were a gift just for her from the entities and/or God.

Many people experience the current as a tangible force of energy that moves them into an altered state. I felt it as a deep pulse and a kind of presence—of love, of spiritual power, something hard to define or describe—during my initial stays. Perhaps the description of the current as a force field comes closest. There have been many times when, by the end of the session in the current room, I will feel like my hands are glued to my thighs (where they have been at rest, palm up) and my feet are glued to the floor by some invisible substance. It takes considerable effort to begin to move them. And I often find it difficult to carry on normal conversation—or to even talk at all—for a good half hour after coming out of the current. My mind is still in a state of somewhat suspended animation during that period and my body feels light and almost insubstantial. My heart generally feels filled with love and my spirit with joy, even ecstasy, as if I had just emerged from a period in some divine realm whose traces are still wrapped around me.

Sometimes, however, I am unable to settle down in the current. My mind is bouncing all over the place, my is body restless; every noise in the room is a distraction, the bodies of the people on either side of me too close, the room too hot or too cold, the music too loud or not to my taste, the staff person overseeing the room talking too much or not enough, and on and on *ad nauseum*. This type of distracted state has happened to me in the past while meditating, so I am not unfamiliar with the phenomenon, nor are most people who practice meditation. During those kinds of sessions in the current I pray to God and the entities for help. And mostly I do my best to have faith in the process. Maybe I am getting close to some new level of awareness and my ego/mind is resisting. Maybe the entities are working on mc at some new depth and the work is kicking up some debris. Maybe the collective energy of all of us there that day is more chaotic. But a sense of underlying faith that all is unfolding according to plan helps me through those difficult sessions.

For people who have a practice of meditation, I recommend using it when they initially begin their sessions in the current. Meditation helps calm the endless internal chatter, allows the body to quiet, and I believe helps us to be more accessible to the work of the entities. Even a simple focus on the breath will do.

For others, using various kinds of visualizations may be helpful, something that is offered verbally by the staff in the first current room—but in Portuguese, which most foreign visitors will not be able to take advantage of. Most of these visualizations that the staff talks us through include the use of color. They suggest—usually toward the latter half of the session—to visualize yourself sending waves of cleansing purple light, first through your own body, then to your own home, your family members, friends, through all of the *pousadas* in Abadiania, through the entire current room, then through the other rooms and buildings of the Casa, and finally, through the medium Joao's body in order to help re-fortify him after his work of that session.

People can also experiment with other kinds of visualizations to help quiet the mind and to support them in their healing process, including sending various colors of light energy through their own body, seeing their body totally healed, being filled with and surrounded by white light, feeling their heart receiving love, etc.

And doing some kind of energy-gathering practice at the beginning of the session in the current can also be very helpful. I have included some such practices in my book *The Return of Spirit,* and teach them to those group participants who are interested in using them to augment their healing process at the Casa. A simple example is to take a slow in-breath while seeing yourself pulling energy from the earth up through your feet until your body is filled with this energy, then exhale and relax. Repeating this process eight or more times at the beginning of the session can give you additional energy for your healing time in the current. *Energy follows our intention and attention,* so using both for the purpose of filling yourself with reserves of power is a productive exercise. And because the Casa is located on a power place with a lot of crystalline energy in the earth below it, doing this exercise in that particular place can be extremely invigorating!

Some people also use part of their time in the current not only to pray for themselves, but also to pray for and send energy to loved ones—or to the others there at the Casa—who need healing. Often these prayers and efforts have tangible results in regards to improvement in the recipients' health, as does putting written prayers for people in the triangle in the main hall or giving photos of people to the entity. There have been studies that show that prayer is a real healing force. People in hospitals recover more quickly when others have been praying for them, whether the patients were aware of these prayers or not (which eliminates the placebo-effect theories in regards to the power of prayer). So praying from the current rooms of the Casa, where there is already so much energy supporting the work, can only do good.

It was during my second trip to Abadiania and the Casa that I first asked Joao in entity to help me be a more effective healer myself. The entity told me he would help, and said I should go sit in the current (which is often the entity's response to my various questions over the years).

That day, as I sat in the current, the entity began to communicate something to me telepathically that would help me to assist in the healing of others sitting in the current or walking through on their way to speak with the entity. I was "told" to visualize three different-colored balls of light, one to be held in my left hand, one in my right, and one placed over the crown of my head. Once I had all three energy balls in place, I was then to visualize a rainbow over the entire Casa, and to hold the entire energy/visualization through as much of the session as possible.

I responded to these instructions, and immediately felt a tangible weight in each hand and a sensation of light over my crown chakra. When I brought in the rainbow, I felt as though it was both an energy of protection for everyone there as well as a bridge between this world and the spirit world of the entities. Many Native shamans of the Americas say that it is across a rainbow that shamans travel back and forth between this world and other worlds.

Since that day I always use the triangulation of colored lights and the rainbow to "set up" my energy for the work in the current, and often use it for doing individual and group healing work elsewhere as well. It has been a powerful gift from the entities and one for which I am grateful. I also have been guided to use my energy in other ways in the current from time to time.

Sometimes as I sit in the current while the lines of people from the main hall begin to file through the current rooms on their way to see the medium, I will be "told" to do various things, such as use my hands to direct waves of cleansing energy down through the room and the people, or to send certain kinds of energy to an individual in the line, or to use my breath in specific ways. I sense that the "instructions" or directions to do these various actions come from the guidance of the entities in combination with my own intuitive guidance.

Sometimes I focus a great deal on sending energy to the medium Joao's body, particularly on days when there are a large number of people waiting to be attended to. I also send energy to those who are receiving visible and invisible operations.

There are some sessions in the current in which such an intense presence of the Divine manifests that we are all collectively transported by it. Some people begin to shake, others to weep, and I can almost hear the beating of celestial wings rushing through the room. The air itself seems to swirl with unseen beings. King Solomon and a host of saints seem to be in the room with us, and all of us sitting in the current are collectively raised up into an experience of the ecstatic. At the end of such sessions, my fellow human beings seem to be literally glowing from within for hours afterwards.

One day I had an unusual visionary experience. I was sitting next to a young woman from New Zealand, and we had both entered and sat down in the current together. Soon after closing my eyes, I entered a trance-like state and began to see a series of images of an elderly Maori native lying in a strange canoe-like shape, and—later in the vision—thousands of arms reaching up out of a sun-baked mud flat. The elder identified himself as the spirit of a Maori who had died but was not at rest, nor were the thousands of spirits reaching up out of the earth and wailing for me to help them. He said he and the others had not been properly "sung over" at their deaths, and so had not yet been fully released from this earth plane.

I told him I was very sorry to hear that and wondered how I could help him. He told me to tell the woman next to me of my vision after the session, and that she would know who to talk to about his situation when she returned to New Zealand. I said I would do so. But when the thousands of other spirits began clamoring for my help, I began to feel overwhelmed. I'd assisted "trapped" or "earthbound" spirits move on to the Light in the past, but only one at a time. The sheer numbers of these unhappy spirits unnerved me.

So I began to call on the help of the entities of the Casa, Jesus, the saints, and all of my personal spirit guides to help all of these suffering spirits. I told them I couldn't do this one on my own! I felt the help arrive—hundreds of helpful assorted entities—and very quickly all of the Maori spirits were lifted en masse from their trapped state to the next plane of their journey. I could sense and almost hear some of their own ancestors chanting in the background, welcoming them home at last.

After that session in the current ended, I told the young woman next to me what I had experienced. She asked me to describe in detail what the elder was wearing—his necklaces, markings, the strange "canoe" he was in, etc. I told her what I could remember. She said she had a bit of Maori ancestry herself, and would do what she could for his spirit when she returned to New Zealand.

When she arrived home, she contacted some Maori people she knew, and described to them my vision and its details. They confirmed that what I had seen were indeed traditional colors, markings, necklaces, etc. of the Maori people. Furthermore, they told her that after the Europeans had increasingly disrupted the traditional Maori lifestyle—as they have done almost everywhere with indigenous peoples—many Maori were not allowed proper ceremonies at the time of their deaths, including the singing of special songs. Apparently the people that my friend contacted held a special ceremony for the spirit of the Maori elder who had never been properly "sung over." Hopefully he is now at peace.

It wasn't until over a year later that the entity said something in the main hall that shed some light on why I might have had that particular vision of those spirits who seemed to have been connected with the young woman from New Zealand. The entity said that every person who comes to the Casa brings with them at least one—if not multitudes—of accompanying spirits seeking the help of the entities and their "spiritual hospital." These accompanying spirits align themselves with the individual by virtue of ancestry, energetic harmony, or even past life connections. They know they will get the help they need at the Casa that will allow them to progress on their journey. And so they follow that person there. Perhaps the young woman from New Zealand who had some Maori ancestry had been followed to the Casa by the many Maori spirits that I saw in my vision who were seeking help.

I mentioned earlier that I had asked the entity to help me become a more effective healer and medium of healing energy in one of my early visits to the Casa. I will relate some other stories of their response to this request. In the interviews recorded later in this book, you will find more examples of how the combined power of the current and the entities has helped other people develop their own spiritual and mediumistic abilities.

During my second trip to the Casa, I emerged one afternoon from a long and powerful session in the current room. I did not feel like returning to my *pousada* right away, and so I lingered at the Casa, sitting for a while just outside the main hall.

As I sat, still slightly in a trance state, one of Joao's volunteer staff rushed up to me. She asked, "Are you a medium?" I was so startled by the question that I said, "Well, I don't know. I usually don't think of myself that way." She said, "I need to find a medium," and went running off. As soon as she left, I started thinking about the many times I had indeed communed with various spirits, including helping some make their transition to the next plane. In the past I had also received advice from the spirit world on how to remove "obsessive spirits" from the living so that the latter might be healed of various afflictions, etc. "I *am* a medium!" I thought to myself. Why hadn't I just told the woman that I was? I supposed it was because I'd always thought of my work more in shamanic terminology, but by the definitions used in Brazil, this was mediumistic work.

As soon as I had that realization, the woman came back and said to me, "You are a medium. Come with me!"

I followed her indoors to the room that served both as the third current room and the one used for the invisible surgeries. The room was empty except for a young couple waiting there with a boy who appeared to be about seven years old. The woman who had led me to the room told me that well after the afternoon's sessions had ended, the couple had arrived with their son, who had some sort of neurological problem, and that they were seeking help for him. Someone had told Joao of the family's arrival, and he had asked his assistant to find a medium to transmit healing energy to the boy. The entities would be there to help.

I stood behind the boy who was seated on a bench next to his mother, and placed my hands a few inches over his head, palms down. Then two other people entered the room, stood at a slight distance from the boy and raised their hands toward him to prepare, as I was, for transmitting healing energy.

Joao's assistant began to pray to God, Jesus, and all of the entities of the Casa for healing for this boy. She invoked the entity of King Solomon very strongly. As she did, I began to feel a powerful and fiery energy surging through my body, and I identified this energy as being transmitted through me by King Solomon. It felt like flames were passing out of my hands and into the little boy, and my body was vibrating from the power. I too prayed initially, but then simply tried to stay "out of the way" so that the energy could work through me unimpeded.

After a few minutes, the boy, who up until that point had seemed unable to communicate on any level or make any kind of eye contact, suddenly turned his head around and gazed up into my eyes for a long moment. He then turned back around and I continued to send him love and the energy that King Solomon's spirit was pouring through me. I found myself placing a hand on the boy's head, then his neck, feeling like something was guiding me to do so. After a bit, the boy turned around and looked into my eyes once again, and then took my hand and brought it down to his chest, right over his heart! It was an incredible moment for me. We stayed that way for a few minutes, and then the woman from the Casa said some closing prayers of thanks and the session was over.

We all felt blessed and the parents were weeping softly and thanking us. The little boy was smiling. I smiled back and gave him a brief hug, then left the room and went back outside.

For a good 30 minutes after that session, the fiery energy continued to course through me. The power was truly awesome, and I just sat down on a bench and let it flow. It eventually subsided, bit by bit, but for a good hour more I felt like I was in a slightly out-of-body trance. I was so grateful to have been given the opportunity to serve in such a way, as well as for the chance to feel King Solomon's power first hand. It was also the beginning of a new phase of my own healing work.

Up until then, I had done various kinds of energy healing work, including Reiki and polarity therapy and some work that was more shamanic. But today was the first time that I felt that an entity with healing abilities had worked through me in this kind of mediumistic way. Since that time I have done more and more of this type of work, both at home and some at the Casa.

Several times I've been asked by the volunteer staff of the Casa to come into the third current room and transmit healing energy to someone needing the extra infusion of it. Each time I have felt honored and grateful for the opportunity.

But one event stands out above all the rest.

On that particular day in November of the year 2000, some emotional baggage from my childhood had been surfacing. At the time, a Saudi Arabian sheik was visiting the Casa for treatment and several American doctors had been enlisted by the medium the day before to assist with his healing. I had been hearing stories that morning about how powerful that had been for the doctors, and the "inner child" part of me was feeling a bit left out of all of the excitement. Yes, I confess, I had fallen into the trap of "I'm being left out" emotions that I had felt so often as a child.

This was embarrassing and annoying as I'd hoped I'd left that particular issue behind me, and it was aggravating to have it come up again so strongly. However, I also realized that this was part of my emotional healing process, so when I went into the current room in the afternoon, I began praying to be able to release that portion of my old pain.

After about 15 minutes in the current, I'd begun to feel some of that pain lifting. Suddenly, I heard a familiar voice next to me and a warm hand took mine. I opened my eyes to see Joao in entity there. I stood up, and still holding my hand, he led me out of the second current room and into the third. I felt an incredible amount of love and tenderness flow through me as I walked with the entity. I had no idea what was going on. My only sense of the situation was that the entities had felt my pain and were going to help me somehow. Once again, I was to find out how well they read my mind and how accurate their response was.

As I was led into the third current room, I saw one of the American doctors who had been asked to help with the sheik yesterday standing at the head of one of the cots. A few other people whom I didn't recognize were gathered along the side of the cot, and the entity led me to the foot of the cot. As he let go of my hand, he told me to begin to transmit energy to the man who was lying there on the cot. It was the Saudi Arabian sheik.

I didn't have time to be surprised by the way in which the longings of my "inner child" had been responded to, nor did I have time to laugh at my internal struggles of just minutes earlier. It was time to get to work, to take advantage of this opportunity to serve and to learn—which, in fact, had been the deeper essence of my longing when I'd heard the stories of the American doctors.

Like the others standing around the cot, I raised my hands over the prostrate form of the sheik, who was already in a state of spiritual anesthesia. I closed my eyes, set up my "triangle of power," and began to focus my energies on him.

I heard the voice of the entity telling the sheik's translator that he was now going to transmit energy through those of us who were standing around the cot. I began to feel the now-familiar pulse of energy flowing through my body. At first, the energy was fairly subtle, and I focused it out through my hands. I then began to pull energy up from the earth and down from the heavens and felt the pulse grow stronger. After some time, I heard the entity ask the American doctor what she was "seeing." She described seeing a knife working on the sheik's eyes. Then all was quiet for a while as we continued to send energy.

Once again, after a few minutes, the entity asked what the American doctor was seeing. She described seeing a white feather moving around. By this time, I was already feeling more energy surging through me, and my body had begun to vibrate a bit. But as soon as I heard her words, it was like a jolt of power surged through me and I felt and "saw" the presence of my many Native American spirit guides hovering above me—shamans, medicine men and women, powerful beings of light all hovering over me.

My body began to shake all over from the energy they brought with them. They were all chanting *"omitakuye oyasin* - for all my relations, for all my relations" over and over. And then, emerging through the host of Native spirits, came the entity I recognized as King Solomon. His presence was even more powerful, and he said he had come with a message that I was to communicate to the sheik. I was to tell the sheik that he was supposed to play a key role in bringing peace. King Solomon didn't say anything more specific, although I sensed that he meant peace in the Middle East.

By then, tears were streaming down my face from the intensity of the vision. I felt like I was in the midst of an energy that could potentially have a huge impact in the world, and that I was to be a messenger from the spirit world to ours. I promised I would communicate the message.

King Solomon then faded out of sight, but the Native American spirits continued to send energy through me. My right arm began to move without my conscious volition as if my hand held a needle and was stitching up something in the etheric body of the sheik. The overall trembling increased. Finally, the entity came up to me and took my hand and led me away from the cot. I opened my eyes and saw that the others had already left. The entity took me over to the sheik's translator and put my hands in his. He asked the translator what he felt and the latter said, "Her hands are freezing cold."

I was really surprised by this statement—which was true, but I hadn't noticed it until then. Usually when I do healing work, my hands get very hot. But apparently cold hands are not uncommon when people are doing healing work in deep trance states.

Then the entity led me back to the second current room to where I had been sitting earlier. I was having trouble walking as my body was still shaking so violently. Once I sat down, I thought that the trembling would calm down since the healing session on the sheik was over. But instead, it continued unabated. My hands began to fly around again as if I was operating on people—cutting, stitching, I don't know what all.

Not only that, but the entities of the Casa began speaking to me in my mind. They told me that it was my destiny to continue to weave different paths of spiritual knowledge together. In Brazil, along with attending the sessions at the Casa, I had also become very involved with another spiritual healing group since the first trip there: another mediumistic group that followed a somewhat shamanic path called Umbanda. At times I had wondered if there was any conflict energetically between the work I was doing at the Casa and with the Umbanda group, even though I was always told at the Casa that people of all paths and religions were welcome there. But I had still wondered about it from time to time. The entities were now telling me that this was part of my destiny, my path. I was grateful that that concern could now be laid to rest.

After an hour or so of all this spiritual intensity in the current, toward the end of the session I felt like I was suddenly enveloped in a huge whirlwind of energy, and my entire torso began moving in circles. This vortex of power continued for some time until gradually, I heard people speaking and knew the session was almost over.

I began slowly coming back to myself. My face was wet with a combination of sweat and tears that had been flowing off and on for the past hour. I felt completely overwhelmed. But I had a message to deliver, and after drinking some of the blessed water that was being poured for everyone, I rose unsteadily to my feet and went to find the sheik.

As soon as I was outside the building, I turned to the right and started moving toward the garden. I saw the sheik sitting on a bench with his translator, but I was so shaky I had to sit down before I could go to him. Some friends of mine came over and stayed with me for a while until I was steady enough to try again. They helped me walk over to over to where the sheik was still sitting, and

I then spoke through his translator and conveyed the message from the Native American spirits and King Solomon. Halfway through describing the experience, I began to weep again. I don't know what the sheik made of all of this, but I was finally able to finish speaking about what had transpired and that he was supposed to play a powerful role in bringing peace.

He bowed his head slightly, and then looked up at me and said, "If God gives me the strength, I will do what I can do."

I nodded, and then left and went back to my *pousada,* escorted by my two friends who helped me negotiate the ten-minute walk. For the rest of the day I was in somewhat of a daze.

A few days later the owners of my *pousada* were able to get a copy of the videotape of the healing session with the sheik. As all of us standing around the cot had had our eyes closed, I hadn't even been aware that the session had been filmed. I was amazed at what I now saw. Joao in entity had been fairly active during the entire session. He would move close behind the American doctor, and she would begin shaking wildly. Then he moved behind one of the other women standing by the cot and she almost swooned. The entity held her around the waist and moved her in slow motion circling patterns that continued even after he'd let go of her. I saw the moment when I began shaking wildly, and it was a bit strange watching myself in this state. But it was very obvious from seeing the tape that the entity—or entities—were choreographing much of what was going on energetically. Energy surged from person to person as the medium moved close to that person or touched him or her. It was truly fascinating to watch.

A few days later I left for the U.S. and home. As always, I felt I had been given more during this last stay in Abadiania then ever before, and would need time to integrate it all.

However, I think that on the day I worked on the sheik, something powerful was set in motion by the entities in my energy field, a process that did not stop when I left Brazil after that trip in the late autumn of 2000.

When I got home, I began to go through an increasingly intense period of strange physical "symptoms." A number of times daily I felt like I was on the verge of fainting, and experienced a kind of overall weakness. It wasn't an ordinary kind of weakness, as I would feel fine when I took my daily 45-minute walks, but when I was not walking the feeling would come back. I was also having problems breathing normally. I kept feeling like I couldn't get a deep breath, and this became increasingly frustrating and worrisome. Generally very healthy and energetic, I was baffled by what was happening to me day by day. I even went to a doctor to get tested for lung problems, asthma or emphysema, but all the test results came back normal.

Not only were the above challenges going on, but my sense of my overall physical body was that it was becoming insubstantial. Much of the time my body felt like a field of fiery, pulsing energy. I began to wonder if I was suddenly dying of unknown causes.

One event was particularly frightening. I was driving my car on the freeway, and suddenly the breathing problems intensified, the sense that I was going to faint increased, and I finally had to pull off to the side of the freeway. My hands were shaking and my entire body was vibrating. I was eventually able to get to my acupuncturist, who was certain it was a panic attack. This diagnosis baffled me as I had not been feeling any sense of panic till after the symptoms developed, at which point I again began wondering if I was dying.

During this entire period of some weeks, the only times I would feel free of symptoms temporarily was when I was doing healing work. I saw a number of people during this time both individually and in groups. I would conduct sessions in which I would act as a medium for the entities of the Casa, calling upon those entities to assist with the work. I had been doing an increasing amount of this kind of healing over the past year, and during this particular period the results of the work became more and more powerful.

One patient, who had had a painfully protruding vertebra for decades and was planning on taking early retirement soon as a result, had a "miraculous" healing during a group healing session with me. Her eyes were closed as I sent energy to the group. At one point she felt her chair tilt back and had the sensation that a knife had plunged into her back. She opened her eyes and saw me standing across the room and no one behind her. She closed her eyes again and the sensation increased. Throughout the next day she continued to be in pain, but the following day when she awoke, the pain was gone. And when she looked in the mirror, the lump of the protruding vertebra was also gone and has not returned since. I was certain that she had experienced an invisible operation by the entities, and this was later confirmed through x-rays that left her doctors baffled.

This same woman brought her son and daughter to a following session. Her son had a terrible cough and I spent time working on him, although the cough did not subside during the session. However, by the next day it was gone and he has not had one since, which is unusual for him as he used to suffer from allergies that made him vulnerable to frequent colds.

The daughter had a rare and large brain tumor when she arrived for the session. Out of 70,000 people with the same kind of tumor, none had ever been healed and all had died because of it. In her case, in the days following the healing session, she began to have strange spasms go through her body several times daily over a period of weeks. Her mother finally took her for an MRI to see if the tumor had grown. To the surprise of the doctors, the results showed that the tumor had split in two and that both halves had begun disintegrating. They were most excited as nothing like this had ever occurred in all of the other recorded cases of this kind of brain tumor. Over the next few months, the spasms that the young woman had experienced following the healing session began to diminish and finally disappear. Her mother is certain that the spasms were caused by an influx of energy pulsations from the entities that were slowly breaking up the tumor.

Some of the people I worked on individually experienced a decrease in physical symptoms, and one man who had been confined to a wheelchair for years began to find it easier to stand up following our sessions. Even his physical therapist noticed the improvement. Another client went into a state of deep trance during her session. I was pleased about the power of the work, intrigued that my own symptoms would temporarily abate during and right after the sessions, but baffled and concerned by the fact that the rest of the time they were as strong as ever.

After weeks of this disturbing and puzzling physical state, I returned to Brazil on Christmas day. A group of people had decided that they did not want to wait till my next scheduled journey to Brazil in March, and so we set off from Miami only three weeks after I had returned to the U.S. from my last trip!

My strange symptoms continued even after several sessions at the Casa. During the third session, while my group was sitting in the current, I got in line with a pile of about 60 photos that we all had brought of loved ones requesting healing from Joao/entities.

As I waited in line to give the photos to the entity, my body began to tremble slightly. The shaking intensified the closer I got to the entity. It was not fear, but it became so pronounced that the pile of photos slipped out of my hands and fell to the floor. Embarrassed for the disruption, I scrambled to pick them up, and then turned to the man next to me. I asked him if he would carry the photos for me and help translate a somewhat complicated question for the entity.

He kindly agreed, which was fortunate as by the time I was in front of the entity I was shaking so violently I could no longer stand, and I collapsed to kneel in front of the chair where the entity was sitting. He looked at me and said that I was shaking because of the spiritual work the entities were doing with me.

As he wrote out the prescriptions for the people in the photos, I asked if I could tell him about what had been going on with me. He smiled and said to go ahead. So I described the past few weeks of "symptoms" and he smiled again, telling me that the entities were preparing me to do powerful spiritual work, and that this preparation was the cause of my various symptoms. He said that after I took care of getting the prescriptions filled for the people in the photos, I should spend as much time as possible in the current room during the remainder of my stay. I thanked the entity for the information and help, and then left with the pile of photos and prescriptions, still feeling rather wobbly.

During the course of the next few weeks in Abadiania, some of the breathing difficulties subsided a bit, as did the feeling of weakness. I don't think I was at my best as a group leader during this trip, and felt a bit unhappy afterwards that my energies were more focused on myself than was usual. However, I felt especially blessed that one of the group members during that trip was Patti Conklin, a well-known medical intuitive and psychic with tremendous healing abilities herself. I have included an interview with her in a later section of this book, as she has had her share of "miracles" and also had some interesting perspectives on the work at the Casa.

Toward the end of that interview, Patti gave me her own sense of what was happening with my energy and the disconcerting physical symptoms. She said what she "saw" was that my overall energy was going through an increase in vibratory rate and that my heart chakra was opening more, the latter being the cause of the feeling of the pressure on my chest and of my difficulty breathing normally.

Patti's diagnosis, along with the words of the entity, assisted me in relaxing more about what was happening to me and put a positive slant on it all. The weeks prior of thinking my physical body might be dying also gave me an opportunity to face "death" once again and to do an inventory of what kind of quality of life I wanted to experience until that transition arrived, however sooner or later that might be.

After two weeks in Abadiania, my group left and I stayed on an additional week—as I often do—to spend some time just for my own work. On the Thursday of the last week there, I went to the afternoon session in the current. As soon as I sat down, I began to suddenly feel the extreme weakness that I'd felt for those weeks prior to this trip to Brazil. Over the next fifteen minutes or so, I had to keep putting my head between my legs to keep from passing out. I began praying and asking God and the entities what to do. This time I truly felt like I was dying, like all of my energy was rapidly leaving my body.

As I prayed, I suddenly had the image of the little *cachoeira*—the beautiful waterfall near the Casa that one could go to for cleansing with the permission of the entities. I thought to myself, "I have to get out of here and go to the *cachoeira* or I'm going to die." For the first time ever since coming to the Casa, I left the current before the session was over and bolted for the area where the taxis lined up just outside.

One of the drivers took me straight to the parking area near the *cachoeira*. I walked down the path and as soon as I arrived at the oasis, I tore off my clothes and clambered up the rocks to the waterfall. Earlier that morning there had been a major tropical rainstorm, and the water was coming down several times harder and colder than usual. Nonetheless, I stood under the waterfall for about fifteen minutes with the icy water beating down over my head and body until I finally felt solid again and my energy restored.

The next day was my last at the Casa for that stay. I was feeling a bit weak again and was again experiencing some breathing difficulties. So I decided to pass by the entity once more before I left, as I was still disturbed by what had happened to me in the current the prior afternoon, and was dreading returning home to possibly another extended bout of staggering around and having trouble breathing.

Once again as I approached the entity, my body began to vibrate. When I knelt in front of him, I told him briefly what had happened the day before and that the symptoms were back again full force. He just shook his head like a patient but slightly exasperated parent, and said, "We are working on you." He then told me to go sit in the current and that he would transmit some energy to me.

No sooner had I sat down in the current and closed my eyes than a burning hot wave of energy passed through the crown of my head and through my entire body. After a few minutes of this, I began to weep—not from pain, but with relief. It was obvious that the entity was following through on his promise, that he was transmitting energy, and that everything else he had told me was also true. My faith deepened yet again, I relaxed about my overall situation, and this time I knew that if I felt any more symptoms like before, that rather being frightened, I would be grateful for I would know that something positive and powerful was being done to and for me. And I was glad, because I'd already seen the results of the increase in healing energy flowing through me just prior to this trip, and was excited about the potential benefit for others from the work the entities were doing on me.

The current of the Casa de Dom Inacio is a powerful resource for personal healing, for spiritual growth and for enhancing one's own healing abilities. Over the past twenty-plus years, probably hundreds of thousands—if not more— people have sat there just as I have. Everyone's experience is unique, and we cannot compare ours with anyone else's.

For those who are blessed to be able to make the journey to the Casa, I encourage you to spend as much time as you can in the current. No matter how uncomfortable or restless or distracted you may be in any given session, have faith that you are being given an incredible opportunity by being able to simply be there. Pray for yourself and others, do what you can to quiet your mind, ask for healing and guidance, and then do your best to surrender to this Divine current and the loving work of God and the entities.

And when you return home from your journey and wish to continue your contact with the entities and their work, simply sit on a chair with your hands and legs uncrossed. You might want to place your hands resting palms up on your thighs if this is the position in which you usually sit in the current. Ask the entities to be with you. Then close your eyes, see yourself there in the current room of the Casa, and you will be there in spirit. I have done this myself on numerous occasions in order to reconnect with the energy there. It is simple, it is real, and it works

Chapter 6: The Power of the *Cachoeira*

The buildings of the Casa are located on just a small part of the land that was purchased by Joao at the edge of Abadiania. Many people are grateful for the beauty of the physical location of this healing center and for the exquisite waterfall that exists on the land —approximately a kilometer away from the area where the main hall and associated buildings exist.

During most of the year, in addition to the mango, jack fruit and avocado trees that grow in the town and on the grounds of the Casa, there is fairly lush vegetation growing on the rolling hills surrounding it. Much of the time, all is shades of green as far as the eye can see, but during some seasons the vista is dotted with purple and fuschia, yellow and orange as some of the flowering trees explode into color. And for a few months each year during the very dry season, the hills turn brown and remind me of New Mexico. I love them in all their seasons and spend an hour almost every day I'm there walking among them and filling myself with the rejuvenating energies of Nature.

Frequently I encounter herds of the beautiful white Brahma cattle that graze peacefully in the hills. They are shy and usually leap out of the way to make a large path for me to pass through as I walk. Often I am accompanied by flocks of parrots flying overhead, the ubiquitous turkey vultures spiraling in their endless search for food, the occasional toucan, hummingbird, hawks, flocks of chattering birds whose names I don't know, and even, once, a beautiful pair of bald eagles. Multicolored butterflies abound: medium-sized ones with orange stripes, tiny lavender ones that circle around me, and the occasional large, iridescent blue ones that take my breath away and that I have seen on occasion at the *cachoeira* (pronounced ca-shoo-ay-ra).

Usually, when I go to the *cachoeira*, although it is possible to take a taxi most of the way there, I prefer to walk, focusing my intention step by step with the sense of a sacred pilgrimage. As I pass the small parking area where the taxis will await the people who have gone to cleanse themselves in the pure waters, the path begins to narrow, the vegetation becomes more lush, and the murmuring sounds of the stream intensify.

About 50 feet before reaching the *cachoeira* stands a small tree at the side of the path that I was introduced to my first time by one of the volunteers of the Casa. It is the guardian tree of the area. I always stop there, whether I am alone or bringing a group, and speak to the tree, asking its permission to enter the *cachoeira*, and invoking the nature spirits of the area and the entities of the Casa for assistance, healing and protection.

Once I have paid my respects and feel the "way" has been opened, I proceed along the narrow path, down and across a wooden bridge, step over the stream onto the first of many large rocks, and arrive in a magical oasis.

The waterfall itself is at the far end of a large, circular opening in the vegetation. Trees surround the entire area, velvety moss grows along the large gray rocks that form tiered layers leading upward to the base of the ten-foot high *cachoeira*. The water moves downward from the falls, flowing between the rocks, forming a pool at the base of them and then continuing out of the area and out of sight.

For me, the feeling of being in this magical area is like being in a hushed and very sacred cathedral. But it is one constructed from trees and ferns, flowing water and rounded rocks, with a celestial blue dome peeking through the arch of vegetation above, rather than from stained-glass windows, hand-hewn stone and man-made cement vaulted ceilings. And in this natural sanctuary small birds chirp the hymns of celebration rather than being provided by an organ's grand and booming tones.

One must have the permission of the entities to come to this piece of heaven on earth. It is not just another tourist attraction, and no one is allowed to take photos there. We come to the *cachoeira* for healing, cleansing and strengthening on all levels. And men and women must go separately, whether in groups or individually. This policy of the Casa was created to make clear that the focus for being at the *cachoeira* is not romantic liaisons, and so that the element of mixed-gender bathing would not be a distraction.

The first time I went to the *cachoeira*, I sensed that it had once been a sacred place of the indigenous people who used to live in the area. Since then, each time I arrive there I usually sing some of the Native chants I know to honor these ancestor spirits as well as the spirits of Nature who dwell there—especially the various water spirits.

Then I call upon the power of God and of the sacred guides and angels of anyone present with me at the *cachoeira*—or, if I have gone there alone, my own guides only—and especially upon the healing entities of the Casa de Dom Inacio.

Then I—or we—clamber carefully up the rocks, which can be slippery, to the base of the waterfall. One by one, we step under its powerful cascade and begin our cleansing.

During the first few moments, the cool temperature of the water—often in contrast to the typically warm daytime temperatures in this part of Brazil—is a bit of a shock. But for me and for most people, the sensation of cold quickly is transformed into a feeling of pure energy. I often feel like I have been suddenly transported into another world as I stand under the rushing waters, cocooned within a sweet and energizing force field and embraced by the eternal Mother of life.

I have frequently wept there—in bliss, or as a release of ancient grief or sorrow locked within me until that moment—mingling my tears with the sparkling drops of water racing over me. And sometimes I have laughed with pure, childlike delight. The pounding of the water on my back and shoulders is better than any Jacuzzi for releasing muscle tension, and I will adjust my position to make sure the water hits just the right spots!

After stepping out of the waterfall, I wait—either alone, or for the group participants to finish taking their turn—and then see if I feel in need of further cleansing. If so, I will re-enter the *cachoeira* as many times as it takes until I feel I have completed what I am there for that day. There is no rushing the process in this timeless place of beauty, and each person is welcome to spend as much time and as many immersions in the water as she feels is necessary to do.

Toward the end of the last chapter, I described how I felt like my life was saved by the power of the *cachoeira*. In a relatively brief period of time, the sensation of energy leaking out of me was reversed and I felt restored.

Each person who goes to the sacred waters has his or her own personal experience. When I take groups of women there, by the end of our "session" everyone looks radiant, almost translucent, like goddesses emerging from a sacred baptism—which indeed it is. Like myself, many weep, laugh, or are taken into a deep sense of peace. Many report experiencing a profound sense of healing as well as a long-lost reconnection to the spirit of Nature.

I believe that in addition to the work of the entities and each person's intention to release any disruptive energies from their being at the *cachoeira*, this reconnection to Nature is profoundly healing in and of itself. Most of the people I bring to Abadiania live in cities, lead hectic lives, and rarely take the time to go out into the countryside and simply be in Nature. The lack of doing so creates an energetic imbalance in our lives. Our eyes need to be able to look out—unobstructed by man-made buildings—into vast expanses of forest or desert or mountains, out into endless blue skies or lakes and oceans. Our skin and hair need to feel the wind caressing them, blowing upon them. Our noses need to be able to smell scents other than car exhaust or the ever-more-powerful colognes manufactured for men and women alike. We need the more delicate perfumes of rain-drenched earth, green and growing things, even the healthy aromas of fresh animal dung.

And our spirit needs to feel its connection to the non-human spirits of our fellow inhabitants here on earth. We city-dwellers can begin to think that our only company in this life is human. We can easily forget how tied we are to the cycles of the moon, the passage of the seasons, the stones, plants and animals here with us, the gifts of water and soil, the sun and stars above us.

Over the years, I have taken many groups on wilderness vision quest retreats for the very reasons above. When we forget our interconnectedness with the web of life, with the totality of creation, we become unbalanced as individuals and then as a collective. We then feel isolated, separate from Nature, and as a result we begin to mistreat the very resources that sustain us. We pollute the air, the water, and the soil without a thought to the consequences to our own lives, to future generations, and to the rest of the web of life here on earth.

I have written at length about the importance of our spiritual connection to Nature—and how to deepen it—in my books *The Return of Spirit* and *A Season of Eagles*. The first book includes a variety of spiritual exercises you can do to that effect, including the option of going on a vision quest in nature.

Making the journey to Abadiania is not exactly the same as going on one of my wilderness quest retreats. Rather than camp, we stay in simple but comfortable *pousadas* where our meals are served to us. But the fact that the town is small, slow-paced, and that you can be out roaming the hills within minutes from whatever *pousada* in which you are lodging provides a wonderful opportunity to reconnect with nature. You can watch the beautiful sunsets, the frequent and glorious rainbows, the rising of the moon and the shooting stars, the curtain of mist that hangs over the valley most mornings. You can go on long walks in the hills and collect beautiful chunks of quartz, little crystals, and other multicolored rocks that are strewn on the earth in abundance.

And you can go to the jewel-like oasis of the *cachoeira*.

Before concluding this chapter, I'd like to share one more story about the powerful effects of the *cachoeira*. A friend of mine who had been to Abadiania several times felt particularly drawn to go often to the *cachoeira* during one of her stays. I was in Abadiania during her visit, and she told me that within a several-day period she went to the waterfall four times. Each time she went, she felt that she received powerful teachings and healing. She also felt highly charged with energy by the end of the fourth time at the falls.

After this last visit to the *cachoeira*, she was at her *pousada* and dinner was announced. As always, she took her plate, filled it with food from the buffet-style table, and sat down to enjoy her meal. Just before she reached for her first forkful of food, she—and the others at her table—heard a loud, cracking sound coming from nearby. The source of this sound was my friend's dinner plate. It had shattered into pieces in a very explosive way as it sat there on the table in front of her!

Everyone at the table was stunned. First of all, the plate was one of the thick, ceramic restaurant-style ones. It was not freezing cold before my friend heaped her food on it, nor was the food any hotter than usual, so the temperature differences between food and plate did not account for the latter exploding. Besides, usually if a plate cracks because of temperature differences, it simply cracks. It generally does not explode with a booming sound and send fragments flying off at a distance.

My friend's conclusion was that she was so highly charged from her multiple sessions at the *cachoeira* that this energy is what caused the somewhat paranormal event. A few days later she passed by the entity in order to ask his opinion about the event. He just shrugged nonchalantly and said, "Oh, it was just energy."

I do believe that the *cachoeira* itself is one of those unusual power places, one that the entities of the Casa use to help people in their healing process. Our planet Earth has many power places, each with their own unique configurations of energy, and many of these places can be tapped into for a variety of spiritual and healing purposes. I will always be grateful for the many experiences and healing I have had at the lovely *cachoeira*, a true power place on the land of the Casa de Dom Inacio.

Chapter 7: Joao Teixeira da Faria

It has been extremely difficult to gather much information about Joao's personal history. He keeps his personal life very private and shares little about it in interviews. Robert Pellegrino-Estrich has done a nice job of summarizing what he was able to learn about Joao's life in the fourth chapter of his book *The Miracle Man*, the only other book written to date in English about Joao's work.

I will offer a brief review of what I do know. Joao was born in 1942 in a small town in the interior of Brazil in the state of Goias. His father was a tailor, and Joao's family—devout Catholics—suffered tremendous hardships economically, as have many Brazilians then and since.

As a child, Joao demonstrated a developing psychic and clairvoyant ability, as well as a very independent and rebellious spirit that managed to get him expelled from several schools. He only managed to receive two years total of elementary school education. This may have been a kind of blessing. The fact that his head wasn't filled with a lot of intellectual information about "how the world works" may have allowed him to be much more accessible to the spirit world in his later life as a medium.

Not only did young Joao get expelled from school, but once he started trying to find jobs, he was frequently fired in rather short order, again, due to his temperament.

After he experienced his visionary encounter by the river with the spirit of Saint Rita of Cassia—the glowing woman—and his first mediumistic incorporation at the nearby spiritual center, he stayed at that center for several months. He received some Spiritist training there, becoming more familiar with concepts about the spirit world as well as reincarnation, and he continued to do his healing work.

Joao then began to travel throughout Brazil, occasionally gaining brief employment but primarily doing his healing work. This work was done under great duress. Frequently, as soon as the news about his miraculous healings would circulate around a city or town, some disgruntled doctor, priest or other authority would fabricate a reason to have Joao arrested, and then he would be forced to move on once again. Accusations against him of practicing medicine without a license or practicing witchcraft arose frequently.

During this period of wandering, he encountered Ze Arrigo, the man who was the subject of the book *Surgeon of the Rusty Knife*. Joao and Arrigo had a lot in common, and the older man in a sense took him under his wing for a while. Arrigo was by then functioning as a trance medium healer himself, incorporating the now-famous entity "Dr. Fritz."

Like Joao, Arrigo lived in humble circumstances throughout his life and was also basically uneducated. For twelve years before he began working as an active medium, Dr. Fritz's spirit had pursued him relentlessly, insisting that Arrigo become a medium of healing. For those twelve years, Arrigo resisted the call, appealing to psychiatrists to cure him of what he worried might be insanity, and to priests to help exorcise what he thought might be some malicious demon haunting him. Nothing worked, and he suffered severe headaches and mental anguish over his situation.

Finally, in 1947, he surrendered and began to work as a medium for the entity Dr. Fritz, and his headaches disappeared. Dr. Fritz revealed himself to be the spirit of a surgeon in the German army who died in World War I and who wanted to continue serving humanity from the spirit world.

While incorporated, Arrigo would perform unusual physical operations like Joao's—also without physical anesthesia. He would often prescribe strange medicines that the pharmacists, when called upon to fill them, would scratch their heads about. Many of the medicines had not been used since World War I! And some of the combinations of them seemed most bizarre, even though they worked well for "Dr. Fritz's" patients. However, when other medical doctors would try to use these same prescriptions on their own patients for treatment of the same maladies, they had no effect.

I would imagine that it was comforting to both Arrigo and the young medium Joao to know each other, for both, in similar ways, had been set apart from "normal" life at the direction and insistence of the spirit world.

Eventually in his travels, Joao gravitated north to the state of Bahia, known still today for its high percentage of people of African heritage. Among their Umbanda and other Macumba temples and gatherings, he was able to do his mediumistic work with less interference, since the practitioners of those paths already did trance medium healing and Joao's activities did not attract so much attention there.

After eight years of being a wanderer within his own country, Joao was able to experience some relief from the endless persecutions and material insecurity under the unusual embrace of the military. He worked as a tailor for military staff for nine years, continuing his healing work for the military personnel and experiencing a rare period of protection and worldly comfort.

Eventually, however, the entities pushed him out of this oddly feathered nest and back into the world of the underprivileged. It was at that time that his spiritual advisor and famous medium Chico Xavier guided him to begin his work in Abadiania. Shortly thereafter, the Casa de Dom Inacio was established, and the suffering masses began to arrive from all over Brazil to seek healing. After the death of Ze Arrigo in 1971, the needs of the ill and impoverished Brazilians increased, and for years Joao would see over a thousand people daily at the Casa. And when he would on occasion travel to other cities in Brazil for a few days, he would often see 20,000 or more people within a three-day period, and still does even today.

The persecutions have not completely stopped over the years. Although Joao has not been beaten nor thrown in jail in some time, in the first half of the year 2000, Joao and the Casa were once again threatened.

I was there at the Casa when this occurred. On that morning, I noticed a group of very serious-looking people standing just outside the main hall. The session began quite late and there were no physical surgeries. People were moved very quickly past the entity and the session was a short one.

The afternoon session was similar, and I saw Joao afterwards and became rather concerned. I had never seen him look like that before. He appeared so pale and drawn I began to wonder if he was seriously ill. By the time I got back to my *pousada*, I asked the owner if she knew what was going on.

She responded by telling me a disturbing story. Apparently there was a fairly well known Brazilian priest who was on his own personal mission: to try to shut down any kind of spiritual healers and healing centers in Brazil. Joao was the current focus of his attacks, and the news that the priest was sending a bunch of officials to the Casa had apparently been known to Joao for several weeks. The week before, I had seen some military and police officers at the Casa, but had assumed they were there for healing. But in fact, they were friends of Joao who had rallied to come protect him and the Casa should the priest's "investigators" show up.

The timing of Joao's allies was off by a week. The following week, assuming that the "storm" had blown over, none of them were present. And then the priest's committee arrived, intent on immediately shutting down the Casa. They moved ruthlessly through the soup kitchen, inspecting for any possible hygienic infringements—and finding none—then on to the area where the herbs were sold, and finally through the main hall and the current rooms of the Casa itself.

They were unable to find anything illegal or substandard in their searches, although apparently they insisted that the method of distribution of herbs be changed—which it has been since then. No one knew if these people would be

73

back again the next day or on some future day to try once again, but for now the Casa was still functioning.

Joao had not wanted the hundreds of people gathered for healing that day to worry about what was going on, and so the whole situation had been kept under wraps. I only found out because I was so worried and because the owner of the *pousada* trusted me not to spread the word until after everything was resolved and more secure. However, I did gather everyone who was staying at the *pousada* that night for a special prayer for the medium Joao and the Casa, and just asked everyone to send Joao energy and prayers for protection.

I personally was angry and worried. Why was it that a priest could not make space in his heart and mind for the possibility that God has used individuals as powerful vessels of healing throughout the history of humankind? Why was he so threatened by this display of God's love?

I knew the answers but it took me a while to calm down and to remind myself that as long as God and the entities wanted the Casa to continue functioning, it would.

Few of us can imagine the kind of dedication to a mission that Joao has taken on in his lifetime. Not only has he faced ongoing persecution and attacks, but in many ways his life and much of his time is at the command of the entities. The difficulty in having any kind of personal life is staggering, although Joao has been married and has children. But even on the days when he isn't holding sessions at the Casa, there is often administrative work for Joao to oversee there, or he will set aside time to spend with the volunteer staff who serve at the Casa with so much love, or he'll need to deal with the many other endless details of keeping the Casa functioning in the way it needs to. And Joao still occasionally travels to other parts of Brazil to heal, leaving after the Friday sessions are over and returning in time for the Wednesday morning session to begin, after treating thousands of people per day in a faraway city during his weekend.

Even harder to imagine than not having much of a personal life is a life in which the person simply isn't there a good half of the time or more. As I just mentioned, not only does Joao spend much of three days a week incorporated by the entities, but he sometimes does healing sessions throughout the weekends in other locations. And the latter pattern was much more true in the past during the earlier days of the Casa. Not only did he travel more during that time, but the numbers of people he attended at the Casa were often over a thousand per day, which necessitated him working from early morning into the evening hours.

I have often seen Joao after the morning or afternoon sessions at the Casa, and it appears to me that he still has one foot in the spirit world for some time after the sessions end. I don't think there is always a sudden transition for him from being incorporated back into normal consciousness.

A man who has known Joao for many years told me that even on the days Joao isn't working at the Casa, sometimes he is taken over by the entities for reasons of charity. Once, according to the story, Joao was on a walk in the city in which he lives. The entities suddenly took over, incorporated in the medium, and had him remove his watch and give it to a man who was half-starved, so that the latter could sell it and buy himself some food. When Joao returned to his normal consciousness, the man was thanking him for the watch.

I sometimes really wonder what it is like to have this kind of discontinuity of "linear" time and experience going on regularly. The closest I can imagine is going to sleep in one location and waking up hours later in another, over and over again.

Despite the fact that most of the powerful work that is done through Joao's body is the work of the healing entities of the Casa de Dom Inacio, I have learned over time that Joao the person is also a man of his own paranormal powers. As I mentioned earlier, he was gifted as a psychic and clairvoyant as a child, and those gifts have undoubtedly stayed with him. However, in his work in Abadiania, he also uses other paranormal abilities. In my most recent trip to the Casa in August of 2001, I received a first-hand account of a demonstration of these abilities and personally witnessed some of the aftermath.

August is a warm, dry month and the daily breezes swirled the red dust of the iron-rich earth throughout the town of Abadiania during the month I spent there that time. There were many people attending the sessions at the Casa, including several groups of Americans that I brought during that month. In addition, there was a visiting French healer and his wife who were staying for an extended visit. This healer had received permission from both Joao and the entities to do healing work on those people in treatment at the Casa who requested it.

Some people spoke highly of the Frenchman's work, while others were ambivalent. One of the healer's claims was that he was removing or exorcising negative entities—obsessive spirits—from people.

One morning, word of these claims had gotten back to both Joao and the entities, both of whom felt that the Frenchman did not really have the ability to do this kind of work and that he was deluding himself and others in making this claim. So Joao decided to give the Frenchman the opportunity to prove or disprove his claim.

Joao called together about half a dozen people plus the French couple to come to his own private cottage on the Casa grounds. He told the Frenchman that he liked him and respected his work. Joao simply felt that the Frenchman needed to be clear what he actually was and wasn't capable of doing.

Joao then told the group of people that he consistently—through exerting his own spiritual power and with God's help—was able to keep closed a particular spiritual portal that existed above the Casa and surrounding area. If left open, this portal would allow all kinds of negative entities to attack and create problems for those coming to the Casa seeking healing. Joao kept it closed for the protection of all those "under his wing."

But on this day, Joao said, if God permitted him to do so, for purposes of a demonstration for the French healer, he was going to open the portal and let into his cottage some negative spirits. He would then ask one of those spirits to choose someone from the group to temporarily attach itself to, and then would give the Frenchman the opportunity to rid that person of the negative spirits.

Joao then made a gesture with his hand, said a few words, and spiritually opened the portal. Once it was opened, he commanded that one of the spirits choose someone there to attach itself to. Immediately Carlos, one of the Brazilians present who volunteers at the Casa and who generally has a mild, sweet disposition, turned into a raving lunatic. He began throwing furniture around, including Joao's television which shattered on impact, tore off some of his own clothing, and seemed to be propelled around the room, crashing into objects and creating total chaos!

In the midst of this, Joao told the French healer to give it his best shot, to do whatever he did to exorcise negative spirits. The Frenchman began praying and using some personal healing tools to try to clear the "demon" from Carlos. After a few minutes, there had been no result whatsoever. More furniture was being thrown and Joao's cottage was being thoroughly decimated. The other people there began begging Joao to close the portal, shocked at the violence they were witnessing.

But Joao said he wanted to give the Frenchman a bit more time, and allowed things to continue for a few more minutes. Finally he told the Frenchman that his prayers and his work were having no impact, and that the latter simply didn't have the capability or the power to do what he had been claiming he could do.

Joao then put his hand on Carlos' head, said a few words, and immediately the negative spirit departed Carlos' body and all was still. Carlos regained awareness, looked around, and had no idea what had just transpired. He had absolutely no memory of what he had done while "possessed" by the negative entity, and was in a state of shock. For the rest of the day and into the following week, he was dazed and having trouble with his concentration. His body was bruised from head to toe and he was limping and in pain for a few days following this demonstration. He also had numerous cuts and scrapes as a result of the violent spirit possession. The rest of the group participants—including the Frenchman—were shaken and deeply impressed by what they had witnessed, and following the session, the Frenchman stopped his claims that he was removing negative spirits from people as part of his healing work.

Joao rarely offers demonstrations of his personal power. He maintains a humble attitude about the healing work that takes place through him year in and year out, now spanning more than four decades, and reiterates over and over that he has never healed anyone, that it is God who heals. Nonetheless, Joao the man is uniquely gifted, and all who come to know him have respect for his personal gifts as well as for his powerful mediumship.

For myself, I thank him for his dedication, honor him as a fellow human being, and frequently send him energy so that his body can continue to sustain the demands of the intense work he does in service to those in need.

And now, I want to introduce you to some of the other people who have experienced the miraculous benefits of Joao's mission and of the entities of the Casa de Dom Inacio.

Josie RavenWing

Part Two: Stories of the Miraculous

*"**Love is who God is and who you are, as well.** The seed of everything you need is already within you. If you would receive a miracle, be still and receive the manifestations of love. The fact is, you take most miracles for granted. Life is full of them and never without them. **Love is the source of all miracles—it invokes their presence.**"*

Glenda Green, *Love Without End*

Josie RavenWing

Chapter 8: Interviews with the *Filhos* (Sons and Daughters) of the Casa

I conducted these interviews while in Abadiania. The people I interviewed are all profoundly involved in the work at the Casa, many of them volunteering their time there on a daily basis three days a week. Most of them endured serious health challenges before first going to the Casa, including illness, injury, and drug addiction, and all have had powerful physical and/or spiritual healing through the blessings of the entities.

Leonora

Leonora is a lovely woman with long blond hair who divides her time between her volunteer work in the infirmary of the Casa and running the small pousada with her husband Charlie, who also works at the Casa. Many people comment that she looks and moves like an angel, yet I have found that in addition to her angelic appearance, she is very down-to-earth and has a wonderful sense of humor. Here is her story.

"I came to the Casa the first time in 1994. A woman friend of mine already knew of the Casa and invited me to join her on a trip there, knowing that I had already been seeking medical attention for some time for a serious skin problem. The word got around about the upcoming journey, and a whole group of us ended up going together by bus. None of us really knew much about the Casa.

"When we arrived here in Abadiania, we stayed at a very old hotel that was totally filthy and disorganized, the food wasn't so great, and we were nine people in each room. This was pretty typical at that time.

"Once we showered and got relatively settled in, we went over to the Casa for the first time. In those days it wasn't like it is now. Things were fairly disorganized, there weren't the big covered areas to wait in, and there were about 1,500 people there that day. We were told to get the 'first time' tickets, so we did, not really knowing what they were for. Fortunately, there were about 15 people in our group who had spiritual background—mostly in Spiritism—

including myself, and this background later helped us have some kind of comprehension of the kind of work that was taking place at the Casa.

"As the session opened, Sebatiao—or Tiao—as he does to this day, gave the opening orientation and explanations. The difference was that at the time there was no stage. He had to clamber up on this little wood platform so he could be seen by the people in the main hall and those overflowing another sixty feet out to where the bathrooms are located. He explained about the remedies and the lines (first time, second time, etc.) and the surgeries, as he still does.

"It was extremely hot as the long line of people scheduled to have operations that morning waited to enter the room in which they would receive them. Finally Joao came out, incorporated, and, as there was no stage, he was just standing on the floor of the main hall like the rest of us, with those closest crowded around him waiting to see the physical operations on the four people Joao had brought out with him. Fortunately, a few other people from our group and I were right there in front.

"Joao performed the operations, including one with the hemostat up the nose. The one that impressed me the most that day was done on a woman. It was different than the others in that the medium did not touch her physically. He simply passed his hands outside her body a few times. Then he lifted up the woman's shirt, and there was a scar from the invisible surgery that had just transpired! This was really overwhelming for me and opened me up a lot. Witnessing that 'surgery' made me realize that while Joao's body was indeed incorporated by one entity, there was an entire team of other entities hovering around, some of whom had operated invisibly on that woman with an invisible instrument, some who were assisting in other ways.

"After the operations, the entity looked at the woman who had originally invited me to the Casa and said to her, 'You go to my current.' Well, when I heard that I got really upset and thought that my friend was being sent away as some kind of punishment, that she'd done something wrong. I rose to her 'defense' and told the entity, 'No, no, she can't leave!' The entity wouldn't even look at me, and my friend just acquiesced to the entity's direction and went into the current room.

"When my line eventually got to the current room, I saw my friend sitting there in meditation and started to calm down. Again, the day was extremely hot, there were so many people - many of whom were seriously ill - and the whole situation was very challenging. Anyway, as I finally passed through the first current room, I saw all of the mediums sitting on the benches there, but I really didn't understand the purpose of the first current room in the way that it's explained to us now. I just figured that the people were there for meditation.

"But one thing I do want to say is that despite the crowded conditions and all, in the main hall and on into the first current room, I experienced a tangible presence, especially in my heart, and I was very clear that it was the presence of God. I didn't connect that energy as specifically coming through Joao, but more that it was due to the presence of so many people coming to the Casa with their faith in God that helped inspire this powerful love of God that was there for each and every one of us.

"When I reached the second current room and got closer to the entity, I became very emotional, filled with feelings of joy and hope and tears and inspiration. I got to the entity and he didn't look up or take my hand as he had done with others, but just wrote out a prescription and words for me to return for a cleansing, a work on my skin condition. So I moved on to the third room where the cots are, and I sat down to receive the energy.

"The second day, I returned and was told to sit in the current. I ended up sitting only a few feet away from the entity. I could hear what was being said as people passed by the entity. I heard one woman ask the entity to work on her teeth. Moments later, we began to hear all of this pounding, as if with a hammer. The man sitting next to me finally opened his eyes to see what was going on, and he then turned and said to me, 'Oh my God, Joao has this hammer and he's pounding away on this woman's teeth. This is terrible!' I told him to be quiet, but he couldn't contain himself. I then opened my eyes and looked too, and the entity was staring at both of us but didn't say anything. The woman he was working on wasn't screaming or anything, despite this seemingly brutal work. Finally, the entity asked the woman, 'How does this feel now?' She ran her tongue over her teeth and said, 'No, it's not quite right yet,' so the entity went back to more banging and hammering with his instrument. It sounded like someone pounding nails into a wall! The man next to me had continued to exclaim to me during the process, 'How can this be?! She doesn't have any anesthesia but she doesn't seem to be in pain. What's going on?!' After a while, the entity again asked the woman how her teeth felt, and she said, 'Oh, it's good now!'

"The entity then had the woman talk to everyone in the room. She said that her teeth had been crooked for years. Her dentist had put braces on them four years ago but they still hadn't straightened out. The woman had been coming to the Casa for about two years for a variety of things, and this time she'd wanted the entity to really focus on straightening out her teeth. That's what he'd been doing. And now she could feel that her teeth were completely straight and she said that she'd felt absolutely no pain during the process. It was really amazing.

"When I went home, I began taking the herbal remedy—at that time it was in tea form —that the entity had prescribed for me, and over the weeks I noticed several effects. I felt like the herbs and the entities were working on my emotional body and were helping bring my own power and potential up to the forefront, so that when I spoke to people about the Casa, I was able to transmit some kind of energy from my heart. It was beauty and power, not only from my own being, but also some of the energy that I'd experienced at the Casa.

"Prior to going to the Casa the first time, I'd been on strong medication for some time for my skin condition. I felt that even though at the time I was still taking the medication, the tea was cleansing some of the negative effects from it out of my system.

"So a few months later, I went a second time with the group so that I could receive the cleansing 'surgery' that the entity had told me to come back for. By then I felt a bit more comfortable and familiar with the Casa. I wasn't quite sure, however, what to focus on when I went for my operation, but I decided I should focus on the illness that was causing my skin problems.

"To give you some background, four years before I first came to the Casa, I'd discovered a little lump on the back of my foot. I went to my doctor who operated on it and took it out, at which time they discovered the nature of my illness.

"So when I went for my operation at the Casa, I decided to put my right hand on the back of my foot, since that was the place of origin of the discovery of the illness that I had. After my operation, I went to the soup area. I was feeling a very strong desire to help out in some way as I'd been given so much energy. So even though I had just had my operation and really wasn't supposed to exert myself, I just thought, 'Well, I've been operated on, and that's really great, and now I want to do something.' It turned out that exerting myself trying to help out in the soup area wasn't such a great idea, because pretty soon I began to feel really unwell, got very cold, and broke out in a sweat.

"One of my friends happened to see me and told me, 'You're not supposed to be doing this. You were just operated on. Go back to the hotel and rest!' I hadn't really realized up to that moment that it was important for me to do that, so I went back to the hotel and undressed so I could take a shower before lying down to rest. Once I undressed, I happened to look down at the area on the back of my foot where I'd placed my hand during my operation. To my amazement, there was a large rectangular area extending up the back of my leg, about two inches wide and four inches long. It was completely red, and it really stood out because the rest of my skin is was very white. I yelped, 'Oh my gosh, that's from my operation!'

"So then I had to go show a bunch of other people, because I was so excited and also because I knew some of the people there at my hotel still didn't quite believe in the invisible operations. They were all very excited too. Finally, I went to bed—it was late morning—and completely crashed into sleep until about six in the evening.

"I'll tell you another story about that trip too. There was a woman in our group who was very overweight—she weighed about 275 pounds—and she had diabetes. She had a lot of other medical problems too: she'd been operated on many times for a heart condition, had had numerous liposuction procedures and then problems afterward with the incisions not healing due to the diabetes. So this woman went by the entity the next day. He asked her if he could operate on her. He told her she had received an earlier medical operation that hadn't been entirely successful, and that he wanted to complete it successfully. So the woman told him yes. Then the entity asked her if he could make an incision as part of the operation. She told him she'd had problems with prior incisions and that her skin didn't heal back together normally. The entity told her not to worry about that, that he'd take care of it, and asked again for her permission to operate. She said yes, on the condition that she would be able to leave the operation walking on her own two feet. She was so heavy that she was worried that if she collapsed, it would be too difficult for anyone to carry her to the infirmary.

"The entity agreed to her condition and began the operation. He made an incision that was about ten inches long on her lower abdomen, then reached in, moved his hand around, removed a few things, then closed the incision with only nine stitches. The woman was a little lightheaded after the operation, but didn't collapse and was able to walk out of the room with someone on either side of her, supporting her.

"She then went back to the hotel, where she told everyone about her experience. She showed them her incision, and it was incredible because the incision was already dry and the skin was already beginning to knit together. Not only that, but when this woman left the entity, she said she felt as if she had stepped onto a magic carpet and was floating out of there as light as a feather. She said it was as if the entity had temporarily taken all of her weight off of her.

"Before our group left for our homes in Vitoria in the south of Brazil, the entity asked to speak with us and said he'd like our help. Apparently Joao was planning on doing several days of healing sessions in Vitoria beginning that weekend, and the entity wanted to know if we would be willing to help assist people when he arrived. We agreed to help.

"So we had arrived at the Casa on a Wednesday, we left Thursday after the sessions and got home on Friday. Joao arrived and treated people there Sunday, Monday and Tuesday. He/the entities treated 20,000 people over those three days!

"The way we set it up was in a big covered pavilion, and Joao sat on a chair on a small stage to receive people for treatment. People were lined up all around the block waiting for their turn. I was still very new to the work of the Casa and was still in treatment myself for the problem on my foot, and my foot was still pretty sore before that weekend. But during those days of sessions in Vitoria, I felt no pain at all, even thought we were working from six in the morning until

10 at night and I was helping people—sometimes half carrying them—to get up and down from the stage.

"On the last day the police came and stopped the work, although they didn't officially arrest Joao or take him away. As usual they cited the problem as being practicing medicine without a license. They did give him time to negotiate a solution, but before that happened it was very upsetting to all of the people who were still waiting there for treatment. I suggested to everyone that they all pray that the situation be resolved in a positive matter, which we then all did.

"What ended up happening was amazing to me. The city official who ended up signing the papers that allowed Joao to finish the day's work was my uncle! And he hadn't even known that I was involved with any of this, nor did he know that I was there that day. So when I heard his name announced over the loudspeaker and that everyone was thanking him for his help, I was quite overwhelmed and very grateful that it was someone from my own family that was responsible for this wonderful turning point!

"After that, everything continued on smoothly and we finished the day of treatment.

"The next morning I returned to the pavilion to look for the things I'd loaned to make things nice for the sessions. When I arrived, I saw that on the floor of the pavilion were a lot of papers. Most were prescriptions for the herbal remedies that people had dropped because either they didn't understand that they were supposed to take them to the 'pharmacy' area where they could pick up their herbs, or they didn't understand the value of taking the herbs so they just didn't get them.

"I felt kind of sad that none of those people had gotten their remedies, because I already knew how powerful they could be. I started asking some of the other people around to help me pick up the prescriptions. Then I saw this older man looking at all of the papers on the ground. I asked him if I could help him, if he had lost something.

"'No,' he said, 'I came here yesterday with my daughter who hasn't been able to speak for years and who has a great deal of trouble sleeping at night. She took some of the remedies last night and slept well, and when she got up this morning she spoke—with some difficulty—but she spoke for the first time in years! She asked me if I would come back here and get more of the remedies for her.'

"The man's eyes were full of tears, and I told him that he should just pick up whatever prescriptions he wanted to pick up from the floor. Fortunately there were still people at the temporary pharmacy packing up the leftover herbs, so I told him to just go over there and get some for his daughter. So the man picked up some prescriptions and I went with him to the pharmacy and asked the people to please give him some remedies, which they did.

"So despite my original feeling of sadness that there were all of the prescriptions on the ground, for this man it ended up being a blessing, one that extended to his daughter who was already being healed.

"After that weekend, I'd return to the Casa every now and then for more treatment and then go back home to Vitoria again. This went on for about four years, with me going every forty to sixty days to the Casa. Over the first few years I never spoke to the entity or asked him for anything specific. I knew that I was being worked on. Sometimes I would think about staying there longer or what it would be like to live in Abadiania. But I was engaged to be married and my fiancé was also from Vitoria, plus I worked and my whole life was there.

"Then, on one trip to Abadiania, the entity asked for me and a couple of other to people to go before him. So I went, never having really spoken with the entity before that time. I was still receiving treatment from both my medical doctor and from the entities. When it was my turn to go before the entity, he told me that my treatment was over and that I was cured. He said it was now time for me to begin my own mission. So I said to him, 'What mission? I don't know what my mission is.' The entity told me that I was to start helping my brothers and sisters who were wounded and who had the same illness that I'd had, and that Dr. Augosto would help me.

"Then Dr. Augosto, who was the entity who was talking to me, told me his own story. What I'm going to repeat for you now is not verbatim, but I'll cover the main points.

"Dr. Augosto told me that he lived long ago in a prior incarnation and was basically a barbarian who carried a lance and had killed his fellow human beings. He passed through other incarnations, slowly evolving, and in one incarnation was a rubber harvester, taking the rubber sap from the trees. Now he was one of the *'tribunal de Jesus'*, helping humanity through the medium Joao and in other ways as well. He said a lot of other things that I don't remember at the moment, although I know that they are all within me somewhere. He spoke for five minutes with me and then spoke with the other people he'd called before him as well.

"For about one more year, I continued to come to the Casa from time to time even though the entity had told me I was cured. I finished taking the series of drugs from my medical doctor as well. One day toward the end of that year when I was at the Casa, there was an announcement made that volunteers were needed to work in the infirmary, so I went. There was another young woman there who had also volunteered, and she said she'd been working there for a few months and that she too had been thinking about spending a more extended stay at the Casa. This was June 9, 1996.

"I kept thinking about that again when I went home, but still felt there were so many things tying me to Vitoria, including the fact that I was still engaged to my fiancé there. But shortly after returning home from that last trip, I broke up with him, quit my job, took care of other loose ends, and one month later, on July 9, I arrived in Abadiania with my suitcase and a great desire to serve, to help others. I was there with a very clear heart and ready to do whatever was needed.

"Once I moved here to Abadiania, I made many friends. Since that time I've always worked in the infirmary. I've dressed many wounds, taken care of many incisions from the physical operations and helped many others who have had surgeries too. I've given hope and faith to those there in need of it and helped however else I could. Even in the face of much pain and suffering on the part of others coming here for help, I've always been able to bring happiness and a spirit of optimism to them.

"One time someone invited me to go to Australia to work. This woman was very fond of me and felt like I was like a daughter to her. So I went by the entity and he said to me, 'This offer from this woman and her love for you is one of the gifts of the Casa. This particular gift is all of the friends that you are making here. Each one is like a link of a chain that is increasing.'

"I feel that my chain of links is very long now.

"I could fill volumes with all that I have experienced at the Casa, books of healings and miracles. When people come to the Casa, they enter another world, an alternative reality of love and healing that people have sought for so long. I've been living in this world for a long time now, and it's very close to what it would be like to be living on a purely spiritual plane.

"What I have learned here is compassion and charity, the true essence of mediumship. If you touch someone with compassion, you are a medium. A medium is a link between the spirit world and this world, and my mediumship is to bring that love and compassion through to others.

"The work of the entities is very individual and depends in part on what the people need and what they merit at that time in their life. Sometimes people arrive here with a great deal of mental negativity and they haven't really created a space in which the entities can help them. That's why their treatment may take a long time, because a lot of inner cleansing and opening needs to take place before their healing can be complete.

"You asked me what I recommend to those people coming to the Casa from other countries so that they can best prepare themselves for the work here. I would say that first they need to realize that we are all God's children, and then, they need to look at all of the mental and emotional baggage that they are carrying and start emptying it out, releasing any negative thoughts or obstacles to their connection to God's love. If they can make those preparations before they embark on their journey to Abadiania, they might be healed before they even get here! Love and faith are the only luggage they need to bring here—or anywhere, for that matter.

"Once people are here and begin spending time in the current, when they sit in the current and close their eyes they should review what it was that motivated them to want to come to the Casa in the first place. Then they should begin releasing all negativity, all bitterness, and ask God for what they need. At times when I myself get moody or out of sorts, what I like to do is go to the current and visualize God embracing me and letting me know how special and loved I am to God. Then I focus on all of the positive things in my life and how I want to serve God, and that brings me back to a good place in myself once again. Then I feel better, leave the current, and go back to work again in the infirmary.

"Every day, we can get up and do something to serve God. So let's do it! There are so many suffering souls, so many filled with hatred and bitterness, and we need to love all of our brothers and sisters, even our enemies, because God sees their need. Often those who are the hardest for us to love are those we most need to love.

"It's the people that I've met at the Casa, especially those I've dealt with closely in the infirmary, who have given and taught me so much. It's not Joao, it's not even the entities who have been my biggest teachers here, but rather it's the people and the love that's come through me and them that has taught me the most.

"Sometimes people come here and they want to leave all of their problems at the Casa. But that's not really the purpose of coming here, in my perspective. The real purpose is for them to learn to overcome their own negativity. One of the biggest problems of humanity is our negativity and false pride. We each need to be responsible for changing ourselves, and through our own efforts to make ourselves better people.

"Many people come here in pain. The Casa is a hospital for souls, and many souls that are ill gravitate here for healing. I've seen that people's pain is, in a certain way, the remedy, for it's that pain that catalyzes them to change and to open up to healing themselves."

Elenice and Edson

Elenice first came to Abadiania with her husband Edson to seek treatment for him. He had sustained a bullet wound in the head from a 38 gun five years prior to this interview, and the doctors had told him that because of the trauma to the parietal area of his brain, they could do nothing more for him. At the time when he first came he was very thin, weak, couldn't hold his head up nor walk, could hardly speak and had various digestive problems, all as a result of his injury. The day of this interview, he appeared to be of robust health, was speaking normally and had been walking with a bit of help from Elenice.

During their first trip to Abadiania four years ago, they met others who had been healed of various serious conditions, and became convinced that Edson would one day walk again if he received regular treatment there. So they moved to Abadiania and have lived there ever since in a lovely house on the edge of town with a large, beautiful garden.

When I asked Edson what the results had been for him in any area of his healing, he said that psychologically he's improved 1000%, and physically about 80%. He says whereas in the past he'd had no hope of ever walking normally again, today he knows that he will, that it's just a matter of a little more time. Also, after the injury, his eyesight measured 45% in the right eye and 40% in the left eye. An eye exam a year ago showed that his vision had improved to 100% in the right eye and 80% in the left eye. He said that by now the left eye could have improved even more. After the accident he couldn't even sit in a chair. Now he can sit fine, and he has his balance and coordination back again. His spiritual doctor at the Casa, the entity Dr. Algosto, told him that he would one day walk again perfectly.

When Edson first arrived, he was on a lot of medications for his condition. In another interaction with Dr. Algosto a short time after moving to Abadiania, the entity took away all of his medications at once. This is very unusual behavior for the entities. Typically they will advise the person to slowly decrease the amount of medication they are using, but Dr. Algosto said he wanted the good challenge of helping Edson go through a "cold turkey" experience. And Edson suffered absolutely no adverse reaction from the process.

Elenice never asked for anything for herself, although the entity did prescribe the herbs for her, and she says she feels wonderful. She says that if it weren't for the work of the Casa, however, she doesn't know if she would have been able to go on after her husband's injury and poor prognosis.

Elenice says that for her, the Casa is everything, including family. Edson— who was a dentist before his injury - also wants to stay in Abadiania permanently, and his wish is to serve as the dentist for those people at the Casa who need dental work once he is able to do so. He said he had been a real party animal before his injury, into drinking and the material pleasures of life. He also told me that before he came to Abadiania, he had no real faith, although he and his wife would occasionally go to mass, but that since arriving in Abadiania for treatment he is certain of God's existence.

Edson feels that being in Abadiania is the best place for a person's growth, and Elenice said that she has truly learned how to live since moving there. Both of them feel that the intensity of energy coming through the medium Joao and the entities is steadily growing stronger over the years since they've been there.

Elenice said that over the past four years they have seen new entities joining the spiritual *falange* of the Casa. She feels the "older" regulars are making space

90

for these newer ones to come and work. There is one entity who she's experienced on occasion who doesn't give his name. When she asked him once who he was, he simply said, "My daughter, they call me Love."

As Elenice told me about the occasional appearance of new entities, I recalled a recent story I had heard from someone at the Casa who had witnessed the following event.

One day during a session, a new entity suddenly incorporated in the medium Joao as he sat in the second current room. This entity said, "Where am I?" One of the staff people told the entity that this was the Casa de Dom Inacio, and that Joao served as a medium for various entities who wanted to do healing work for those who had come seeking it. The entity was silent for a moment and then said something like, "Oh, all right, I can do that," and then proceeded to do healing work on those who were there for the duration of the session. As far as I know, he never identified himself and I don't know if he ever reappeared after that session.

I myself was present once when a new entity incorporated in the medium Joao, in late November and early December of 2000. This entity identified himself as Francisco Xavier, and said he had been St Ignatius' (Dom Inacio's) first follower when the latter established the Jesuit sect. Xavier was an extremely dynamic entity who, over the next two weeks, appeared frequently and did many, many visible surgeries and other demonstrations of his abilities. Since that time he has shown up again on occasion and always does powerful healing work.

When I asked what Elenice and Edson would like to tell people who were about to come to the Casa for the first time for healing, Elenice said she would tell them to have faith in God, for without that, they have nothing. But even if they don't have faith, she said they should come anyway because their faith will grow little by little once they arrive. She also advised having patience and love. Elenice has seen people arrive at the Casa full of anger and hostility from their life experiences, and become loving, peaceful people after experiencing the healing energies of the Casa.

Edson and Elenice have changed from being in a state of hopelessness four years ago to feeling that they now are constantly receiving tangible energy and blessings from above. Elenice said "It's like living in paradise."

Tania

"The first time I came to the Casa it was to accompany my husband, who was suffering from a deterioration of the retina. I also brought a picture of my father, who had six brain tumors. He was near death, and I just wanted him to be able to die in peace and not have any more pain.

"I wasn't going to go by the entity—I was just going to have my husband take my father's photo by the entity. But I started feeling so much love there at the Casa, so after my husband was recovering from his spiritual operation, I took my father's photo to the entity myself. I didn't say a word when I got there—I just held an image in my mind of what I wanted for my father. The entity asked me if I would return in 40 days, and also asked me when I was going to start thinking of myself, and not just of others. I told him probably never, that I'm always this way. But the entity told me three times that he was going to help me. Me. Even though I wasn't asking for help for myself, he said he'd help me.

"The entity also prescribed the herbs and the energized water for my father. My father began taking them and soon was free of pain, even though his doctors had morphine on hand for him in case he needed it. He passed away, still without pain, from a cardiac arrest some time later.

"I returned to the Casa again and was told to sit in the current. I moved to Abadiania shortly thereafter. I've been here ever since that time three years ago. Once I moved here, I began attending all of the sessions at the Casa and my husband received the work there too. Sometimes the entity asks me to arrange a cot for people in the operating room; other times to represent others for surgery, and other things too. At this time I work primarily in the recovery room—the infirmary - taking care of people after their operations. The main work that goes on in there is love, just like everywhere else in the Casa.

"In regards to my husband's progress, after two years of attending sessions, the entity told him he hadn't started working on his eyes yet, that he was still preparing my husband for this work. Nevertheless, the problem has stabilized and my husband is able to get around fine with his daily tasks.

"My son Marcello is studying medicine and he has been to the Casa three times. Last week the entity had him come on stage during the physical operations and suture one of the incisions. He would like to say something too."

Marcello: "I don't feel that there is any conflict between spiritual medicine, like at the Casa, and conventional medicine. They can actually complement each other. And since there are not enough medical doctors who are mediums, we need more mediums who can do healing work."

Carlos and Rosane

Carlos: "We first came to Abadiania in 1997. Two months earlier my father-in-law had come here to the Casa to receive treatment for cancer, so we decided to come live here while he received his treatment. We also decided to work here, and began building a *pousada* where we would be able to both live and work. We made this move here entirely on faith that everything would work out!

"After we were here for about two months, I finally decided to go to the Casa myself. Neither Rosane nor I had any real physical problems. I went primarily out of curiosity that first time, as we'd been hearing about all of these unusual operations and that the entity sometimes foretold people's futures with great accuracy.

"The first time I passed by the entity, he didn't say a word to me—he just handed me a prescription for the remedies. I thought to myself, 'Well, if he's not going to talk to me, I'll just go back in the afternoon and talk to him!' So I went back in the afternoon to tell the entity about our *pousada* and that if there was any way we could help out people coming to Abadiania, we were available. I was all ready to give the entity my little speech, but when I got in front of him, my throat completely closed up and I couldn't get a word out! The entity just looked at me and smiled, and said, 'You don't have to say anything. I know everything already.' Well, that was my lesson of the first day!

"During that first year we were mostly working on getting our *pousada* built, and we'd go sit in the current at the Casa once or twice a week until the time came when both Joao and the entity told me to start working at the Casa. He said, 'Do whatever kind of work you want to do here, but just do it with love.' My first work there was to help organize the lines of people getting ready to see the entity. On the days where my help wasn't really needed for that, I would go sit in the current.

"This year—three years later—I was given the work of caring for the *cachoeira* (the waterfall that is part of the Casa grounds and used as part of treatment, especially for cleansing/purification work). When I first started doing this work, I was kind of nervous, worrying about insects and snakes and wanting to make sure everyone would be okay there. But I gradually became more comfortable there, and I always feel the presence of the entities and spiritual energy when I'm at the *cachoeira* now. And whatever I ask for there, I always end up receiving.

"For Rosane, the entity gave her the work of cooking at the *pousada*, and to do it with as much love as possible. She has done this, although now that we have our baby, she doesn't have as much time to be involved with the cooking. And shortly after she became pregnant, the entity predicted the date and time of birth of our daughter. He was accurate within two minutes of her birth!

"Even though Rosane and I really didn't have health issues when we arrived here, both of us have felt an overall improvement in our health. And three years after Rosane's father began his treatments at the Casa for his cancer, he was pronounced completely cured and was told he could leave Abadiania if he wanted to. He left, and is doing great now.

"Also, before Rosane and I came here, we really didn't have a clue about what spirituality was. We were Catholic by habit and would go to church now and then, but that was about it. We didn't have any idea what meditation was, and I feel like I really didn't know what it was to truly love someone before I came here. When people stay here for a while, they begin to let go of the material world and discover the deeper values of friendship, a sense of community and family. Rosane and I feel we have friends all over the world now, between those people we've met at the Casa and those who have stayed here at our *pousada*."

Rosane: "I agree, and I try to do everything here with love, whether it be the cooking, the cleaning, or the way I deal with people. People feel happy in that kind of environment, and that's what we are trying to provide here."

Carlos: "I'll tell you something else that I've experienced since I started going to the Casa, but I want to make sure you communicate this well to your readers so that they won't misunderstand it. Sometimes I've experienced that the entities will put people who are here through various challenges, even sometimes creating certain difficulties, as a way to test people's faith and teach them about themselves."

[*Author's comment: I am quite familiar with this methodology from various spiritual teachers I've had throughout my own life and through studying world religions and many spiritual traditions. From Zen masters to Native American shamans, they all seem to have studied similar teaching methodologies in this regard! Apparently the entities have also read the same manuals. When I asked Carlos how he knew it was the entities doing this kind of thing and not simply the normal course of life's developments, he simply said that he and others had experienced this and seen it happen a number of times and that he was certain about it.*]

Carlos: "One of the things we've noticed in the people who come here is that over time, they stop complaining so much. When you come here, you see people in circumstances and with health issues even more serious than your own little aches and pains, so the latter assume a different perspective and don't seem so important in comparison.

"You asked us if, over the three years we've been in Abadiania, we feel that the work of the entities has increased or diminished in power or has stayed the same. In our perspective, depending on the people who are here in a given week, sometimes the work seems much, much stronger with a lot more surgeries, etc., and then it will stabilize to a more 'normal' level again. We feel that part of this depends on the level of faith of the people coming to the Casa and also on how well they have prepared in advance of coming here. But it also depends on the entities on any given day. Some of the entities do primarily diagnostic work and the prescribing of the herbs, etc., while others arrive and *boom*, they are very active and operating like crazy! You were here, Josie, when one of those entities came in November (2000)—the entity Francisco Xavier.

"I also wanted to say that some people arrive here seeking help at the last stages of serious illnesses. Sometimes the disease is just too far gone for the entities to be able to keep the person's physical body alive, but nonetheless, they do spiritual healing on those people—like they do on everyone—and often make it possible for those people to have less pain during the remainder of their lives and to have a more peaceful transition when they leave their bodies behind.

"The entities won't lie to people who they can't help. If they can't heal the person's physical body, they'll tell them so, but they'll also tell them they'll make them as comfortable as possible and help them with their crossing. If the entity tells someone who comes for treatment, 'I can heal you,' then the person can rest assured that that will happen. If the entity tells the person that he or she is preparing to die, or if he tells a person who is seriously ill that he or she should just get the blessed water, or that they should go home and be with their family, that means that the entities can't reverse the progress of the person's disease and that they will simply help the person prepare for his or her crossing.

"On the other hand, we've seen people healed of so many kinds of diseases here, including every kind of cancer as well as AIDS. And even if people's illness is extremely advanced, it still might be valuable for them to come to the Casa, as only God knows what might be possible in their healing. And if nothing else, they will receive spiritual help from the entities for whatever part of their life still remains.

"One other thing I wanted to say was about the entity Dom Inacio. When he incorporates in the medium—which is rarely—he makes a large sign of the cross, and sings this particular tune that he loved when he was alive, and he also limps. When he was alive, he was in the military for a time and sustained a bullet wound to his leg, so that's why he limps. This is how we recognize him.

"To close, I want to tell you that once when Dom Inacio incorporated in the medium, he told us, 'All my children will eventually come to this Casa. Those who come here have been chosen and are very blessed and fortunate and privileged to be here.'"

Elizabeth

"Ten years ago, I discovered that I had a fast-growing brain tumor that was compromising my neurological brain functions. I began frantically going from one doctor to another, hoping for a different—and more positive—opinion. But the doctors all concurred, and told me I would need a personal caretaker as I was rapidly losing my coordination and soon wouldn't be able to take care of myself. I was also losing my memory to the point where I couldn't even remember the names of my own children or close friends. My sense of direction was deteriorating to the extent that I would get lost easily, even in familiar places. I also experienced a strange sense of detachment: I stopped missing people or worrying about anyone.

"My doctors said there was nothing they could do for me. At one point the effects of the tumor became so extreme that I collapsed at home. I remember lying in bed, hearing the voices of my colleagues from work —who were certain I was dying—saying good-bye to me, and I was unable to open my eyes. I then realized I *was* dying, which surprised me, as I'd always been certain that I would die very suddenly in a car accident rather than as a result of this kind of slow deterioration.

"But I didn't die that day, and soon thereafter, a colleague of my sister-in-law told me about Joao de Deus and suggested I go see him. I decided to go, but my family didn't believe in Joao and were not at all supportive about the journey. As a last request to my former husband, I begged him to put me on the bus to Abadiania, which he reluctantly agreed to do.

"So I embarked on the journey into the unknown. Before leaving, I stopped taking all the medications my doctors had given me, as I felt that when I arrived at the Casa for treatment, I wanted the entities to see my condition as it truly was, not masked by drugs.

"The 48-hour trip by bus was like a journey through hell. Although my condition remained stable and the thought of seeing Joao seemed to fill me with extra reserves of energy, it was an extremely grueling trip. My fellow passengers were in various stages of health crises, and our group looked like it was being transported from a war zone. People had all kinds of diseases including open skin cancers. Many passengers were vomiting during the trip and the smells in the bus were awful, and yet, everyone helped each other out during those intense days of travel.

"Perhaps because of my confusion from the brain tumor, I had somehow expected the bus trip to be a very short one. But then one day, two days, and into a third day passed and I began to think I might collapse before arriving at my destination. When we finally arrived in Abadiania, I just looked around and thought, 'This is where I'm going to die.'

"On our first morning of sessions at the Casa, I was standing in the main hall where the orientation speeches are given. Joao came out on stage, incorporated, and began to do some surgeries. At one point he looked out at me, left the stage and came over to me, put his hand over my head and said, 'Don't let anyone cut your hair.' It took some time afterwards for me to understand what the entity's words meant. When a person is about to have brain surgery, they shave the person's head just prior to the operation. The entity was telling me not to go to a hospital for brain surgery. During the course of my treatment at the Casa, I never received an operation either—visible or invisible—and yet, ten years later, I'm still alive and well.

"That first day, and then the next and the next, the entity would tell me to sit in the current. I became increasingly angry, as most of the people around me were being told by the entity to have operations at the Casa. I kept wondering 'Why not me?' On the last day of my first stay in Abadiania, I thought about posing this question to the entity as I waited in line to see him. The entity that session was Dr. Jose Valdivino. When I got to the doorway of his room, he smiled at me and said to me, 'Your treatment is to take place in the current room. Have patience and perseverance, and you will learn a great deal in the current, and not only for your physical healing.'

"Later that day when it was time to leave Abadiania, I felt reluctant to go. Although I was still feeling symptoms from my illness, I also felt as strong as an Amazon and was afraid I would lose this strength if I went home. In fact, after I returned to my home, I had several more crises that sent me back to the hospital. During one of the hospitalizations, they started preparing me for brain surgery. At that point I suddenly remembered the entity's words and fled from the hospital. After that, none of the doctors wanted to be responsible for my treatment, as I wasn't cooperating with what they felt I needed. They had told me I had about 1% of a chance to survive the surgery, and that even if I did survive it, with physical therapy I *might* learn to speak again. Those prospects didn't look very good to me.

"So I decided to simply continue my treatments at the Casa, and started going there once a month. My healing began to progress, despite the fact that my inner critic kept telling me that what was going on, both with others and with my own healing, couldn't be real. On my third trip to Abadiania, in order to try to confirm or lay to rest my doubts, I sneaked into the entity's room in the morning to examine the tray of instruments used in the physical surgeries, to see if they were some kind of trick instruments. After checking the instruments and not finding anything unusual about them, I slipped into the current room to sit for the session. But the entity came in, took me by the hand and had me go out into the main hall with him and assist him in the surgeries by holding the instrument tray.

"I felt so ashamed and embarrassed that my hands began to shake, shaking the tray as well. I realized that the entity knew I had checked on his instruments out of lack of faith, and I felt badly. That afternoon I wouldn't even go into the main hall during the opening speeches. I just stood outside trying to stay invisible while at the same time trying to watch what was going on when the entity came out and began to do surgeries. To my dismay, the entity saw me and left the stage, walked through the hall and up to where I was hiding outside, and said, 'Daughter, I told you your work is in the current room.' So I went there.

"The next day I decided I would go in the first current room and kind of hide in the back corner. I sat down, lowered my head, and prayed I could just be invisible there. But in a while, I suddenly felt a hand on my head, and the entity said to me, 'Daughter, come and work.' He had me go out into the main hall to hold the instrument tray again. And again I was shaking all over.

"The first operation the entity did that day was the one in which he pushes the hemostat up the patient's nose. At the end of the hemostat was a cotton ball that he dipped in a small bowl of water. He put it part way up the patient's nose and then paused, just as I had the thought, 'My God, he's doing this and it's not hurting the person.' The entity dipped the cotton in water again, and put it in my mouth to taste, saying, 'That water is not anesthesia; it's love.' He then proceeded with the operation.

"Every time I returned to Abadiania after that, the entity would have me either hold the instrument tray or work in the current room as a medium of transport, helping take the illness out of various patient's bodies, passing it through my own to cleanse it, and then releasing it. At that time I knew nothing of this kind of work on a conscious level, but I was asked to do it anyway. Due to my lack of understanding of transport mediumship, at first I was afraid, but gradually my fears diminished.

"Over time, as I became increasingly involved in helping others and reading about spirituality and healing, I began to forget that I was ill. When I returned home after some months of visits to the Casa, I saw one of my medical doctors and he said to me, 'How is it that you are still alive?' Not only that, but some officials from the bank where I had worked before becoming ill insisted on going to the hospital with me one day. Months earlier I had given them medical documents showing my condition and describing my inability to continue working due to my illness. But because of my undeniable improvement, they began to doubt the validity of my earlier claim. The doctors assured my colleagues that the original documents had in fact been real and that they couldn't understand my progress either.

"After four years of monthly treatment at the Casa, my doctors were unable to advise me what to do. My tumor was still there, but was obviously shrinking. Six years after beginning treatment at the Casa I had another MRI. Although the tumor was still there, it had shrunk to three centimeters—about one tenth its previous size—and was no longer compressing and compromising the rest of my brain in such a way as to cause the many severe problems I'd had had prior to the work of the entities.

"As I continued my treatments at the Casa, I began to experience a strong drive to move to Abadiania, but the entity told me it was not time yet. So I started going there every 15 days instead of once a month. For me, the energy there was like a spiritual water that quenched my deepest thirst. But on the material side of things, everything was falling apart. I had lost my job, my property, my marriage, and the entity had recommended that my children stay with their father, so in some ways I felt I had lost them as well. But the entities told me not to be afraid, because they would take care of my children.

"I got to a point when I had nothing left and didn't know what to do. One day during that period, I was walking on the beach, wearing my shorts and a T-shirt and carrying a bag with a few other articles of clothing. I suddenly decided to go to Abadinia, and got on the bus and took off. When I arrived at the Casa for the first session of the day, the entity smiled at me and took my hand and said, 'Now you will stay here to live'.

"My first thought was, 'Oh, no, not now!' Every other time I had come I had brought a big suitcase with lots of clothes, my CD player and music, and all kinds of personal stuff. And this time I'd just come with a tiny little bag of clothes. I told the entity that I had no car, that I'd need to rent a house but had only 93 *reais* with me (about $50 U.S.), and how was I going to manage? The entity told me that to start with I would live on the money I brought with me. I told him I had to go back home and get some more clothes and money, but the entity said, 'If you go back home now, you will disincarnate.'

"Not wanting to die yet, I remained in Abadiania and was allowed to stay at different people's homes for a while. I would go to the Casa on all the working days and sit in the current. Then I began searching for work and found a job in Brasilia, which was about a two-hour drive each way from Abadiania. I was promoted rapidly in my job where I worked in sales. I wanted to move to Brasilia so that I wouldn't have to commute so much, but the entity told me my home was to be in Abadiania. I finally was able to rent a house here. But I started to miss one day of sessions a week at the Casa, then two and finally all three days of sessions and was getting more and more work in Brasilia.

"Then everything began to fall apart. I'd been getting commissions on my sales, and suddenly one day my boss refused to pay me—for no reason at all. I then began trying to sell my car to get more money, but every time I'd try to do so I'd get in a car crash. Finally one day the entity told me that I had manifested things very quickly on the material level, but that I wasn't making enough time for the entities to do the spiritual and healing work, and that's why things were falling apart.

"At that point I was already with Luis, my husband now, and the entity said, 'Why don't you both work in Abadiania'. I responded, '*What* work in Abadiania?!' He said that Luis and I should work with people and that we should build or run a *pousada* where people could stay when they came to Abadiania. Well, at that time I only had three *reais* (about $1.50 U.S.)!

"Later that day I passed by a building on the street here, where the owner was sitting with her head bowed looking very sad. I asked her if she needed anyone to work for her and she said no, that she wanted to rent the building to someone. I told her I'd like to rent it but that I didn't have any money. But the next time I saw the entity he told me Luis and I should rent it for three years. He said for the first year we'd be working very hard and we'd have a lot of problems; that in the second year we'd progress a lot more, and by the third year we'd start making some money on it.

"Thankfully, we were able to work out a contract with the owner that allowed us to pay rent at the end of each month rather than the beginning, so that hopefully we'd have enough accumulated earnings at the end of the month to be able to pay the her. I'll never forget our opening day. We had just enough money to buy a few tomatoes and a bit of steak for our first two lunch customers, as well as some beans and rice I'd cooked earlier. Then more people arrived, but we had no more food. So Luis stood in the doorway as people came to sign up and pay for lunch. As soon as they'd pay, he'd slip me the money and I'd go running out the back door to the store to get a few more tomatoes and steak and a bit of salad materials! That was our opening day.

"A year and a half later, in June of 2000, Luis was starting to attend sessions at the Casa as well as trying to settle up his business affairs in Brasilia where he'd lived and worked before. The entity said that was fine, but that he was not to use any of that money for our ongoing living expenses in Abadiania. We kept having tremendous financial problems, to the point that one night we just sat in front of our *pousada* and cried. We concluded that we'd just have to give up the *pousada* and move to Anapolis to try to find work.

"But to our surprise, the next morning very early, Joao knocked loudly on the door, waking us up. I came to the door with my hair a mess, saw Joao who was standing there with two lawyers, and he said, 'Are you thinking of leaving?' I said, 'Oh, no, no.' Then Joao called for Luis to come down and asked him if *he* was thinking of leaving and he said yes, that it just wasn't working out for us here. Joao then said that the entity had told us to stay here and that we must stay here, and that we should pass by the entity again and tell him what was going on.

"So we did at the next session, and the entity said, 'Now you must go back to the south of Brazil where you lived before you came here, sell everything, and bring the money back here to Abadiania. Just go there, finish it all up and bring the money back.' We did, settled everything, came back and ended up buying the *pousada*, and more people started coming to stay there. The entity also told us to start coming more to the Casa to work, and that we should always have a smile for everyone.

"So we did, and we're still here, trying to learn what we're supposed to be learning, and I will only go back to conventional doctors if the entity tells me I need to do so for some reason. And I'm in touch with my children, who are also receiving various kinds of help from the entities. So I don't worry about anything anymore. I have peace and my faith, and I'm very happy. If I start working too much at the *pousada* and not spending enough time at the Casa, the entity calls me back there again so I can stay balanced.

"To finish up, I just want to tell people that being here is like being in a 24-hour-per-day university, and that we are always being taught something in one way or another. The work is ongoing!"

Tuca and Norton

Tuca and Norton are both professional actors in Sao Paolo: Norton in movies and television, and Tuca in the theater. Norton first came to the Casa about two and a half years prior to this interview, and Tuca six months prior.

Norton first came because a friend gave a photo of him to the entity for spiritual help, and the entity said that he wanted Norton to come in person. And a year ago Norton got the herbal remedies for Tuca to help her with depression and panic attacks. She noticed that her depression and panic attacks disappeared very soon after beginning to take the remedies and that her way of thinking began to change in a positive direction.

When Norton was about nine years old, he was sitting beside a river and received a vision of Indians. That was the beginning of a series of accurate premonitions and clairvoyant experiences. As time went on, he began to study the Spiritist work of Alan Kardec as well as Buddhist philosophy. Despite his studies and his innate gift of clairvoyance, he was surprised that the entity had asked him to come to the Casa. The first time he visited the Casa and saw Joao, he immediately felt love for the man. Joao addressed him as his son and Norton has felt that Joao has been like a father to him ever since.

As for Tuca, she went to a Spiritist center for the first time when she was eleven, but didn't really understand what it was all about. When she was 16, while taking some courses in energy work, she discovered that she had "healing hands." She used her gift for four years and then stopped until she began attending the sessions at the Casa.

Since then she feels more at peace within herself and more loving toward herself and others, has a clearer perspective on her life and herself, and feels her intuitive nature is getting stronger. She says even the constant traffic jams in Sao Paolo where she lives don't bother her any more.

And since attending sessions at the Casa from time to time, her mediumistic abilities have been developing rapidly. Two days prior to this interview during a session at the Casa, Tuca had her first experience of mediumistic incorporation. She and Norton were working on a person who had requested their help, and she began feeling a great deal of energy. Suddenly she had another spirit inside her, one that had been attached to the patient and that had been causing him problems. She began shouting and kicking, but the whole time she was conscious and knew it wasn't really her, but rather an obsessive spirit. She was finally able to spiritually cleanse it and send it on to the Light. Tuca had a similar experience with a man who had cancer. Due to these experiences, she says she now knows she is a medium of "spirit transport."

Norton too has felt more peace and love, and has had a different view of the world since first going to the Casa, as well as noting an increased opening of his third eye and spiritual vision. However, it hasn't been a smooth ride for him. He says that along with the opening of his vision and the resulting sense of responsibility he feels to live more impeccably, the intensity of temptation to do otherwise has increased. At times he feels he is at the bottom of a dark pit struggling with a fondness for whisky, with the loss of his prior girlfriend, fighting with his father and losing ground professionally. During the worst of those times, the entity spoke to him one day at the Casa and told him, "I can help you in both your spiritual and professional life, but if you continue to drink, I won't be able to help you grow."

Despite this statement, Norton continued to drink off and on during the last two years and suffered professionally and financially, due, in his words, to "not behaving himself" in the way the entity had advised. However, he says that in the last two weeks here at the Casa, (at the end of 2000 and the beginning of 2001), the grace that he has received has more than made up for the last two years of struggles. He wants to work with Tuca to help cancer and AIDS patients, and the entity blessed them in this work and told Norton to take nine special stones from the sacred *cachoeira* near the Casa. The entity said that they were to place these stones on the area where they found illness in their patients, and that the stones would help pull the energy of the disease out of their patients' bodies.

These past two weeks have been powerful for Tuca as well, and Norton feels that she is now able to "see" even better than he does. Tuca can now see illness and health in others' bodies. A few days ago the entity showed her a photo of a dog and asked her, "What do you see?" She told him she saw a dog. Then the entity put his hands over one part of the photo, removed them and then asked her again, "What do you see?" And this time she saw a black dog with cream-colored stripes, with a demon looking out of its eyes and a cow's head staring out of its neck. She said it was truly disgusting looking. The entity said, "Daughter, do you feel fear when you see this?" Tuca said no, she didn't. Later on in the session someone else was passing by the entity and with her eyes closed she suddenly saw the cancer in his body. She said she pulled it out of the man as if she was peeling a mask off of him, then bathed the cancer with white light and love, and it disappeared.

Tuca said that before beginning to attend sessions at the Casa, she had had only had one such experience and it was during the time she was taking the class in energy work. She was working on a woman with cataracts and saw an image of the problem, extracted it from the woman's body, and the woman's vision began to improve.

In their work, neither Tuca nor Norton ever use the word cancer. Instead, they substitute the word "spider". "that person has a spider" rather than saying "that person has cancer." They do this so as to divert—for themselves and the other person—all the negative and fear-based thoughts and emotions associated with this disease so that they can all sustain a more positive focus.

She says that in healing work, you can't force something to happen, but if you are coming from the heart and from a place of love, healing will take place, because that love comes from God.

Toward the end of the interview, Norton said he was "told" in meditation in the current that God did not create disease—it is we human beings that have done so with our thoughts. Norton continued to say that we don't "catch" diseases from others, but that we create them in ourselves from our thoughts and fears. He feels that it is possible to be around the worst of infectious diseases, or to even touch people with leprosy, and not "catch" their illnesses if one is not afraid and comes from a place of love. Norton cited Jesus and Mother Teresa as examples of the latter.

When it comes to their thoughts and attitudes toward healing, both Norton and Tuca reflect the predominant energy and philosophy of the Casa de Dom Inacio: that the energy of love, which is God, is the most powerful healing force of the universe.

Joao Vasco

"I first heard about the medium Joao's work from a man in Lisbon whose stepfather knew about Abadiania, and this man suggested that I go to receive help at the Casa de Dom Inacio in Brazil. At that time I was heavily involved with hard drugs—heroin and cocaine.

"At first I didn't follow up on the suggestion. I had started with soft drugs when I was 16, and by age 18 I tried heroin for the first time and then used it again and again, and then cocaine, and I just went on that way. I would go to detox centers and be clean for a while, and then would go back to my habit again. This went on for years. One year I had a really good summer, stayed clean, was progressing with my university studies, and then in September had a blood test and found out I had both hepatitis B and C. I reacted really badly to that news and went right back to heroin. By then I was messing up not only myself, but destroying my family as well. My family members were at the point of telling me, 'If you're going to keep taking drugs you're going to have to leave home.' It was around that time that the man told me about the Casa. I felt I had nothing to lose, and I decided I would go to Brazil without really knowing what it was that I was going to.

"I arrived at the Casa in May of 2000, and it's now January 2001. I came here with my mother, who stayed here with me for the first three weeks. At the time of my arrival, I was a hard core materialist who had been studying philosophy at college and who thought he knew everything. I was also a Marxist/Leninist and communist and thought I knew it all. The first day I was in Abadiania I heard people talking about spirits, about the entities, and my first reaction was, 'I want to go home!' Not because I didn't believe in it, but because suddenly I *did* believe.

"The first day I went to the Casa was a Monday—not even a working day there—and I was so impressed I suddenly believed and knew that the work there was real. All of my previous ideas just went out the window, especially when I went in the room with all the discarded crutches and wheelchairs from people who had been healed there. When I left the Casa a while later to return to my *pousada*, I kept shaking my head, because I couldn't find my prior ideas anywhere.

"Despite all this, on the first morning of sessions that Wednesday, I didn't participate. I just went to the Casa at the end of the session and took the soup. But someone invited me to come that afternoon, and I said, 'Okay, I'll go.' So I did, and when I entered the first current room on my way to see the entity, all of my defenses crumbled, especially the defense against God's existence. All I felt was, 'I believe, I believe.' The love there was incredibly powerful, and by the time I entered the entity's current room, I was almost fainting from it.

"I looked at Joao's body sitting there in the chair, incorporated by the entity, and I thought to myself, 'That's not just a man there.' I finally arrived in front of him, and he just gestured and said, 'Go sit in my current.' So I turned and began walking toward one of the benches in the room to sit down. But after a few steps, the entity spoke out to me, and as I turned to look at him, he said, 'I will help you.' I can't tell you how important hearing those words was to me. I sat in the current and I felt like I was floating in the air.

"And yet, as overwhelming as that first day was, it didn't stop me from trying to convince my mother to take me home as soon as possible. Originally, when I arrived at the Casa, my intention had always been to go back to Portugal at the earliest possible moment. Because, you see, my problem wasn't only the drugs, but it was also a spirit obsession, although I didn't know that at the time. The second time that I went past the entity, a woman from my *pousada* went with me to ask for me how long I should stay in Abadiania, as I could not speak to the entity for myself in the initial stages. I did want the treatment from the entities, but my idea was that I would stay in Abadiania for a little while and then have the entities keep treating me when I went home. The first thing the entity told me was that I would stay here a few days and then I could go home, and then maybe come back again some other time for a bit. So I thought that was just great. But as I look back, I think the entity was telling me what I could accept at that moment in order to help me relax more into the work day by day.

"Twenty days later, my mother left for Portugal without me! The entity had not yet given me the okay to leave, but by then I felt fine about staying a little while longer.

"Josie, you asked me if I struggled at all with a desire for drugs since I've been here, and no, I haven't, not really. The thing that I did keep struggling with was this obsession about returning to Portugal, but over time I've understood that this was a manifestation of the obsessive spirit that has been attached to me as well as of my own personal tendencies to obsess over things.

"For the first few sessions at the Casa, I sat in the current rooms. But then Sebastiao talked with the entity about me (for I was still unable to speak for myself with the entity during the first months here), and the entity said I needed to be treated daily in the third room where the spiritual operations take place. So I spent many weeks lying down on a cot in there during the daily sessions.

"It was during that period that the entities were working really strongly to heal my physical body as well as to do the major work on helping me with the obsessive spirit, although that obsession work is still ongoing. At first I didn't understand much about de-obsession work, but as time went on and I talked with people and did some reading on the subject, I reached a better understanding.

"During my first session in the operation room, my consciousness was lifted out of my body and I was taken to this place where I saw an angelic being with wings, which I assumed was my guardian angel. I remember traveling with her in the air, and then I was put on a bed in this other realm. I felt so much love that I just wanted my angel to let me stay there. The entities began really working on me. I could still feel my body down below me in the operating room, and it began to experience this kind of magnetic burning. I had one hand on my chest, and it felt like it was fused there. The entity or angel kept comforting me during this process, trying to make it easier for me. This experience happened several times after that during the sessions. Then, during one session, I was lifted up again and my angel came, but this time she was doing all of this nasty stuff. I can't even describe to you how nasty it was. I could hardly stand it. I wondered if it was just me projecting those images out of guilt and shame for my past actions. But I felt this strange presence behind my head and it started bringing up all of these awful emotions to the point where I couldn't even pray for myself. At the same time, I could hear people in the room beginning to pray for me, and my body was just writhing with anger and intensity. When the session ended and I got up from the cot, it was like something else had taken over me. I was completely full of arrogance, and just looking for a fight. I was finally experiencing part of the force of the obsessive spirit that of course had some things in common with my own issues and personality.

"For an extended period after that session, I couldn't stand to look at myself in the mirror. The feelings of arrogance and hostility continued, and it seemed like it was only when I was around my mother that I could relax a bit. All of this was a manifestation of the interaction between the obsessive spirit and my own. I can't hold the 'obsessor' entirely responsible, because, as I have learned here, it is the corresponding qualities and weaknesses within my own being that allowed the other spirit to be able to move into my energy field in the first place. That's how it works.

"Anyway, after that session, I felt compelled to walk over to the Casa that night. I got as far as the gate, but just couldn't bring myself to go through it. So I was standing there clutching the metal grid and just writhing again with that same agony I'd experienced in the treatment room. I remember a car drove by that was broadcasting a prayer, but I still just couldn't get free of the imprisoning energy to go through the gate.

"That happened to me a few times. Now all of this intense work with the obsessive spirit was very early on in my treatment, and I was still on morphine pills to help me through the pain of the heroin withdrawal. I was having a lot of trouble sleeping, and that same night when I couldn't walk past the gate of the Casa, I tried to sleep in my mother's bedroom in hope that I could relax more there. But I started shaking a lot and this frightened my mother, so I had to go back in my own room. It was a very tough night. I was having convulsions, and I finally asked my mother for a sleeping pill.

"In retrospect, I think that not only was I dealing intensely with the obsessive spirit that night, but I believe that the entities were also cleaning the worst of the drug withdrawal symptoms out of my system in one fell swoop. Because in the morning, after sleeping maybe one hour at the most, I awoke with the birds singing, and feeling really clean and clear. I was able to eat breakfast without experiencing any nausea. And I didn't need the morphine after that. So a drug withdrawal process that otherwise might have taken one to two weeks and with a lot of physical pain was burned out of me in one night through the work of the entities. It was truly a miracle.

"When my family in Portugal heard about this, they were really surprised. They asked my mother if I still wasn't taking morphine pills and she said no, that I didn't need them any more. It is such strong work that goes on here. I remember going through withdrawal several times in Portugal and spending four days without sleep in total misery. To have it all over with in one night was amazing. Yes, I still have nights here when I don't sleep well, but that is a normal part of the treatment here and many people experience this once they begin their sessions at the Casa. Once the entities start working with you, they don't abandon you, don't leave you alone, day or night, whether you are still here in Abadiania or have gone to some other part of the world.

"Although I completed the drug withdrawal process early during my stay here, the de-obsession process has been slower. This is because when a spirit has been attached to you for a long time, in a sense it has become a part of you. You identify yourself through and with that relationship. And in my case—and probably in that of others—this obsessor was a spirit of someone to whom I did something really wrong in a prior life, otherwise it wouldn't be obsessing me and being so angry with me in this life. So first I need to ask forgiveness and to apologize to that spirit, and eventually it needs to move on, because the relationship is not good for either of us.

"But I too need to let go of that spirit. I remember one morning here I woke up and felt completely stress-free and thought that finally the de-obsession process had been completed, as up to that morning, for years I always woke up with lots of anxiety and stress within myself. I kept looking for the stress and it just wasn't there that day. The stress and anxiety had been coming from the obsessive spirit, and now it was gone! But I think in one way, I called it back to myself. I was used to it and felt very strange and disoriented without it. So there is still more work to be done on that issue. That spirit and I each need to work on ourselves, and then there is work that needs to take place between us. This is the place to do it, though. I heard someone say at the beginning of one of the sessions at the Casa, that the Casa is one of the biggest de-obsession houses in South America. I don't know enough about other places to be able to compare, but it wouldn't surprise me if that were true.

"The de-obsession process is going on 24 hours a day for me, but I experience the most intensity of that work from the entities during the night when I am sleeping. My spirit travels out of my body and goes to meet with the obsessor to work things out. The entities are working with that obsessive spirit (as well as with me), confronting it, teaching it, whatever is needed. I also experience more intensity with this aspect of my healing on the 'non-working' days of the Casa. During those days I don't have the structure, the shelter of the Casa, so more stress and other things come up that I need to face and deal with in order to become stronger.

"Anyway, after that initial period when I was put on the cot in the third current room during every session, I started working more in the first current room for a while. By the end of September—four months after I arrived—the entity told me that the work of my physical reconstitution was complete. So then little by little I was given some work at the Casa so that I could give back some energy there. I started helping people with their initial orientations, sometimes passing by the entity with them and translating for those who needed it. For months now I've been doing more and more translation, sometimes passing by the entity ten times a day. This is a real change from my first months here when I couldn't speak to the entity at all! But it happened so naturally and gradually that I never really noticed.

"And all of this interactive work with people has been a very important part of my own healing process. Social reintegration is typically a big problem for ex-addicts, as they've often been de-socialized for years. So for me, this is a very good way to move back into human society in a positive way. Doing this translation work at the Casa is part of my treatment.

"For me, the deepest healing I received at the Casa was regaining my faith in God, and really knowing that life does not end with the end of this earthly existence. A few months ago the entity Jose said that the main work of the Casa is the development of each person's spirit, and that the body is the vehicle that spirit has chosen for its continued evolution. He also said that when a person comes to the Casa, he or she brings at least one other spirit with them that is in need of treatment here. It might not be an obsessive spirit, although it could be. But it could also be a spirit that aligned itself with the person in order to come receive the spiritual help here.

"Anyway, understanding the infinite quality of the life of the spirit and knowing that all things happen for a reason—to further our development—has been the core of my healing here. I also have faith in God for the first time since my childhood, and I now know that love is eternal. This is very healthy for the spirit to know."

Sebastiao

Sebastiao, or Tiao, is the lovable secretary of the Casa who handles many of the administrative duties of the Casa and gives the opening orientation at each session. He has been with Joao since before the Casa was established and has a strong psychic link with both Joao and the entities. He is a powerful medium himself, although he rarely speaks of this.

He graciously took time out of his extremely busy schedule to participate in an interview. We sat on the outdoor veranda of the Casa, facing the rolling green hills, birds cheeping in the background and a soft breeze blowing, and I began to ask him some questions. Our interview was conducted in Portuguese, and I have done the best I could to translate it accurately—in content at least, if not word by word.

"Tiao, how was it that you came to meet Joao?"

"When I was in my teens, I was in seminary school preparing to be a priest. But at age 15 I left the seminary. Over time, I developed a relationship with a girlfriend, which was nice, but I kept thinking that there something more to life, and I kept looking for it.

"One day I was in Anapolis with my girlfriend and we were walking down this street. We paused in front of a doorway, and this woman came out and told me I could go in, that it was my turn now. I didn't know what to think, but I went in anyway.

"Inside was a man, who looked at me, gave me a prescription for some herbal remedies, and told me to come back later and talk to someone named Joao for a consultation. So I got the herbs, feeling somewhat baffled, came back later, and the same man told me to come back the next day and talk to Dr. Augusto.

"The next day I returned and the same man looked at me and told me to come back the following day and speak with yet another doctor. This went on for a few days until I finally realized that the "man" I kept talking to was in fact the medium Joao de Deus, and that each day I'd seen him I was in fact speaking with a different entity that he had incorporated. It is now 29 years later," he joked, "and I am still waiting for my private consultation with Joao!"

"Since first meeting Joao, has there been any kind of key turning point in your life that you would like to share?" I asked.

"Yes. Some years ago here at the Casa, a family arrived with their eight-year-old daughter who was blind. The parents got in line to go see the entity and the little girl was left with me. After a while, she took my hand and insisted that I take her to go see the entity too, so we got in line together and I took her past the entity and then back to the office where she could wait for her family to rejoin her.

"A while later, I checked back in the office and the little girl was crying hard, with all of her family there with her. I stormed into the office, thinking they were being mean to her and ready to defend her. But I was very wrong about that, as she soon made clear.

"She told me that when we walked together into the first current room, she saw two men there. One was wearing pants, and the other was wearing what she described as a skirt. It became evident to me that she had 'seen' the entity Dom Inacio in his robes, and one other entity as well. We had passed by Joao in entity in the second current room and been told to go on to the third current room to sit for a few minutes.

"In the third current room, she told me that the two men were there again, and that the peeled what was like a dark piece of tape from her eyes. After the men—the entities—did this, she was suddenly able to see perfectly. The reason she was crying when I found her in the office was that she was completely overwhelmed by her experience—and so was I when she described it to me!"

After a few blissful moments of contemplating this miraculous story, I shifted the subject of our interview slightly. I told Sebastiao that over recent visits to the Casa, I had become more aware that there were several kinds of volunteer mediums helping in the current rooms, and asked Sebastiao about this.

"Would you describe the different kinds of mediums that work here, Tiao?"

"First, there are three main categories: conscious, unconscious, and clairvoyant mediums. Among the conscious and unconscious types, there are mediums of transport, mediums of incorporation (like Joao), and mediums of energy transmission who can do energy passes."

I was very familiar with the latter category, as I had, by the time of our interview, already had the opportunity to visit a number of spiritual centers and healers in Brazil, and many of the spiritual healers and mediums would, as part of the healing, take their hands and move them through the energy field of the patient, often snapping their fingers at the end of each "pass" to shake loose any negative energy they might have accumulated. I have done these kinds of passes myself and can attest to their potential effectiveness.

Tiao explained that mediums of transport were those who were able to help the entity remove obsessive spirits from patients at the Casa by sending them to the light. These same kinds of mediums also were able to take away illness and pain by transforming them into light energy. After hearing some of my stories about how the entity had enlisted me to help patients at various time, Sebastiao told me that I was a medium of transport and incorporation.

He went on to describe how Joao is an unconscious medium of incorporation, in the sense that his own personal awareness and memory of what he does while incorporated is absent. On the other hand, conscious mediums of incorporation maintain their own awareness, even when another entity is present in their bodies and working through them.

He gave me an example of the latter.

"A few weeks ago the famous medium Rubens da Faria, the current 'Dr. Fritz' medium, came to the Casa seeking help. Rubens is a conscious medium of incorporation, and Dr. Fritz does many physical surgeries through him. The problem is that Rubens himself can't stand the sight of blood and suffers a great deal when Dr. Fritz is doing the surgeries. So Rubens came here to the Casa to see if the entities here could help him to be able to do more invisible surgeries, the way the entities often work through Joao, so that he wouldn't have suffer so much.

"Joao himself was not here that day. He had been detained on a trip to Portugal. But I called him to let him know that Rubens was here. He said that Rubens should sit in the entity's chair in the second current room as people filed by for healing, so Rubens did.

"Apparently Rubens went into trance during that time, and when the session was over and he came back to himself, he asked rather anxiously if he had performed any physical operations on anyone while he was in trance. He was very relieved to find out that he hadn't."

So perhaps Rubens received the help he sought at the Casa.

"Tiao," I asked next, "have the mediums who volunteer at the Casa been trained elsewhere prior to coming here, or are they trained directly by the entities as they sit in the current? Or do they already have gifts of mediumship before they come to the Casa and if so, do the entities help strengthen their natural abilities?"

"All of those things are true, depending on the medium. The mediums do not receive any formal training from the entities of the Casa. But the entities do help them develop their gifts. Many of the Casa mediums came here with serious illnesses, and part of their healing has been through working as mediums in the current rooms."

"Have you found that many people, who would ordinarily have been diagnosed as having mental problems such as schizophrenia, are actually mediums who are in contact with the spirit world but who don't realize they are mediums?"

Sebastiao nodded. "I have heard the entity tell such people that they are not crazy, that they are mediums and that he will help them develop their mediumship."

I thanked Sebastiao for his time. He concluded by telling me that his one regret is that he is usually so busy at the Casa that he doesn't have time to really get to know the many people who approach him with questions and for help, and he fears that sometimes he may be too abrupt due to the overwhelming demands placed on his time and energy. But my experience of Sebastiao is that he usually has a ready smile, a gentle manner, and serves the "house of Love" well.

Chapter 9: Interviews with Visitors to the Casa

Some of the following people were participants in the various groups I have taken to the Casa, and I have identified them as "group participant," while others are people I met while at the Casa.

Group Participant Beth

Beth has had her share of miracles throughout her life. Here is her story.

"I've had a lot of health challenges ever since I was young, beginning with allergic asthma as a child that disappeared in early puberty and reappeared when I was 18. I've also had chronic fatigue and a variety of problems with my bladder and reproductive system.

"As I've developed spiritually, I've come to a perspective that, although these things have been painful, they have helped me grow and learn in various ways.

"One of my most life-changing events took place in Monterey, Mexico in 1998, while I was there on vacation with my husband and two young sons who were seven and eight at the time. We drove to an area near some waterfalls and a guide offered to take us up the mountain to the falls on horseback.

"At first, this seemed like a wonderful idea, but part way up the mountain, I noticed I was beginning to have a difficult time breathing. At first I thought this might be due to the altitude, but as my breathing worsened, I decided to have my husband and the boys continue without me, and to go back down the mountain to the car with the guide to see if my inhaler was in the car.

"As I rode the horse back downhill, I realized that I was having an allergic asthma reaction to the horse itself. So I got off the horse and continued stumbling down the path. I kept hoping my inhaler was in the car, but another part of me knew I'd left it back at the hotel. Nonetheless, I kept going as I didn't know what else to do.

"At a certain point in my struggle to reach the car, I suddenly felt my intestines totally let go. I immediately knew what this signaled. When there is not enough oxygen coming into the body to support the heart and brain, the body will shut down other systems in order to divert the available blood and oxygen to the heart and brain.

"I was aware that this was a signal that I was very near death. I began to pray as I stumbled onward, asking that I might just make it to the car. But when I finally did, I found that indeed, I'd left my inhaler at the hotel. I had gone as far as I could go and was about to collapse.

"I was hanging onto the car, still praying, while some people called an ambulance, and I began to see a white light. I knew I was right at the doorway of death.

"Earlier in my life, although I was not raised Catholic, I had had some kind of intermittent connection with the Virgin Mary. As I stood there, I remembered that the Virgin of Guadalupe was the patron saint of Mexico, and I began to pray not only to God and Jesus, but to the Virgin as well. I told them that I just couldn't die, that I had two young sons that needed me to raise them.

"As I stared at the white tunnel of light that was growing clearer and clearer, I saw the Virgin of Guadalupe step between me and the other side. She extended her hands toward me, and actually handed a breath to me. And for just a moment, I could breathe again. She moved out of the doorway to the other side, but when I began to gasp for air once more, she moved again in front of me and handed me another breath, which I gasped in.

"Finally the ambulance came, and I continued to focus on the Virgin. All the way down the mountain to the hospital, she kept handing me breaths. The medical staff finally was able to get me on oxygen and after a brief period of passing out, I could breathe normally again. The Virgin had saved my life, and the next day I visited the shrine of the Virgin of Guadalupe and gave profound thanks.

"My next major health crisis involved the growth of a fistula, which is like a tube of tissue that somehow forms between one organ and another. This one went from my bladder to my uterus. I didn't know what was going on at first, but I was in a lot of pain and kept getting infections, and was living on pain pills for a while. Finally my doctor diagnosed a fistula, and said that the only way to deal with it was through major abdominal surgery, about equal to the intensity of getting a hysterectomy, in order to cut and cauterize the fistula. And the recovery period for such an operation is generally six to eight weeks.

"I had no medical insurance and very little money at the time, and this would have been my fourth major surgery, so I was basically hysterical over the situation. And it wasn't something you could just put a bandage on and it would eventually go away. Fistulas just don't do that, and if you don't deal with them medically, you run the risk of massive infection and sepsis throughout the body as a result.

"My only—and temporary—alternative was to go on antibiotics until I could save up enough money to have the surgery. So that's what I did, not liking to do so because of the side-effects of being on antibiotics long term, but not having any other option that I knew of at the moment.

"During that period, Josie told me she was going to the Casa de Dom Inacio. She was aware of the health issues I was dealing with, and asked me if I would like her to take my photo to the Casa so she could show it to the entity and request healing for me. She was going to be leaving in a week, so as far as I was concerned, her timing was perfect!

"Anyway, she took my photo to Brazil. I was still on a regime of taking antibiotics for a week, then going off of them and waiting till the symptoms of infection would start to return, and then going back on the antibiotics once again.

"On the third evening of Josie's stay in Brazil while I was at home washing dishes, I suddenly felt this warm current of energy come over me, and I immediately felt surrounded with love. It was a very intense sensation, like I was being filled with warm honey. I stopped what I was doing for a few moments, laughed a bit to myself, and then went back to washing the dishes. A few minutes later, I had to stop again as the sensation was so strong.

"I thought to myself, 'I bet Josie is praying for me from Brazil'. I decided to lie down on my bed and meditate on this and enjoy the experience, which was becoming increasingly overwhelming. I left the dishes and lay down, and had a very blissful experience of joy and love. Eventually I fell asleep and slept through the night.

"The next morning when I got up, I mused on my experience of the night before and decided to email Josie in Brazil, thanking her for her prayers. She was going to be away a few more weeks and I wanted her to know what I'd experienced.

"About that time, I ran out of the antibiotics and was in the waiting mode again. After about four days, I realized that I was not having any pain yet, nor any signs of infection either. I thought, 'Hmmm, that's interesting.' I wasn't having any 'leaking' from the bladder through my uterus either. And the symptoms never came back.

"When Josie returned from her trip, I told her in person what I'd experienced the night of the current of love, and found out that that had occurred the same day she had taken my photo to the entity. I finally realized that the entities of the Casa were actually healing me.

"I did have one 'slip' after that. Josie had brought me the herbs that the entity had prescribed for me, enough for several months. I was still taking them when she went back to Brazil with her next group. During that time, I had been staying with the simple diet restrictions that went with the herbs—no alcohol, pork, etc. But one night while she was away, I attended a birthday party for a friend and toasted her with a glass of champagne.

"The next day, all of the symptoms of the fistula came back full force—pain, signs of infection, leaking, etc. A few days later I emailed Josie in Brazil to inform her of my lapse. Apparently she got the email right away and went by the entity the next day, told him what had happened, and begged that the entities forgive my lapse and heal me again. She also requested permission to represent me for an invisible surgery, and was allowed to do so.

"Once again, all of my symptoms disappeared and have not returned since (and it has been a year now). So all of this made it quite clear to me where the healing energy was coming from!

"About half a year later, I was able to make the trip to Brazil and the Casa with one of Josie's group healing journeys there.

"Before that time, I once again had a problem with an ovarian cyst. Some years earlier it had gotten so bad that it had to be treated medically. My doctors told me at that time that if it ever flared up again, I would have to have a hysterectomy. For some years I had been able to control the problem with nutrition—particularly with soy products—but about 10 days before leaving for Brazil, some of the symptoms of the cyst suddenly returned. I began having irregular bleeding and pain over that area of my abdomen. I got very worried, as I couldn't afford to have a hysterectomy and was also a bit concerned about traveling in this condition.

"I arrived in Brazil and two days later was standing in front of the entity, who told me to come back two days later for an invisible operation. Until my 'surgery,' the entity said I should spend time in the current room during the morning and afternoon sessions. I did so, and the energy in the current room felt very familiar to me due to my prior experience the evening I'd had to stop washing dishes. It was very warm, loving, and enlightening.

"The morning of my surgery, I joined all of the others having invisible operations in the third current room, or operating room. We were instructed to keep our eyes closed and put our right hand either over our heart, or if there was one specific physical area we wanted healing for, we should put our right hand there. I figured the session would be the kind of light, blissful experience I'd had in the current rooms over the past few days.

"So I closed my eyes, put my right hand over my sore ovary, and began to open myself to the energy. At the same time I began to silently pray and affirm to God and the entities, 'I thank you for my healing, I receive my healing now, I thank you for the healing that I am receiving,' over and over. I noticed that the area under my right hand was beginning to feel warm and tingly, and I thought, 'Well, that's working.'

"So then for some reason I decided to move my right hand to my heart—I guess for all of the other things I wanted healing for—and continued praying and saying my affirmation. Within moments of moving my hand, I began to feel a wave of intense nausea come up, and it kept building and building. As the nausea continued, I felt movement inside my abdomen, as if invisible hands were tugging at something, and kind of a fluttering feeling.

"The nausea was getting so intense that I couldn't handle it, so I moved my right hand back to my abdomen. That seemed to help—for a few seconds! Then the nausea returned a bit, but not so bad as before. But then I said to myself, 'If I'm going to do this, let's just do it all the way and get it over with.' So I moved my hand back to my heart, and the nausea came back so hard that I began moaning and falling over. My ears started ringing and I started to pass out, and I felt I wasn't going to be able to handle it any longer. I opened my eyes and put my hand down on the bench to steady myself, and one of the volunteer staff women came rushing over with a bucket in case I had to vomit.

"I leaned over but was kind of fighting throwing up, and then I just collapsed on the floor. So the staff people carried me to the recovery room and put me on one of the beds, and I then slept for the next few hours. When I woke up, one of the women brought me some of the blessed 'medicinal' soup that they serve at the Casa after the morning sessions, and I was able to eat it.

"I lay down for a little while more, then decided to get up, pick up the herbs that are always prescribed to those receiving surgery, and go back to the *pousada* to rest. When I got up, I noticed that my abdomen was extremely sore. I got my herbs but was kind of staggering around and in some pain. Unbeknownst to me, Josie had checked on me when I was in the infirmary and had been told I'd be there a while still. She waited outside and then checked in there again about fifteen minutes later. Somehow, she hadn't seen me when I left, and she went rushing back to the *pousada* to look for me.

"Fortunately, one of the women in our group saw me staggering around after I got the herbs and helped me get back to the *pousada*. I don't think I would have made it without her help. I was truly in a post-operative state and the spiritual anesthesia had worn off by then. I got back to my room and was really in a lot of pain, feeling as if I'd had an incision made inside my abdomen.

"I was able to sleep most of the day and into the next morning, but by abdomen was pretty sore for the next three days. However, the morning after my operation, the bleeding from the ovarian cyst had stopped and that situation has been fine ever since. So I had yet another major healing from the entities.

"I also felt like I received some healing at the *cachoeira*—the waterfall of the Casa. Josie took the women in our group there, and as I stood under the water, I said 'I release all negativity and ask that it be replaced with the white light of God as well as with health, peace, protection and love.' As I did this, a lot of

116

things let go inside of me. Tears began to flow, and I felt as if I was being cleansed inside and out, and on many levels.

"Between that experience and the work in the current and my operation, I felt some very profound emotional and spiritual healing took place as well as the physical healing. There had been places inside of myself—emotional and spiritual—that I had not been able to access for about ten years as a result of some trauma that had taken place during that time. Even years of psychotherapy and other work had not been able to release the blocks and trauma before going to the Casa. There were places of low self-esteem, an inability to get in touch with anger, and a feeling that parts of myself were actually missing.

"Since returning home from the Casa, little by little these parts of me have been coming back. It's almost like the entities performed what some people call a 'soul retrieval' for me. I feel more confident than I have in years.

"I feel that the healing at the Casa takes place on all levels, and I am very grateful for the profound help that I received both long distance and while I was there."

Lloyd Youngblood

Lloyd is a gifted healer in his own right who lives in the U.S. and has been studying powerful healers and healing systems for many decades.

Although his academic background is in history, political science and business administration, Lloyd has had a keen and long-term interest in the metaphysical. He said he didn't begin his healing work until he was 50—in the early '70s. He is also a member of a professional dowsing association, and uses his dowsing rod to measure people's auras and other energy fields.

Lloyd first met Joao in the mid-'80s, when author Bill Cox invited Lloyd to join him in Brazil on a journey in which they would research various spiritual healers. Joao was one of the healers they visited. During those days Joao was still traveling extensively, and Lloyd and Bill would meet him in various cities where he'd be attending to the multitudes day and night, sometimes seeing tens of thousands of people over a several-day period. Understandably, Joao would often become exhausted and frequently Lloyd would send him energy at the end of the day to help him out, something that Joao appreciated.

It was also Lloyd that inspired Joao to begin blessing the water that has become a part of the Casa treatment since that time. Lloyd had seen Joao bless water that the latter would then use in his healing work. He decided to measure the energy of this blessed water with his dowsing rod after one such session, and was given Joao's permission to do so.

He first measured the energy field of a bottle of water and found it—upon measuring it with his dowsing rods—to extend about one to two inches outside the bottle. Then he had Joao hold the water in his hands and asked him to transfer his personal energy into the water. The energy field extended to five or six inches. Then Joao incorporated one of the entities and held the bottle of water once more. This time, the energy field extended out between six to ten feet from the water, which was unusually strong. It was this discovery that led him to suggest that Joao in entity bless water for people to use as part of their healing process.

During that same journey, Lloyd saw Joao in entity do numerous physical surgeries, during which he would remove tumors and other substances from the patients' bodies. This made a dramatic impact on Bill and Lloyd both, as it has done for many people over the years.

During a subsequent visit, Lloyd measured Joao's energy field, first before incorporation, then afterwards. Before incorporation, his energy field expanded 18 to 24 inches outside his body, which is normal for a reasonably healthy person. Once Joao was incorporated, however, the energy field expanded to over thirty feet, indicating that a new and powerful energy field had joined with Joao's.

In the fall of 1999, Lloyd made another journey to Brazil to see Joao. I was there at the time, but never met Lloyd directly. However, I was able to buy a video of an unusual session at the Casa in which he played a key role. The following has been transcribed from the video footage.

Lloyd (on stage with Joao): "Thirteen years ago someone took a photo of Mr. Joao doing a healing on me. In the photo you can see me fine, but where Mr. Joao was standing there was only light. I'm giving him a copy of that photo as a gift."

Lloyd then measured Joao's energy with his dowsing rod before Joao incorporated. It showed that Joao's aura extended a good four feet from his body. Lloyd then measured one of the patients standing on the stage awaiting surgery, and the man's aura radiated less than a foot from his body.

Then Joao incorporated several entities, one after another, each of whose auras Lloyd measured with his dowsing rod. The first was Dom Inacio himself, whose aura extended around 35 to 40 feet from the medium's body. The next was Jose, whose aura was slightly smaller; then Dr. Augusto de Almeida, whose aura was about the same as Jose's. Then came a rare "appearance" of King Solomon, whose aura was somewhat larger than that of any of the other entities, and finally, Dr. Oswaldo Cruz, whose aura was slightly smaller than that of Jose and Dr. Augusto. The difference between the largest and smallest was only a matter of several feet.

Lloyd told me in our interview that the largest measurement he'd ever taken of Joao's aura during incorporation was during one of his trips to see Joao in the '80s. At that time Joao's aura measured a good 70 feet from his body. Lloyd also measured the energy field of a patient just before and after the latter had received a visible surgery, and the patient's energy field had expanded from zero (before) to 73 feet after the operation. Lloyd commented, "I cannot account for the increased amount of this unusually powerful but unknown (to me) ingredient. Perhaps it actually represented more than one entity's energy at that moment, plus Mr. Joao's, plus the 'inspired' hopes and prayers of the client."

I asked Lloyd how he saw as the role of faith in the effectiveness of healing. He told me that in his experience, faith made a difference—at least in the healing work he does himself—particularly when the patient is aware that Lloyd is working with him or her, whether it be face to face or via his telephone healing sessions. In those cases, he feels that faith and belief are very important, and that negative thoughts and doubts can truly interfere with the healing process.

However, occasionally people ask Lloyd to work on friends or family members who, because of their skepticism about spiritual healing, would never make an appointment with him for a session. With these people, who are not consciously aware that he is helping them, he is able to heal them in about 60% of the cases, which is a very high rate of success. He says that with such people who are without faith, who are unbelievers, he is able to circumvent their conscious mind and telepathically touch their subconscious mind in such a way that it accepts the healing.

In response to my question about what else might make a difference in the effectiveness of spiritual healing work, he said that the soul's purpose can effect whether healing occurs or not. For example, with some people, their soul has chosen illness or injury as a way to learn and develop in this lifetime. And for a soul that has completed its purpose, it is free to leave via whatever means, whether it be through an illness or a car accident or whatever.

Lloyd also feels that disease is not something that God created, but rather, it is something that we humans create as a response to life's various stresses, stresses that often include early childhood emotional problems and traumas. However, some of our illnesses and injuries have, in his experience, roots in former lifetimes as well. With his gifts, if the cause of such a challenge is not from this life, he is able to look back through a person's past lives to find the origin, and he then can more effectively begin the healing work.

In conclusion, back to the subject of spiritual healers, Lloyd feels that no healer succeeds in curing the physical 100% of the time, but that a good healer can average 80% success. Because of lack of daily consistent documentation and follow-up procedures at the Casa, he does not know what Joao's rate of success is.

The only statistic that I, the author, have on Joao's rate of success is from a book in Portuguese in which numerous people who had been to the Casa were interviewed. The statistics showed that 90% of those who had been treated at the Casa felt that they had benefited.

Jan

Jan is one of the many visitors from outside of Brazil who I met at the Casa. I got to know her over several visits to Abadiania as Jan stayed there for some months. As with many others, her illness became the catalyst for great learning and rich spiritual experiences. Here is her story.

"I am 24 years old, and life has been mountain climb for me. The most difficult part of this journey started when I discovered at age 21 that I was HIV positive, and I had no other choice than to choose to die or to live.

"One day I had heard this clear and warning inner voice whose message struck me so hard that I knew I had to go for a medical test. I had to go for four different tests just to be sure each one of them was right, and for me life was never the same again from that point, knowing I was sick and that I would probably die from AIDS. I had watched people on the television with the disease, and just imagining myself undergoing all of those physical changes really scared me.

"I never wanted to die when I was just 21 years old. I believed there was more to life than what I was going through. I became desperate to hear about miracles, stories and world legends of people who had overcome such life and death situations.

"A friend who I was living with never stopped supporting me through that difficult time. However, he himself then found out he had cancer, and he needed a great deal of medical attention until his illness reached a point where his case was beyond medical help. Now we both were in urgent need of help and of any miracle we could get.

"Then God opened a door for us, and we heard about the miracle man of Brazil. Wow. That moment for me was a major turning point. I felt that this man Joao de Deus had the key to my life and I really wanted to go and meet him. And so I did.

"My first glimpse of the entity was already a healing for me. I walked through the line and explained my situation to him, and to my surprise, the fact that I was HIV positive didn't really seem to bother him. The fact that it didn't bother him was part of my healing. At first, I wondered to myself if maybe he didn't really understand the fact that I had HIV and was dying, as he wasn't repulsed by my illness and the only thing he said to me was to come for a spiritual operation the next day.

"After my spiritual operation, I felt so weak that I had to go and sleep right afterwards. And while I was sleeping and dreaming, I began to realize a lot of blessings that God had placed in my life.

"In the weeks following my operation, whenever I would pass by the entity to see if he had anything else to tell me, he would keep telling me to sit down in the medium's section of his current room. It's funny, because at first this made me feel really neglected, as I thought it meant he didn't want to hear what I had to say about my illness. But in fact, what was happening was that I was receiving my healing through concentrating on other people's needs rather than on my own. This is what it is to be a medium of the Casa.

"Sitting in the current as a medium wasn't that easy either. Your mind, spirit and soul lead you to different areas of life and mostly not your own life but those of others. For me I felt sometimes like I had to carry the weight of my family, friends and people dying and living with HIV positive. My feeling was that I wanted to reach into their hearts and show them some hope. In all of the time that I sat in the current, I didn't think about myself that much, nor ever had this sudden moment of feeling that my HIV was gone. I just worked as a medium, concentrating on other people in need.

"The entity will work on other people through the mediums of the Casa, and in that process he made me understand that he was preparing me to do spiritual work (spiritual healing). It wasn't my healing anymore that was the main focus, but the responsibility that I help others.

"Sometimes the entity would take me with him to people who were sitting in the current room needing healing, and he would lay my hands on them. This felt really extraordinary because I never knew what I was doing until afterward when I was seated in the current again.

"The most important experience for me was when the entity had me put my hands behind this lady who had a big growth on her neck—a cancer tumor. The entity was holding me from behind, and he then pressed my hands really hard on this lady's tumor for some minutes. In a while, the tumor felt like it suddenly disappeared! And on that same day the lady was told by the entity that her healing was completed, and she was free to go home. I haven't heard from this lady since that time, but I hope she's doing fine.

"Being in Abadiania was really magical. And many of my most powerful experiences occurred when I was sleeping. During those times, like after my operation, it felt like I was dreaming but they were in fact true dreams that came to pass.

"While I was in Abadiania, I never wanted to confess that I was HIV positive to anyone apart from the entity himself, but after some months there, the word went around somehow. There were some very narrow-minded people I met who were very prejudiced against me because of me having HIV, and they didn't think I was cured. They told me that I should go for a test and then we'd see who was right.

"When I felt strong enough, I went for a test even though I was very worried that I might still have the disease. The fact that I was leaving Brazil for home the same week of the test made me feel a little bit safer, and my interest was just to prove to these guys that I wasn't HIV positive, even though it really was none of their business.

"After two good weeks back home, I got an email from a friend in Brazil who'd gone with me when I went to have the test, and in that email I found out that the results came back negative! I have done some tests here in my own country since that time and they are still negative. I had been HIV positive for three years until my healing at the Casa. My friend who had had the cancer, who also went to the Casa, is also doing fine and wants to go back there again, as do I.

"I am happy and blessed to have met the miracle man of Brazil who has changed my life. I hope this story will give you a reason to give yourself the chance to visit the Casa and to have your life restored abundantly. I have made it, and I have hope that you can make it too. Not only AIDS cases, but anything you are undergoing today could be helped at the Casa.

"I believe in the work at the Casa one hundred percent because I have been there and I have seen for myself what really happens."

Group Participant Patti Conklin

Patti has become an increasingly well known medical intuitive and healing facilitator in recent years. She was a participant in one of my group's journeys to the Casa and has had a most unusual life and a deep connection to God. Here is some of her story.

"Josie, you asked me if I would first share a bit about my own work and gifts: for example, how I experienced my gifts as a child, when I began consciously doing healing work, what kinds of healings I do and what the 'mechanics' are of how those healings work.

"As a child, I was fully 'sighted,' as all children are. But for me, I knew that what I was seeing was accurate. My parents always used to tell me that I wasn't seeing what I was seeing, or they would get frustrated with me because I would mention that there were angels and different entities in the room. But even though they said I was wrong, because of my inner knowing I always knew that I was accurate in what I was seeing.

"When I was seven, I had my first 'visitation' that was not an angel but what I call Father, God, or Creator. I was told three things at the time: that from age 38 to 42 would be my greatest growth years; that from age 42 to 62 would be my greatest contribution to humanity; and that my purpose for being here was to teach people how to become insubstantial [beings of light] without transitioning ['dying']. I didn't understand that at the time, but I kept it in my brain.

"As I was growing up, I felt like I had a split—or dual—life, because pretty much after the age of seven I wasn't allowed to speak in the house and my siblings weren't allowed to speak to me. My parents were just too frightened by what might come out of my mouth due to my ability to see on so many levels. So I entered into a period of silence. Yes, I spoke to my friends at school, but never about this side of my life the sighted part of me.

"By the time I was twelve I was pretty much living on the streets. I was fascinated with people and how they thought, and would literally sit on a street corner for hours and watch people think and watch the words form in the hemisphere of their brain. I'd see the words actually go down to the cellular body and into the structure of the cell itself. I'd also see movies forming about different people's lives as soon as they'd start talking to me. There would be this 3-D imagery of the whole event that they were starting to describe. So if somebody was talking about an event and they were leaving pieces out of the story that maybe they were too embarrassed to tell me, their body would still show it, because the body records everything in truth.

"So I'd just watch these movies that their bodies were showing me, and watch human behavior in general. The streets were my university training, and I graduated from that program before I got my high school diploma at age 16!

"I'll tell you another thing that happened when I was young—about 12. My English teacher had told me I reminded her of Edgar Cayce, and she recommended I go to the bookstore and get a book about his life. So I went, and as I was reaching for a copy of the book, God literally froze my whole body and I could not move. He thundered in my ears and said, 'Stop! Do not contaminate the knowledge and information that you have inside with someone else's thoughts.' I said, 'Fine, just give me back my hand now.' So from that point, I stopped reading, I stopped questioning other people, I just stopped and really wondered if I might be psychotic, even though I didn't think so. More deeply, I knew that my intent in life was to help people understand the spiritual.

"It wasn't like I was having visitations from God on a regular basis during that time, but there were visitations when I needed them most for direction. It wasn't just a feeling that God was there, but God would actually appear and say, 'I want you to go do this.' People ask me how I knew these were true visitations. I think to myself, 'oh, please.' The minute God starts to appear, your whole physical form evaporates, and you become one again with God. And when the visitation is over, you cry like crazy because you're back in your physical form and it's starting to become solid again and you so desperately want to go. It's actually quite painful. It's beautiful when the visitation happens but it's so painful to be left afterwards.

"Some years later, when I was 28, I was driving by a psychiatric center and Father/God spoke to me. He said he wanted me to stay there for three days, and that the doctors there would help me to understand why I was different. And I said 'okay,' pulled into the center, walked inside and told the psychiatric nurse that I wanted to see the head psychiatrist.

"I met with him and told him I needed to stay there for three days and he said, 'Why?' I told him that God wanted me to. I'm sure he thought, 'Oh yeah, we've got lots of those kind of folks here.' We started talking and he said to me that I didn't really appear to be psychotic. I told him I didn't think I was, and he gave me a weird look but told me I could stay anyway.

"The first day I was there, we did a life history. I had lived a very isolationist life. My parents were very uncomfortable with me, were not religious or spiritual, and the gifts that I had were profoundly disturbing to them. So we talked about my life all that day. At the end of the day he told me he was amazed that I was not insane or schizophrenic as a result of what my life had been like. I told him again that I didn't think I was. I told him that when I was growing up, the only 'voice' I heard inside was God's voice, and I knew that as long as I paid attention to that voice I was fine, no matter where I was or what I was doing. I didn't listen to the external voices of the people around me, including my family.

"He finally said, 'tomorrow, we're going to do an IQ test. At the end of the IQ test he said, 'Before I give you the results of this, let's do a brain wave pattern test. Do you mind if I hook you up and start the test?' I said I didn't, so he did the test. At the end he came into the room and asked if I minded if they did the test again. I said no, so we did it again. He came back looking totally perplexed and said, 'I'd like to talk to my colleagues before we talk any more about what's going on with you.'

"The morning of the third day he came into my room and said, 'The reason you feel you are so different from other people is because you are. Your IQ is 168. You're a genius. But beyond that, your brain wave pattern is almost 250% faster than the average person, far beyond what we'd consider manic or schizophrenic. You don't have any of those episodes plus you're too well grounded to fit those diagnoses. The only thing that my colleagues and I can come up with is that we feel because your brain wave pattern is so fast, it's increased everything in your body, including the optic nerve function. As a result, you're able to see energy patterns that the rest of us don't see. Beyond a psychic ability, it's an actual physiologically-based ability.'

"I told him that made sense, and he said that he and his colleagues would love for me to stay another few days so that they could study me. I said, 'No, no, God told me three days. This is the third. I'm out of here!' But the whole experience really helped me to understand myself, because I had to understand my situation analytically, why things were so different for me than with most people.

"I continued to develop my healing work and abilities, but was very careful not to approach people myself, even if I saw cancer in someone's body. God really taught me not to interfere unless it was His will. Once I was in the Far East in an Asian village and saw a mother carrying a two-year-old child who was dying of severe respiratory distress. My hands started heating up like crazy with massive energy flowing through them. I took a step forward because I was going to lay on of hands, and just as I did, Father spoke and said, 'Child, I did not ask you to intervene. Please respect my process.' I stood and watched that child die without touching it. It was agony. My own sons were six and seven years old at the time, and my heart just went out to that mother and child. But as I saw the child's soul rise out of it's physical form, I was amazed to see the joy and the connectedness of the soul to Source.

"I'm 43 now, and I've lost the ability to switch my sight off and on—it's always on now. You know how the Bible says that when people die their entire life passes before them? Well, when I look at you I see everything that has happened to you from that moment in time backwards. I have to release all judgment to do this work, whether I'm working with a Death Row inmate who's about to be executed, or I'm working with the family of a child who's ready to cross over, or with someone who's just wanting more understanding.

"In my work as a medical intuitive, a lot of times doctors will call me when someone has cancer, for example, and it's manifested in several areas of the body and they want to know where it originated so as to treat it effectively. And I can tell them, because for me, there's nothing within the body that is hidden. And you're always going to find an emotional or psychological or spiritual core event that has eventually manifested in the body. This is something that is important for people to understand.

"I've also been called upon by the Catholic Church to do exorcistic work. Contrary to people's fears, there are not very many demonic forces walking this earth. The purpose of a demon is to destroy the physical body that the soul is inhabiting, and that's usually the body of a light being, someone who has come here for a very specific spiritual job.

"Demons are different than what Brazilians call "obsessive spirits." The latter are spirits of humans who haven't fully crossed over—for whatever reason—and are still on this physical plane. When you have mental illness, alcoholism or drug addiction, they all poke holes in the auric field which then allows an obsessive entity to attach very easily. Even having surgery or having a baby under general anesthesia can open your field to the point that you're vulnerable to obsessive spirits. Some people come out of anesthesia with a different personality, or start a drug addiction *afterwards*, and its because an entity has attached itself while they were unconscious. Even feeling unprepared for life and its challenges and going into a deep depression can open a person to those obsessive spirits. From my first week at the Casa, I'd say that 50 to 60% of the people I personally saw there had obsessive spirit attachments.

"Back to the subject of demonic spirits, a low vibration can't exist with a high vibration. So to rid a person of a demonic, I just take my vibration, raise it as high as possible, go into that person's body also, and then the demonic is cast out because it just can't stay. It normally takes me about 10-15 minutes to cast it out and send it back home.

"Dealing with obsessive entities is an entirely different matter. With them, I'll just look them in the eye and say, 'Do you see who I am?' and they just take off. I'll never forget this one entity that actually had his hand around a woman's heart. That one was actually more of a gargoyle. But anyway, I sat down on the woman's bed—her physician was there too—and the entity immediately put its hands around my throat—using the woman's body to do so - and started saying, 'I'm going to kill you!' and blah-blah-blah. And I remember looking into her/its eyes and saying, 'You might want to think again,' and the thing just shriveled and came right out and went away. I don't know why I do those things, but I noticed some of the same things happening at the Casa when some people went in line past the medium. All Joao/the entity had to do was look at them for a moment, and the obsessive spirit would just let go of that person and leave.

"Most of those obsessive spirits go to the Light, because 98% of those entities are light beings who have their path just like we do. There's really no right or wrong, good or bad about the situation—it just simply is. They may have become obsessive/attached spirits in order to take their 'host's' soul to the next level of understanding. We have to see that those spirits are in perfection just the way they are, just as we have to see ourselves that way.

"Our soul is here on earth to learn. It's not fully connected to Source because it's still in our physical being. We've got to be willing to go through the tunnel. We've got to be willing to face the darkness, the fear of everything that we are and of everything that we are not in order to find the Divine, that piece that we originally started out as.

"We've got to have chaos in order to grow. So what we sometimes call darkness is catalytic, not a bad thing. People need to get out of the sadness when they see someone—or themselves—with a serious disease. Sometimes people think I'm cold and unemotional when they've asked me to do healing work on a seriously ill family member and I tell them, 'Well, if healing is in the plan at this point, fine, and if they're meant to cross over, I'll sit with them.' But then they see that I'm really coming from a loving place and that in *my* mind, crossing over is not a bad thing. They are leaving because their work is done. You cannot leave this earth plane until your work is done here. That's why so many suicides fail. Those people's soul work here just wasn't done yet.

"People often have so much trouble with the idea of death. They say, 'Why did that person have to leave? They had so much to live for still,' etc. You have to understand that it's the soul that is running things, and that the soul wanted to go home when it's work was done here. That's why some healings work here at the Casa and some don't, in the sense that the person 'dies.' But there is always healing at the Casa, even if it's on the level of helping the soul strengthen in its resolve to go home. It's not a failure if they're not miraculously physically healed and they still pass on.

"My orientation in my own work with others, is 'Did the soul come through a growth process by being in contact with me?' It has nothing to do with 'Did I heal this person or not.' My main concern is if the soul went through a growth process with its connection by coming into contact with me. And that's exactly the same as with Joao and other people of his caliber. That's the purpose, whether it's within those few seconds of contact with the entity when Joao is incorporated or over a longer period, the issue is for the soul to go through some growth—that's the deeper level of healing.

"Josie, you asked me to describe my way of 'seeing' when I focus on Joao when he is not incorporated, and then when he is. When I see the man in his physical being, what I see is that his cellular structure is becoming weakened, and that is very, very typical. What I mean is this. Our physical forms have become very polluted throughout the centuries and our cellular structure is not used to handling that level of energy—like with the entities that Joao deals with. That's why you'll see people like Joao becoming ill as they get further on in their work, or have strokes or blood clots and so on. On a cellular level it's exhausting to keep moving that kind of energy day after day, year after year, because we've become so polluted. So I see the toll that this work is taking on Joao's physical form, and this has been true for most people over history who have brought through that level of energy. It seems to be an occupational hazard of this kind of work.

"But on another level, when I look at Joao the man (not when he's incorporated), or Pope John Paul, or the Dalai Lama, they are all white columns of light. Joao is fully integrated. Now that doesn't mean he doesn't get ticked off sometimes or go through other very human emotions. We're still in human form and we're still going to be human. But he's definitely just a column now.

"When I 'see' Joao when he's fully incorporated by the entity, his strength is back. In my eyes, his physical form isn't even there any more. He's become insubstantial in form and is fully connected. So when I look at him it's like being able to just see right through him.

"I think it was on my third day at the Casa that I was watching Joao as he sat in the chair with people filing by him for diagnoses and help. That day he incorporated two or three different times—several different entities within a matter of minutes—depending on the person who was approaching him in the line. So in that instant between incorporations, his physical form would be back and then disappear again. That's different than what I do. I'm in both spaces all the time so there isn't so much sliding in and out. I don't have an actual entity taking over my physical form. I am the entity. I think it's got to be extremely demanding on Joao's physical form to have that kind of capability to go back and forth the way he does, and yet it's the whole basis of the kind of mediumistic work he does. He has to be able to get out of ego, because ego has to be non-existent during those mediumistic states.

"You're talking about a very advanced soul in Joao's case, one who has to be willing to completely step out of the way. Because it's not just his consciousness that has to move out of the way—it's his actual soul that does, in order to make room for the entity. You can't have two souls occupying the same body.

"You also asked me what I 'see' when Joao is incorporated and doing the physical surgeries on people, like the eye scraping, the incisions, etc. What I see is the entities going in energetically and removing stuff from the subtle energy fields. What we have to remember is that sometimes, even though we're talking about vibration, if we have the same thought form and it goes to the same part of the body often enough, it actually creates a disease or physical manifestation. So what Joao's doing is removing the physical portion that has already manifested, and what the entity is doing is realigning the whole subtle energy field. Just taking out the physical does not remove the emotional or spiritual core issue. So what I saw during the physical surgeries was the entities taking out the spiritual aspect of that illness from the subtle energy field—whether it's the eyes, or like the woman with the breast incision I saw last week, or sticking the hemostat up the nose. Joao's hands and instruments were removing the physical component while the entities did the other stuff.

"When the entity tells people requesting them that they aren't going to get a physical operation, but rather an invisible one, in many cases it's because there's nothing physical that's manifested enough or in such a way that there's something physical to take out. For example, there was that guy last week who had cirrhosis of the liver. Well, that liver is like Swiss cheese. They can't take out the whole liver, so they're going to have to work on an energetic basis with the illness.

"Sometimes, in fact, often at the Casa, I think, the location of the physical surgery is not where the physical problem seems to be. For example, you mentioned the 'nose job' that was actually to treat the man's hernia. Remember when I talked about those tendrils earlier? That's when you have the core issue somewhere other than the place where the disease or physical problem seems most obvious. I would suspect that what Joao is doing in those cases, then, is going to the point of entry closest to where the core issue was. So even if the hernia is in the guy's abdomen, it's still connected by a tendril to the location of the core issue. The entities have the 'sight' to be able to look in there and find the actual core, which may not be where the 'disease' seems to have most obviously manifested.

"When a person has an invisible surgery at the Casa, it's because they can be worked on best through the subtle energy field without the trauma to the body that the physical surgeries involve. Even with tumors, they can be dissolved through the work on the subtle energy body.

"The thing is, there are so many different aspects to this work. If the person really believes, and has a deep abiding faith that they'll be healed, chances are they will unless the soul's ready to check out. And that's where we get so much of our cancer and AIDS. The soul is simply ready to check out, and that's the way it's been chosen for them to go. In the case that it's that person's time, the entities of the Casa can take away pain so that whatever the person is going through in that process is in the best interest of the soul at that time.

"Back to your question on why some people seem to have rapid, even 'instantaneous' physical healings here at the Casa, while others take place over time or in some cases, may not happen at all. It all has to do with what the soul is needing to learn. If the soul still has work to do and a spontaneous healing is part of the growth of that soul, that's what will happen. If it's not meant to happen that way, it means that this is part of what the soul agreed to come in to do. We need to get beyond our consciousness of looking at a disease and saying, 'Oh, you poor thing', because the soul is growing tremendously within that proces,'

"I look at the people that have the greater hardships and life, and realize that they're the stronger souls, because they came in and said, 'Okay, I'm willing to do this.' Some people feel I'm unemotional when it comes to dealing with the disease process, or they look at someone like Joao and wonder how he can keep seeing person after person and not be effected. But the more you see that everything is perfect, that every soul is fulfilling its purpose, its journey, the less you get so caught up in emotionality over it all. That doesn't mean that some people's situations don't touch our heart, because every once in a while that does happen to me. But it's not a matter of feeling sympathy for them, but rather an issue of, 'did the soul grow?'

"Even in those two seconds when you're before the entity, for example, there is growth taking place with every soul that comes before him. And that's really Joao's and the entities' purpose. The physical surgeries and healings are just kind of the icing on the cake. A lot of people get confused by that. While I've been here, I've heard people comment, for example, on the man who has that huge lump on the back of his neck, saying, 'Why doesn't the entity remove that?' Well, the soul's growth is the primary thing, and if it's not meant to be for that soul's growth, it just won't happen. If the physical and the emotional and soul's purpose are all in the right place, if the milkman had a higher vibration than that man with the lump, he could be healed through the milkman.

"Let's talk about the role of faith for a minute. When people come to the Casa, especially the Brazilians, they come with a lot of faith and belief. They're not coming necessarily expecting miracles, although sure, everyone would probably like one, but they're coming primarily to be blessed. And if the miracle occurs, of course that's wonderful, but if it doesn't, that doesn't erode their faith and belief. This is something I really noticed last week here: the fact that a miracle not necessarily happening right away does not erode their faith. That's how you know their faith in God is absolute: if it's meant to be, it will happen, and if it isn't, it won't. And if it doesn't, they don't assume it means they're being punished. In the U.S., we go through victim stuff, even around our healing. But these people don't, and that's something I really love about them— such a level of faith they have.

"When I teach a workshop, I could literally walk up to everyone there and take out every illness or disease from them, just like Joao can do. The thing is, though, if people don't understand what created the illness in the first place, in a matter of days they will manifest it again. So at the Casa, when healing takes place—as it always does, at least on the spiritual level—and the symptoms don't change, then it has to do with soul's purpose, and soul needs to be with that illness for its own growth. Or, it could be that they need to understand their behavior better before the healing can take place.

"Sometimes I see people here bringing children who are very ill, and often in that case, the child's soul has chosen the illness as a catalyst for their family's growth. So it's not a matter of bringing them here and healing them. It's more a matter, from my point of view at least, of helping the parents understand that they need to be as loving as possible and know that their child's soul is in perfection. And they need to see that their expectation of their child was for it to be as perfect in body as possible, and as a result, they think there's something wrong, when in fact there is nothing wrong with that child and that the child is perfect in every way. The parents need to let go of their perception that something is wrong. To me, that would be the greatest gift that they could receive in coming here.

"You asked me what role I feel that faith plays here at the Casa in regards to healing. Whether it's here at the Casa or anywhere else, the deeper we are into our faith, the more we're working from a place of love: love of God, Source, whatever. And because we're all one on the most fundamental level, when you have that strong faith, it activates the heart chakra and raises the vibrational level in and around you. Then your soul has the choice of tapping into that vibration to help it along in healing the body—or to leave the body.

"Sometimes in prayer groups people will get very emotional about their prayers and from that place be asking God to heal someone's tumor or whatever. All of that emotion creates a very chaotic energy, and besides, that person may need that tumor at that time in their life. When I'm asked to pray for someone, I say, 'Father, please allow this person to feel You in whatever way is most appropriate.' That's my prayer, because illness isn't a bad thing.

"So back to faith, especially with those people in third world countries like Brazil with a lot of faith, people aren't praying so much for individualistic things but more that God touch that person. Their whole heart center opens up and then the soul of the person they're praying for can choose to use that vibration in healing the body, or, if their purpose is done, in assisting the soul to go. If friends and family members of people in comas—or near death in some other way—would understand that there is no ending with death, rather than cause the soul of their loved one torment by insisting it stay in the body when it's really time to go, they could let go of that person and it would be much easier on that soul.

"The power of faith and prayer is incredible, and it could do a lot more than we allow it to do because of our emotional involvement. Josie, you've experienced a lot of vision quests and have dealt with others having visions and spirit visitations. A lot of times after such an experience, people rush to interpret what they saw, which is often their own emotional overlay rather than a true interpretation. It would be better for them to just let the experience keep flowing. The same is true with faith. We would do better to simply have faith in the love and perfection flowing through us from Source than to try to keep interpreting everything that we think is going 'wrong' through our limited data base and emotions.

"The Casa is built in an area that is a strong vibrational power point. When you combine that power with the faith of the people who come here and hold their faith and raise their vibration, it brings the strong energy from the earth even closer to the surface. There are quite a variety of kinds of people who come here, and sometimes I'll watch clusters of people grouping together at the Casa. When you get a group of people who are trying to control the process of healing in some way with their prayers or attitudes, I see the energy around them become very dense. When I'm seeing clusters of people who are more open, the energy is clearer.

"I personally have to be able to walk my talk and be certain that my outer actions—and even inner thoughts and emotions—are in alignment with what I believe. For example, just before I came here to Abadiania, I knew that I had some anger and bitterness within me due to some experiences I'd had recently. And to me, that is just unacceptable. It was a small amount, but it was enough. If I'm not willing to look at it and release it and come back to unconditional love, I have no right to be the teacher that I am. So releasing it is one of my main focuses of healing during this time at the Casa and on this trip. I feel that it doesn't matter what good we're doing out in the world if we're not looking at our own process of behavior: how we interact with others, with society, and most important, with ourselves.

"Josie, you asked me earlier about my perspective on the 'current' at the Casa. I think the current is a combination of what the mediums in the current rooms generate, and the entities, and the fact that the Casa is sitting on a powerful vortex of earth energy—a very strong current or vibration in and of itself. So there is this energy emanating out of the earth, an energy that is present in much of this part of the world. At this point in his mediumship, Joao could probably incorporate anywhere, but this energy here is very helpful to him. The entities themselves are also high vibrational beings and contribute to the current. And the level of faith of the house mediums also contributes to it, as well as the faith of those who come for healing here. The current seems present throughout the Casa, but for me, it seems most substantial in the second current room where Joao sits incorporated to receive people, because that's where the entities are most concentrated. The energy of the first current room seems to have more of the chaotic, fluctuating energy that brings up more of the emotional and spiritual database. So by the time people have gone through the first current room and get into the second current room, there is more capability of healing taking place for them psychologically, physically or spiritually.

"The way the Casa is set up is very conducive to healing, including the energized water served at the end of sessions and the 'medicinal' soup after the morning session which helps ground what took place earlier.

"Again, in my perspective, the most important thing is what the soul has gone through as a result of a person's participation at the Casa rather than what their conscious mind is aware of or the physical aspects.

"There are several reasons why I would recommend coming here to Abadiania. For one thing, the pace of life is much slower here than what most people back home are caught up in, so it forces people to slow down themselves and look at what's going on in their process. The energy here is substantial enough that it will effect everyone who comes here in terms of raising emotional stuff that needs to be looked at, no matter what their conscious reason for coming here. I feel that many Westerners have lost the ability to truly have faith, and I think that when they come here, they can come to a whole new level of faith and get back to trusting in self. They can stop needing to question the 'why' of everything, realizing that there is much more that we don't know than we thought—and that that's great!

"When they see someone like Joao working, especially doing those physical operations, it would literally change their comprehension and shift their paradigm. And that's very important. I believe there will be conscious shifts for every single person who comes here, and even more shifting subconsciously on the level of the soul. Both the curious and those deeply searching can come here to experience a true healer and benefit from the contact.

"Coming here, one gets a whole new understanding of the word healer. I don't consider myself a healer and cringe when people announce me at programs as a fabulous healer. I'm a facilitator and do what Father asks of me, and I give people tools to use for their healing. That's my job. But someone like Joao—or rather, the entities who are really doing the work—is phenomenal. He's allowing his ego to be pushed aside so that the entities can come in and do the work. That's been the humbling experience for me here: to see what I would truly consider a healer. There have been great masters who have walked the earth like Jesus and Buddha and others who have done healing. They've all worked from the Divine and have been pure of heart and have done what Father has asked them to do. But what goes on here is a whole different thing, what with the incorporation work going on. This kind of thing seems to happen more in third world countries around the world, where the people are so much more humble and full of love that healing entities are able to work through them.

"I think if people truly had the understanding of what is really going on here, they'd be flocking here in even greater numbers.

"One thing I've personally experienced here is that I've slept and slept, day and night both. I tell my clients that if true healing is going on, they'll probably be exhausted for a while. So that's been going on for me. The second night I was here, there were three entities in my room that I could see—two male and one female - working on me. I could see their features, which is unusual, because usually I can't see spirits distinctly, and couldn't at the Casa where there were so many entities. And while I'm still processing some of the emotional stuff that I came here to work on, I can honestly say that my anger and bitterness is gone and I'm looking at what my next steps will be. And I also feel I've been rejuvenating from the demands of my work much faster than I've usually been able to do elsewhere. So all in all, it's been a wonderful experience for me."

Chapter 10: Testimonials of Cures Translated from Documents of the Casa

I transcribed, translated and condensed the following testimonials loaned to me with the permission—and from the staff—of the Casa de Dom Inacio. Each testimonial had been stamped and authenticated by a notary public and includes a sworn statement by the person who wrote it that it was true. The testimonials were given freely and the people who wrote them have given permission for them to be shared.

Ilza Wilson of Australia

"...I came to the Casa in November of 1998, and January and November of 1999. In 1998 I'd been diagnosed with cancer in both lungs and the throat, which was still there after a year of chemotherapy and radiation therapy.

"When I arrived in Abadiania for the first time I was very ill and in a lot of pain, taking morphine in the morning and evening. In the afternoon of November 12, 1998, the entity Dr. Augosto de Almeida operated on me. Since that time until today (September 21, 2000), I've taken no medicine, not even for headaches. In November 1999, Dr. Augosto told me that I could have an x-ray and it would show that I was completely cured.

"I returned to Australia and on August 1, 2000, I had an x-ray. The doctors couldn't believe what they saw: I was completely cured. All that remained was a tiny scar in my left lung. I told the doctors what had cured me. One of the doctors wept and hugged and congratulated me. He said, 'I've heard many stories of cures that medicine can't explain. But this is the first time I've seen direct evidence of such a thing and I now know that God is the best doctor.'

Nadir Gumiero Lena of Brazil

Nadir came to the Casa and wrote the following on January 21, 2000. She had a solid lump in her right breast that showed up in an ultrasound exam in April of 1999. Her doctor had recommended a biopsy but Nadir refused and went instead to the Casa for treatment that same month. The entity in the morning session said she should have an invisible operation that afternoon. After the operation she returned to her home, taking with her the herbal remedies of the Casa. Her second ultrasound exam then showed that the nodule had moved from one part of the breast to another.

Nadir returned to the Casa and she received another herbal remedy. After returning home again, shortly thereafter she had a high-resolution mammogram that showed that the nodule was now completely gone.

Ignacio Zanelato of Brazil

On May 14, 1990, Ignacio experienced a major detachment of the retina—84 degrees—that was diagnosed by a medical doctor. Over a five-year period he had a number of operations for this condition, during which the doctors tried to save the retina but which instead resulted in the loss of his cornea. After a corneal implant, the problem was aggravated further when he suffered a major hemorrhage. The doctors became increasingly discouraged and finally told him there was nothing more that they could do for him.

Ignacio took a chance and went to the Casa, received an operation on a Thursday and left for home Friday. On Saturday while he was still traveling homeward, his vision began to clear and he stated, "I began to see this marvelous world again. I thank God for this miracle that occurred four years ago."

Desides Terreira da Conceicao of Brazil, written Feb. 28, 2000

When Desides first went to the Casa, he had no use of one arm and was in a great deal of pain. The doctors had told him the bone had deteriorated and was pressing on a nerve. Physical therapy was only making it worse. He was told he'd just have to get used to it and be on pain medication for the rest of his life. Depressed and discouraged with medical treatment and options, he went to the Casa where he received spiritual operations and the herbal remedies. He is cured and is a very happy man.

Terezinha Zordaus Morda of Brazil, written May 22, 2000

Terezinha had a strange illness. She was constantly thirsty day and night and even five liters of water at a time could not quench her thirst. The doctors could not figure out what to do, so she finally put herself in God's hands and asked that God show her the way.

Shortly thereafter someone told her about Joao de Deus. Terezinha began to frequent the Casa de Dom Inacio and over a three-year period she went 15 times, after which she was told she needed no more treatments. She was cured of the thirst and of many other infirmities.

Maria da Graca Calimam Tomazelli of Brazil, written May 19, 2000

Maria was desperate, with many health problems that were not being resolved by medical treatment. Finally she went to the Casa. She received physical operations on her eyes and experienced no pain, after which she was able to stop using her very thick glasses. Her problems with stomach pain, spinal problems, and problems of the ovaries and uterus have all been cured or vastly improved "through the power of faith and love." Other problems of the liver, veins and feet have also been healed.

Zilda Leoterio de Almeida of Brazil, written May 19, 2000

Zilda went to the Casa for the first time in 1996 with problems of headaches and distorted vision as well as gall-bladder problems and back pain. She was operated on and cured of all of these problems. She says that since that time, whenever she feels something is wrong, she goes to the Casa and is cured of all her problems. She says the work there "is done solely through love."

Normelita Donascimento Farias of Brazil, written May 22, 2000

Normelita suffered debilitating mental illness that progressed to a point where she had to be restrained in order to prevent her from attacking her own children. She had been in this state for 18 years, seeking various treatments in various hospitals, sometimes committed to mental facilities for extended stays. Nothing helped until, accompanied by her husband, she went to the Casa.

She arrived there in physical restraints but went home without them, feeling completely sane. It's now been six years since she went to Abadiania and today she is cured and happy, "thanks primarily to God and my faith and Joao de Deus."

Antonio Fernandes Galvao of Brazil

Antonio was cured of facial paralysis (left side) at the Casa through Joao's work. He suffered this paralysis during the night of December 22, 1999, noticing it first when he got up the next morning to brush his teeth. His doctors told him the paralysis was due to a blocked artery from the heart. They prescribed some drugs and physical therapy, but after four days Antonio felt he was getting worse rather than better. So he decided to go to the Casa, where he had been treated in 1981 for terrible head pain.

He arrived this time on December 27, 1999 and was attended to by the entity on the 29th. He was seen that morning by the entity Dr. Augusto, who said he needed surgery and asked if he wanted visible or invisible. Antonio chose invisible surgery, which he received that afternoon at 2:30pm. Immediately after surgery he began to feel improvement and he returned to his hotel. Upon arriving there he noticed he was already able to blink with his left eye and that his face was returning to normal. He had been prescribed three bottles of remedies at the Casa.

The next day he returned home to Goiania. On January 4, 2000, he went to a neurologist and went through a series of neurological exams. The consensus of his doctors was that he was totally cured and they sent him home with nothing more than a bottle of vitamin B-12. He says he knows he was healed through the work of the medium Joao and the entity Dr. Augusto.

Chapter 11: Further Reflections on the Casa

It is always a wonderful challenge for me to step into another culture or spiritual path, something I have done numerous times. Some of what I have learned by doing so is to suspend my own paradigms and ways of operating and to immerse myself as completely as possible in a new way of being and of seeing things. This approach has served me well, whether in Brazil and at the Casa, on the Navajo reservation where I lived and attended ceremonies for some years, and in the many other places I have been privileged to visit and experience.

Brazil is a predominantly Catholic country, as is much of Latin America. Joao himself was raised Catholic, and many of the Brazilians who attend the sessions at the Casa are as well, although many of them, including Joao, are also Spiritists, and sometimes are members of other spiritual groups as well such as Umbanda or the Santo Daime church.

As a result of the strong Catholic presence, at the Casa you will find pictures of Jesus, Mary and other saints, and the sessions there usually include the Lord's Prayer and the Ave Maria, sometimes repeated more than once during a given session. Nevertheless, people from all races and religions are welcomed equally and without discrimination at the Casa, and I have encountered people there from almost all of the world's main religions and other spiritual paths.

I have noticed that occasionally, some of the Americans who go to the Casa have had some initial level of discomfort with the Catholic influence there. These are usually people who were brought up in one Christian faith or another and who still have unresolved ambiguities about the Church and their own religious upbringing. I feel that their issues with the Catholic overtone is part of their healing process, and encourage them to look more deeply at what it is that is really being offered at the Casa. The people of Jewish, Hindu, Buddhist and other faiths, including shamanic backgrounds, oddly seem to have much less of a problem with the Catholic overlay at the Casa than do many American Christians!

Here is the story of one American's experience of spiritual healing relating to the above issues.

"One day during the waiting period in the main hall, I experienced the beginning of an emotional breakdown. I was taken to the recovery room, lay down on one of the cots and started to sob uncontrollably.

"The volunteer who was caring for me looked at me and asked me what the necklace was that I was holding. I told her it was a Buddhist mala. She smiled at me and showed me what she was holding, and said, "This is a Catholic rosary."

"Suddenly the energy of the Christos came into me. At the age of 18 I had denounced Roman Catholicism, and threw the Christ out with the Roman Catholic dogma. While laying in the recovery room, it was made clear to me through my experience there that the True Christ, the Light, the Christos, is independent of Roman Catholicism.

"So I experienced a re-unification with the Christos.

"During my second trip to Abadiania, I was told by the entity to have an invisible operation the next day, and so that is what I did. On the day after my operation, I was in the main hall and getting ready to go sit in the current room. Sebastiao was on the podium talking.

"All of he sudden he kind of gestured out to me, telling the helper at the door to take me to the operating room. I thought to myself, 'Operating room, second day in a row, what is that about?!'

"When I was taken to the operating room, the female assistant told me to lie down on one of the cots, and so I did. I then must have gone into a non-ordinary state, a kind of trance state in which I was told repeatedly that the light of the Christos was above my head.

"Later in my *pousada* room, a friend visited me. I told her the story of what had happened to me and she looked up and said, 'Yes, you have an aura of gold around your head!' That confirmation was something I really needed.

"These spiritual experiences were of great importance to me. The re-unification with the energy of the Christos was a deep part of my healing process."

Some American visitors to the Casa also develop various agendas initially that are usually irrelevant to their healing process and are probably diversionary tactics of the mind, designed to keep them from focusing on their own personal healing issues. For example, some visitors feel the plumbing should be re-done more like the American system, or that the opening speeches should be shorter or should be simultaneously translated into English, or that the music played should be different, or a variety of other comments or criticisms.

I have been guilty of the occasional critical thought myself. But then I stop and think, "It is I who am the guest here. I am being welcomed into the Casa as well as to Brazil, and it is I who needs to adjust to what I find here, not vice verse!"

I think that if those of us who visit the Casa from other countries would adopt this attitude, we would be able to take better advantage of all that awaits us there and be quite grateful as a result. This is not to say that there is no room for small improvements here and there at the Casa, and indeed they welcome suggestions there. But it is more a matter of focus and gratitude that I am addressing here. If healing and spiritual expansion are what you are seeking at the Casa, that is what you will find, for that is its primary purpose for existence.

One of the things that I have criticized on occasion has been the music played during the sessions in the current rooms. When I first started going to the Casa, the music was generally of the soft, soothing, New Age meditative type. It was very conducive to going into trance-like states and helped me relax and open up in the current.

Then, after about a year from my first visit, I noticed that the music was being played louder and was of a much more lively—and to my ears, somewhat raucous—style. I was not happy with this and had more trouble concentrating in the current. I finally put my suggestion to change it in the suggestion box as well as discussing the issue with the man who was in charge of the sound system and music being played.

He told me that the music was the choice of the entities, not his own personal choice. At first I didn't believe him, and went to yet another person with my complaints. What this person told me gave me a new perspective on the situation.

He told me that many people who come to the Casa with physical, psychological and spiritual illnesses are themselves natural but untrained mediums. Over time, the entities found that such people went readily into very receptive trance states with "spacey" music, thereby leaving themselves too open to possible negative spiritual influences. For this reason, the entities had decided to change the music to a variety less conducive to trance states in order to protect these untrained but powerful mediums.

This information humbled me and led me to realize that often there are good reasons behind the way things are done at the Casa that I might be quite unaware of, and as a result of understanding this, I have been much less prone to be critical of the way things are run there.

The issue of some people who are drawn to the Casa being undeveloped mediums themselves is an interesting one. In Brazil generally and at the Casa in particular, as I have mentioned earlier, many people feel that the cause of most serious illnesses is spiritual: obsessive spirits and other negative spiritual influences. However, sometimes there are positive spiritual forces that can inadvertantly cause illness as well. The latter possibility was explained to me by an Umbanda practitioner in Brazil.

In essence, what this Umbanda practitioner said is that each person has various spiritual guides and mentors that want to express themselves through us. If this expression is suppressed, then that suppression itself can eventually cause illness in the person.

I would conclude, then, that for a natural but undeveloped medium, this would frequently be the case.

Let's take a look at the issue of trance mediumship more generally. From what I have read and perceived, my sense is that most traditional Western psychologists or psychiatrists would look at mediums like Joao, the late Ze Arrigo or the Umbanda mediums of Brazil and come to the conclusion that their mediumistic activities were a manifestation of psychological illness rather than of spiritual talents. From a psychological perspective they would wrongly assume that either these people had multiple personalities, were delusional and hearing voices, or were simply repressed and "acting out" aspects of their personality that they were unable to express under ordinary conditions. Even Ze Arrigo thought he himself was crazy when the entity "Dr. Fritz" first started speaking with him. He was also ill off and on with blinding headaches for 12 years until he finally surrendered to being a medium. Then the headaches went away. And the issue of whether he was crazy or not was also resolved when he became the powerful trance medium healer whose work, in retrospect, was similar to that of Joao's today.

The viewpoint of mental disorders, as regards to mediums, is understandable within the context of clinical training, which is usually oriented toward seeking out and hopefully ameliorating psychological pathology. Unfortunately, this perspective makes no room for the possibility of an interface between the spirit world and those of us here in human bodies, nor does it make room for the possibility of God giving certain individuals unusual but potentially very useful spiritual gifts and perceptions.

I ask the reader simply to make space for the possibility that not everyone who hears voices or who goes into altered states is necessarily mentally ill. Some of these individuals may in fact be natural mediums who have simply not been trained and whose culture makes little space for the possibility of an interface between the ancestor spirit world and ours.

Part of the value of the Casa is that the entities often help train undeveloped mediums. I have seen this take place on a number of occasions, some of which were discussed in the many interviews. I have even described earlier in the book how I myself have been the recipient of such training.

With many people who have been helped by the entities to develop their natural mediumship, part of the result is that their physical illnesses are healed. So in these cases, the healing is truly a spiritual healing which then positively effects the physical as well.

I believe the work at the Casa is having a huge ripple effect out into our world. The entities have frequently said to visiting medical doctors that spiritual energy healing is going to be the wave of the future in medicine, and that part of the mission of the entities is to transmit some of this energy to and through the doctors who come to the Casa.

Many healing practitioners, including myself, who are already working in the spiritual healing arts, are finding that our effectiveness and the quantity and quality of energy coming through us in our work with others has taken huge leaps through our contact with the entities.

Undeveloped mediums are being trained and then are going back into the world with more abilities to help others.

In addition, all of those who have received healing through the work of the Casa have told countless stories of their experiences to family, friends and strangers, thus subtly permeating the collective field of consciousness, or "morphogenic field," with the knowledge that God is creating miracles of healing through human agents such as Joao. This is increasing our collective faith in the potentials of spiritual healing.

And finally, if many—or even some—people who have been diagnosed as mentally ill are in fact undeveloped mediums in contact with the spirit world, then the work at the Casa can not only help them, but may begin to have an effect on how the Western mental health community might more accurately perceive and better help such patients as well. Perhaps some of the American and European visitors to the Casa who are psychologists and psychiatrists may be able to bring this perspective and assistance to those wrongly diagnosed as mentally ill. I am not saying that all people who have been diagnosed as schizophrenic or with other psychoses are necessarily untrained mediums. But even if some of them are and could not only be relieved of their suffering with proper help and training, but then in turn could help others, it would be an incredible blessing.

Learning about the work of the entities of the Casa has perhaps, by now, begun to sound almost as natural to the reader as learning about "living" teachers and healing practitioners. It has become quite natural for me, so much so that I can almost forget that there was a time when I believed that life and consciousness ended when our last breath left our body. Some of the value of spending time at the Casa and experiencing the tangible presence and work of the entities has been my growing certainty that individual consciousness does not end when the body dies. It simply moves onward in its journey and purpose. For some souls, that purpose is to continue helping the "living" from the spirit world, as is the case with the entities of the Casa.

Knowing that the individual consciousness—and often aspects of the personality as well—continue on has removed most of my fear of death. What little of that fear remains is the slight edge of fear of the unknown, of change, which is something I have in common with my fellow human beings and usually manage to overcome! I believe that many people who have spent time at the Casa have been similarly comforted by experiencing the entities and by the understanding of what their interactions with us really mean.

The potentials of the work of the Casa de Dom Inacio are vast and already having an effect in the world. What future and ongoing effects are possible remain to be seen, but the Casa is an incredible resource for humanity and merits more research. This book is but one more step in bringing additional attention to its potentials and to the frequent miracles of Love that take place there.

Bust of St. Ignatius in the Casa Gardens

Discarded crutches and wheelchairs from people healed at the Casa.

Joao de Deus

Praying at the triangle

Artistic revelation of Joao, healing entities, volunteer mediums of the Casa, and a patient being worked on

People waiting to go see Joao "in entity"

The current room

Joao "in entity" holding his prescription pad

Joao going into trance before beginning a surgery

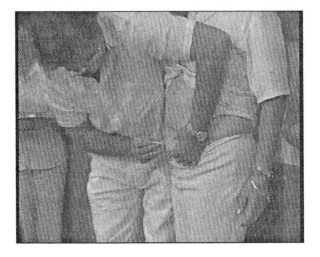

Joao in entity making an incision

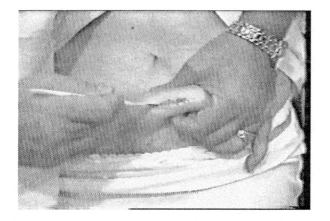

Joao in entity performing an incision that docsn't bleed

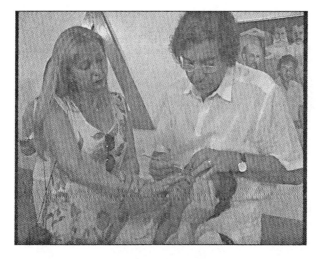

Eye surgery

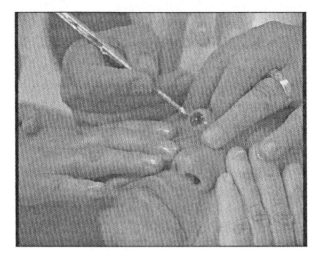

Close-up of eye surgery

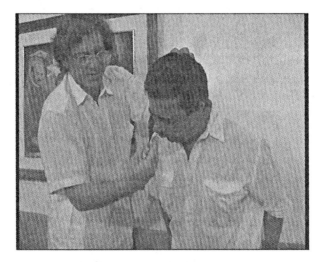

The famous "nose job" operation

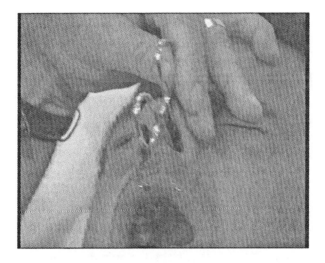

Close-up of the "nose job"

Photo of entities (balls of light) around Joao as he operates (only Joao's legs are visible)

People getting the free "medicinal" soup after a morning session

Author during an unusual sunset after a blissful session at the Casa cachoeira
(waterfall)

Part Three: The Process and Mystery of Healing

Josie RavenWing

The purpose of this section of the book is twofold. Part of it is specifically to help those people who are able to take the journey to the Casa de Dom Inacio make the utmost of the opportunity for healing that is available there. But more generally, it is for all people who wish to embark—or who already have—on a personal journey of healing. My intention is to offer perspectives, references and practices that can be used to support them in their healing process.

I have an overall perspective that life itself is a miracle, an ongoing one that is constantly taking place within and around us. And our body is constantly effecting miracles of physical healing that our conscious mind is usually unaware of—repair of cells, defense against infection and illness—and all of the other daily miracles for which we rarely express our gratitude or even acknowledge.

At a deeper level, I believe that true healing involves more than the alleviation of symptoms. Symptoms are simply that: messengers wishing to get our attention and demonstrate to our consciousness that something is out of balance. If the source of that imbalance is not healed, then there is a good likelihood that even if a given symptom is "cured," it or other symptoms will reappear as further messengers—until true healing takes place.

The process of healing is in many ways a mystery—in my opinion almost as great a mystery as life itself—although there are a number of powerful perspectives on it that have great value. Therefore, it is a humbling process for me to attempt to write this part of the book, and I have procrastinated writing it over and over. I know that I do not have all the answers to this mystery despite decades of pursuing its call. I don't know if anyone here on Earth does. But I will share with you the best of what I have learned, in the hope that at least some of the information will strike chords within you that will help you attain further harmony with yourself and the universe around you. For I believe that such harmony is a major part of the true essence of healing.

Josie RavenWing

Chapter 12: The Dance of Healing

"Healing requires action. It is not a passive event. We are meant to draw on our inner resources, to find the material strength to leave behind our outmoded beliefs and behaviors, and to see ourselves in new, healthy ways…"
Caroline Myss, *The Anatomy of Spirit*

Perhaps because I have spent a great deal of time as a dancer, I enjoy using the metaphor of dance when referring to the active aspect of the healing process.

Many people who come to the Casa de Dom Inacio—and many who don't—have been conditioned to abdicate their healing process to authority figures, whether such authorities be the entities of the Casa, their medical doctors, psychotherapists, or other healing practitioners.

This comes as no surprise—or shouldn't! Most of us have been raised to abdicate at least a certain amount of personal responsibility to outside authorities. "Father knows best." "Don't question your doctor." "Your lawyer will tell you what to do." "The Pope knows what God wants for us."

Now I'm not saying that other people don't have valuable areas of expertise that can benefit each of us a great deal. What I am saying is that we are often encouraged—knowingly or unknowingly—to be passive in our own lives, and to listen first to what outer authorities advise rather than consulting the God-given authority, wisdom and intuition that is within each of us.

In fact, going within in this way can actually be the first active step, or even leap, into the dance of healing. If we can't—or don't—trust our own inner knowing, then we become disconnected from ourselves. That schism itself is something that needs to be healed as it keeps us very vulnerable to various kinds of dis-eases. Until the schism is healed, we often ignore the early-stage messages and messengers of our psyche and body when they attempt to tell us that we are out of balance. Therefore it sometimes takes the louder messengers—heart attack, chronic fatigue syndrome, cancer, depression and others—to get us to finally listen.

When people say that they don't know how to hear their own inner voice, usually they are simply forgetting all of the sounds it has made. The inner voice does not always speak in words, although for some people it does. For others, it comes as a gut feeling: "I just *knew* I shouldn't have gone to that party/gone out with that person/eaten those French fries/gotten involved in that business deal/etc." We can't say how we knew, but we did, and we ignored the voice and then regretted it.

For some people, information will come in dreams. I'll give you a personal example of this.

I was actively involved in a dance company years ago. Well, actually it was several decades ago. Time flies! Anyway, we had been rehearsing a very challenging piece for months and were two weeks away from a performance. In one part of the dance, I had to take a running start, then take off and fly through the air sideways and parallel to the ground for about ten feet, to be—hopefully— caught by my partner. He would catch me in his arms while I was still on my side and parallel to the ground.

After practicing this over and over for weeks, my side began to get a bit sore. I basically ignored this for a few more weeks until one night when I had a "message" dream. In the dream I was being told very loudly by a voice that I needed to go to a doctor right away.

Thankfully I didn't ignore my dream. I made an appointment, got in to see the doctor quickly, and found out after the exam that my spleen was so bruised and swollen that it was in danger of rupturing. Under doctor's orders, I had to refrain from practicing the leap and lift that had caused the injury for a few weeks until two days before the performance. I did cheat a wee bit, in that I practiced the leap in my mind over and over. After two weeks of visualizing the leap and lift and only two days of physically rehearsing it, I did fine. Then I was on stage. And all went well.

There are probably many other ways that people are able to tap into their inner knowing besides gut sense (which some people call instinct or intuition), our dreams, hearing a voice inside of ourselves telling us what we need to know, or receiving an illuminating image "out of the blue." Even messages from what we call our conscience are a form of this inner knowing. There is no one right or only way to perceive. Some wise part of us knows and is trying its best to convey its knowing to our consciousness.

We sometimes label people who have a highly developed "ear" for their inner voice psychics, clairvoyants, channelers or medical intuitives. But the ability to hear and respond is innate in all of us.

However, sometimes our mind does not want to hear the inner voice, and does its best to plug its metaphorical ears. At first you may wonder why we would want to cut ourselves off from a voice that could lead us back to health, to wholeness.

From my own experience and those of many others, I have concluded that reason is this: *by listening to our inner voice, we might actually have to change something in our lives!* And creature of habit that our mind is, the idea of change is most unpalatable to it. However, there is no growth or healing without change on some level, so if we want either growth, healing or both, we must brave the disgruntled mutterings of our mind and—may the Force be with us—dance into the unknown.

Author and medical intuitive Caroline Myss has noted that healing is an active process that requires "...the will to see and accept truths about one's life and how one has used one's energies; and the will to begin to use energy for the creation of love, self-esteem, and health...When a person is passive—with an attitude [toward healers and healing methods] of 'just do it to me'—he does not fully heal; he may recover; but he may never deal fully with the source of his illness."

I have seen the "just do it to me" and "quick fix" mentality so common to us Westerners both in myself and others who come to the Casa de Dom Inacio as well as in our approaches to medical doctors, psychotherapists, and "alternative" healers. We want our miracles and we want them now! But often we don't want to participate in them.

This is not to say that the entities of the Casa can't or don't perform miracles of physical healing without our conscious, active participation. But the more I go to the Casa, the more I sense that the entities catalyze a change/growth process and awareness that is a core aspect of the healing work. The entities often say that they heal the source of the problem, not just the problem itself. As I mentioned earlier, often people sitting in the current rooms or undergoing invisible operations at the Casa will begin to weep or become angry or feel many other emotions that have been stuffed and buried for years—to the detriment of their health. Feeling—which is part of becoming conscious of—and releasing these stored emotions are part of the active process we can then engage in.

On rare occasion, I have even heard Joao in entity scold someone rather vigorously. The reason is usually that the person has stubbornly refused to make the simple changes needed for his or her healing: following the modest dietary restrictions that accompany the use of the herbs prescribed by the entity. The most common of these lapses is the use of alcohol, which is not to be drunk while a patient is taking the herbs. I have heard the entity tell someone passing before him in line, "I cannot help you any more. You keep drinking alcohol [or taking drugs, etc.], and until you decide to stop doing that, go home and continue with your life. When you have decided to change, come back."

So even the entities of the Casa, with their miraculous healing powers, want us to be active participants in our own process of healing. They have said that they can do 75% of the healing work, but without at least 25% of our participation, the process cannot be completed. I'm sure they are more than aware that unless we change whatever has provoked the "symptoms" of illness in the first place, true healing will not occur. And so they do what they can to help us to first become more conscious, and then to become more active.

I have experienced these "nudges" from the entities numerous times in Abadiania. Often it feels like the individual or individuals who most "pushes my buttons" emotionally speaking will be there at the same time that I am. It's almost as if this has been pre-arranged as part of my ongoing healing process. Then I get to look at my issues in the mirror of self-reflection and figure out what I can do to understand and/or release them. I have experienced some of my most truly petty and disgusting emotional moments as well as some of my most ecstatic spiritual moments while under the lovingly ruthless and thorough care of the spirit doctors of the Casa! In both cases I do my best to participate in accepting and releasing the painful emotions and to embrace the ecstatic moments.

In my book *The Return of Spirit,* I suggest that we can all be active participants in our spiritual growth, and I offer many practices on how to do so. In this book, I am suggesting that we do likewise with our healing process.

There are an infinite number of ways in which we can be proactive in regards to our healing. I will touch on some of them in the following chapters.

Chapter 13: The Role of the Mind

"All our thoughts, regardless of their content, first enter our system as energy. Those that carry emotional, mental, psychological or spiritual energy produce biological responses that are then stored in our cellular memory...in this way, our biographies are woven into our biological systems, gradually, slowly, every day."

Caroline Myss, *The Anatomy of Spirit*

It was when I was in my late teens that I first learned of the powerful effect the mind has on the physical body.

At the time, I was studying with a shamanic dance teacher. The classes were not at all what one would ordinarily expect of a dance class, as we, the students, spent the first hour or more lying on the floor! However, we were by no means inactive. Our teacher would begin by having us close our eyes and focus on our breath for some time. Then she would give us a series of images to concentrate on. Some images were of our body being transformed into a thin mesh screen with air blowing through it. Sometimes we would visualize the spaces between the bones and imagine water flowing through them. At other times we would see strings attached to various joints and imagine that some other force was slowly pulling the strings, suspending and moving our limbs.

Eventually, we would come to our feet with our eyes still closed, and continue working with the various images as we began to move. As the years passed, the images we were given to work with became increasingly sophisticated and we were able to use them with our eyes open while performing complex dance combinations.

Over time as I worked with this approach, I began to notice that as I focused on various images while I was still lying down, muscle groups would release all tension. And sometimes as they did so, emotions that had been stored in these muscles some time in the past would also come to the surface and release. Tremendous reserves of energy were also unleashed through the use of mental imagery, in addition to allowing me to move so effortlessly that I often as felt light as a feather. I noticed that my posture and that of my fellow students also began to improve, and that I felt healthier and more vibrant than ever before.

My teacher was one of the early pioneers in this kind of work—the use of imagery to alter the physical body. About 12 years after I first started working with her, I happened to meet a man named Tim Gallwey, author of *the Inner Game of Tennis* and other *Inner Game* books. He too had discovered the powerful applications of the mind and mental imagery. But in his books, these applications were oriented for the use of athletes. Since that time, more and more athletes have found that if they can visualize their performance—move by move at its optimum potential—in advance of the game, the body will then follow suit when it's time to act.

As time went on, this use of mind/body imagery began to seep into the health field. We have now entered a new millennium, one in which many people use a variety of visualizations to both maintain health and to promote healing in areas of dis-ease and injury. A visualization can be as simple as "seeing" a tight muscle turning into a ball of melting butter—for the purpose of releasing the muscle tension—or as complex as seeing images of armies of healthy cells marching through swarms of cancerous ones and blasting them with firebombs.

Dr. Karen Olness says, "My intuition is that whatever energy is associated with the construction of images and the process of thinking transmits a message to a cascade of body processes…changing images does affect physiology."

Not only are we using mental imagery these days to change our bodies and effect our own personal "miracles" of healing, but we are also using verbal affirmations. Verbal affirmations are best constructed as if the affirmed event, state of being, healing, etc. has already occurred. One of my own personal favorites is "I am a being of radiant health, energy and love." There are dozens if not hundreds of books of positive affirmations if you are in need of suggestions. Terms like "the power of positive thinking" are now commonplace, and such methods are being applied toward anything from health issues and improved self-esteem to success in business and financial abundance.

Our knowledge of the power of the mind and its effect on our physical health has expanded significantly over the past 30 years. Using visualizations and/or affirmations, many people have healed themselves of minor to major physical and emotional afflictions. The mind can thus be one of our most powerful allies in healing. It can also take a very destructive role if fed the wrong diet—particularly a diet of primarily negative thoughts and limiting belief systems. Such a diet inevitably has an adverse effect on our health.

Unless we have involved ourselves in some kind of ongoing meditative practice, most of us identify almost totally with the thinking processes of our minds—which for the most part are unruly and have a tendency to slide into deep ruts. This is not true for us when we first come into this world. At that time our mind does not yet have a vocabulary, so we are totally in the moment and perceive our inner and outer world from a state of unfiltered, "innocent perception." We are one with ourselves and with the universe.

Over time, we begin to gain vocabulary, and our world becomes increasingly labeled: "That's a bird, that's a dog, that's daddy, that's your tummy." Then more judgmental labels like "good" and "bad" come into play, as well as concepts of linear time, like "early, late, today, tomorrow." We begin to speak in words and then in more and more complex sentences.

And our talking becomes both external and internal. We start to talk to ourselves—silently, for the most part, but powerfully and almost constantly nonetheless. In this manner, we all become insane.

Now that must sound like a very strange statement. But in a certain sense, it's true. The more we think, the more we become split from our original state of unity and connectedness, and we hurtle forward into a growing state of separation from our deep self. We learn to judge ourselves and others, and to limit what we think we can do and how long *we think* it will take to do it. We create a personality based to a great extent on all that we have internalized of what others have told us about ourselves and the nature of reality.

And the more we talk to ourselves—what we call thinking—the more we believe what we are saying to ourselves. Have you ever really noticed that you are talking to yourself almost constantly? This background noise is so ubiquitous that, like the person who lives by the ocean and after time doesn't even notice the sound of the ever-present surf, we hardly realize we are hearing it.

Often our thoughts can take quite negative turns. Depending—usually—on what we have been told about ourselves or about the world when we were children, we can become expert in even deeper crazy-making. We start repeating to ourselves messages about our unworthiness, our failures, our "badness," or how scary or violent or full of suffering and illness and evil the world outside of us is. And the more we talk to ourselves along these veins, the more we filter out all that does not agree with those thoughts, until our experience of life, ourselves, and the world are all congruent with our thoughts.

And as we judge ourselves, so do we begin to judge others. We form opinions about others based on very narrow bands of perception. How could we not? This is how we are treating ourselves, so it is inevitable that this is how we will treat others. We have exchanged unity and heart for the tyranny of thought and separation.

For many of us, it is not until we begin to attempt some form of meditation that we realize how noisy and pervasive the internal dialogue is, and what a slave of our thoughts we have become. But that realization is a true moment of enlightenment, and has the potential of motivating us to learn to **be** in a different way.   Because when we start to truly hear all of the things we are telling ourselves, we realize how many of them are limiting and far away from the state of love of self, others and life that we long to live in. We finally have come face to face with our belief systems.

Belief systems are incredibly powerful.   On many levels they control our experience. If we believe that satisfying, loving relationships are impossible for us, we will impeccably choose to be with people that will fulfill those beliefs. If we believe that we are doomed to material poverty, we most likely will set things up to assure that state. If we believe that we are incapable of healing ourselves from various kinds of illnesses, or that illness is inevitable, or that we will never be happy, our thoughts and beliefs are powerful enough to manifest all of that. And if the collective around us—whether that be our family, society, or all of humanity—shares the same beliefs, that collective simply adds energy to the belief structure.

Conversely, if we believe that we deserve all of the goodness and bounty of life, we will attract our share of that as well.

Caroline Myss believes that miracles, including miracles of healing, are natural, and she set out to discover "…what we do that interferes with the energy that makes miracles happen…If you are spiritually centered and call back your energy from negative beliefs, you can eat [only] cat food and still stay healthy."

Let's look at the power of mind and belief in regards to three areas: hypnosis, faith, and the placebo effect.

In the state of hypnosis, we are deeply relaxed and our minds are open to a variety of suggestions. The hypnotherapist can suggest that we are three years old, and our voices, gestures, etc. will take on the qualities of that age. On-stage performing hypnotists have suggested to a person that his body is as rigid as a wooden plank, and it has become so much so that a third party can walk across it or sit on it. Experiments have been done in which it has been suggested to the hypnotized person that a flame is being held on his skin, and actual blisters form there. A man who was paralyzed was told under hypnosis that he could walk, and under hypnosis he did. This is yet another example of how our minds can profoundly effect our physical state.

And similar to the effects of hypnosis is the power of our mind through dreams. It is not uncommon for people to have such erotic dreams that they have a physical orgasm as a result, even without any kind of stimulation except that of the mind through their dream.

Faith seems to function similarly to belief systems.   If we believe our particular health care practitioner has the ability to help us, this faith has a strong effect on the outcome of the treatment.

There is a quote from St. Ignatius at the Casa de Dom Inacio. It says, "For those who believe, no words are necessary. For those who don't believe, no words are possible." In one of my readings, I found yet another relevant quote: "I think it was Sir William Osler who said that faith in the gods cures some, hypnotic suggestion, others, and faith in the common doctor, still others." And from yet another source, "When all is said and done, nobody can predict with unfailing certainty what any given mind and body are capable of accomplishing. The patient who has faith, whether in a divine higher power or in the benign hands of a charismatic healer, seems to have a better chance of being healed than someone who does not."

Now this is not the total picture when it comes to healing. I am personally acquainted with skeptics who went to the Casa de Dom Inacio and were healed of physical maladies despite their doubting attitude (the latter of which often reversed itself after the healing!). I also know of people who have been the recipients of long-distance healing work. They had no conscious knowledge that anyone was intervening on their behalf, and yet there was a direct correlation between the timing and efforts of the healer and the subsequent benefits that occurred for the patient. This has been true of the long-distance work of the entities of the Casa, as well as with practitioners of Reiki, Healing Touch, and other forms of distance healing including the power of prayer. There have even been controlled hospital studies showing that when—unbeknownst to the patients—energy practitioners have worked on the patients from another room of the hospital, these patients' rate of healing was significantly higher than for those who did not receive the energy work. The same has been found true for patients who have been prayed for by groups of people. So the role of the mind is significant in the course of healing and in our lives in general, but I cannot say that it the sole factor.

However, the placebo effect is yet another example of the power of mind. Many scientific tests have been performed in this area that indicate the power of belief. If we are convinced that we are taking a powerful anti-arthritic drug, our painful arthritis often subsides, even though the pill is simply sugar or some other non-pharmaceutical product. I read one description of a doctor who had given a patient with a serious illness a new drug, and told him it was extremely effective for his condition. The patient began to improve rapidly. Then an article came out in the newspaper saying the drug did not work at all. The patient's condition began to deteriorate again. Then his doctor told him the newspaper article was in error, and the patient's condition once more improved. And finally, yet another article was published with new evidence on the lack of effectiveness of the drug, and the patient's condition deteriorated so rapidly that he died soon thereafter.

In my readings I also came across a description of a patient who was misdiagnosed as having a fatal illness, which he died of soon thereafter, even though it turned out that the original diagnosis was wrong and that his health at the time of diagnosis was reasonably good. Similar to this is the whole concept of "hexing" or putting a death curse on someone. If the person is told or shown in some way that he has been cursed, and if he lives in a culture where there is a strong belief in the power of curses, he will often die during the period expected for that kind of curse. But if the victim of a curse lives within a culture in which there is no belief in the power of death curses, it is unlikely he will be effected at all, unless perhaps the curse has been thrown by a truly powerful sorcerer who has the ability to effect the energy of believers and unbelievers alike.

Of course, current Western culture performs its own sorcery in this regard. Most of us have been conditioned to believe that we will die of some illness, if not of some injury. And so we usually do. And yet there have been cultures in which it was believed that people could simply choose to leave their body when their soul's purpose in this life had been fulfilled. And so they did.

Our Western culture does seem to be going through some paradigm shifts about illness and death at this time. One might define a paradigm shift as a massive transformation of deeply rooted belief systems. This kind of shift can happen for an individual and for a large group, even for humanity as a whole, and seems to operate on what quantum physicists call the "hundredth monkey" or "morphogenic field" phenomenon. The basic theory behind this type of phenomenon is that when enough people—or animals as well—attain new knowledge or awareness, the latter reaches a state of critical mass that begins to overflow into the collective mind of that species.

This transfer of information from a small group to a larger one can occur without direct communication. The term "hundredth monkey syndrome" came into being in the following way. Apparently a monkey on a remote island finally figured out how to wash a particular local tuber in the ocean and then to split it open with a rock, thus making it easier to get to the edible insides. Soon the original monkey's fellow monkeys on the island learned this new skill. This in itself is not surprising, as it was a case of learning by example. But soon, the monkeys on other islands in the region were observed to be suddenly practicing this same new skill. And physical travel between the islands was impossible for them. The theory is that the element of critical mass—re this new skill—kicked in and was somehow transferred to the collective mind of all the island monkeys of the region.

This phenomenon applies to the human community as well. Within the scientific community, for example, it has been noticed that a new theory or discovery will often pop into the minds of scientists in various parts of the world simultaneously but without prior communication between them.

At this time we have a huge number of baby boomers who have been exploring holistic healing and many spiritual paths over the past few decades. They are beginning to discard the prevalent Western beliefs that say we will be infirm and increasingly useless to society as we age, and are replacing them with beliefs that we can continue on into elder status with vitality and great wisdom to share with the younger generations. And an increasing number are adopting the ancient beliefs that we need not become ill as a way to leave our bodies at the end of this life, but that we can remain healthy up to that point and simply leave when we are ready. I would guess that when that belief system hits critical mass, it will become a reality for many people.

Speaking of paradigm shifts, I believe that the physical surgeries performed by the entities of the Casa are primarily paradigm shifters. They jar our thinking mind and beliefs out of their ruts and make space for the inexplicable. After witnessing the surgeries, people's minds are more convinced of the possibility of a spiritual, "miraculous" healing, and this then creates more potential for that to occur.

I'm going to give you a few more examples of interesting paradigm or reality shifts that have occurred in the lives of some individuals.

The famous former British cellist Jacqueline du Pre was stricken with severe multiple sclerosis. It had been a year since she had been able to play the cello due to her illness when, one morning, she suddenly awoke to find herself inexplicably cured. For four days she played the cello better than she ever had, then suddenly relapsed once more and never played again. Deepak Chopra commented on this phenomenon by writing, "...she transcended her illness so completely that reality simply changed." For four days, the physical condition of her nervous system was altered through the conditions of a major paradigm shift.

Another example of such a shift was the one I gave in the chapter on the surgeries of the Casa. This was the case of the young woman whose sight returned despite the fact that she had no optic nerve function.

And then there are the cases of individuals with multiple personalities. Often such individuals manifest entirely different physical symptoms, allergies, etc. varying from personality to personality. One personality will be allergic to a particular food, but when they shift into another personality, they have no such allergy. In the case of one woman with multiple personalities, depending on which personality she was in moment to moment, in one she would be menstruating, but as she shifted into another personality, she was not menstruating any longer. These are potent examples of the power of the mind as well, and perhaps fall generally under the category of paradigm shifts.

We have now looked at the power of the mind through belief systems, faith, and paradigm shifts, as well as the potential of consciously applied imagery and affirmations to be able to effect our quality of life in various areas. Our ongoing inner dialogue of self-talk—which is largely automatic and unconsciously applied—functions in the same way that consciously applied visualizations and affirmations do, in that the inner dialogue has a direct effect on our physiology. This is actually good news in the sense that once we realize this, once we become *aware*, we can begin to make choices about what we are saying to ourselves. We can begin to substitute positive messages and tapes for the old negative ones. Although this still leaves us within the realm of thinking, consciously applied thought can be used to move us back toward that state of unity once again. And we can even choose to *not* think for periods of time through some form of meditation or "innocent perception."

Glenda Green wrote a beautiful book called *Love Without End* about a series of miraculous events that occurred in her life. Green is an artist who, some years ago, decided to paint a portrait of Jesus, having never done any religious art prior to that time. To make a long story short, she began to perceive the entire portrait as if it was already completed—and in holographic form—in the space in front of her. Then Jesus actually manifested in her studio, and over a several-month period of posing for his portrait, the two of them carried on numerous and illuminating conversations that later became the subject of her book.

Jesus addressed the tyranny of the mind in great depth. In one of their conversations he said, "...from the viewpoint of the mind, **control and understanding are one and the same.** The mind assumes that it understands whatever it controls. This is the central problem...in a mind-dominated world, and the single most important reason to require that the mind be your servant and not your master...The answers to healing your life will be found in the inner strength of your heart."

He then went on to suggest three practices to free ourselves from the tyranny of the mind: "...strengthen all of your positive emotions through daily gratitude and admiration, ...disempower your negative emotions daily through forgiveness,...[and practice] innocent perception;...you do not have to do anything to make this universe divine. All you have to do is to perceive and then to regard with honor that which is already here."

In Green's book, Jesus says that the mind is actually two things. It is "an integrating and transmitting instrument which is basically a complex DNA computer. It centers in your brain and nervous system but actually involves every cell of your body. The second part [of the mind] is an electromagnetic field permeating and immediately surrounding your body."

If this is true, then the first part of that statement validates what some scientists and doctors are now discovering: that there truly is no separation between the mind and body. This makes the issue of more consciously directing our thoughts even more important to our overall well being. And the second part of the statement seems to correspond to the field that some people call the subtle energy body and what others more loosely term the aura.

Patti Conklin, medical intuitive (and subject of one of the interviews in this book) feels that our unspoken thoughts effect the subtle energy body, while our spoken thoughts register directly in the body as truth. This possibility can be used to inspire us to use our words more consciously. For example, we might want to eliminate expressions such as "I'm sick and tired of...," or, "this is a real pain in the neck (or other body parts!)," or "this job is a real headache," or "this is to die for," or any other expression that refers negatively—albeit idiomatically—to ill health in our bodies.

Our words and thoughts do create images, and we have already learned that images as well as affirmations have a direct effect on our physiology. So all of us can take positive action toward improving our health by becoming conscious masters—rather than unconscious servants—of our minds.

You might want to support this process by making a list of your belief systems about yourself, about health and illness, about death, abundance, and any other important areas of your life. Look for where your mind may be holding limiting beliefs. Then do a personal ceremony to release each one. This could be as simple as writing each one on a piece of paper, and then burning it as you say the words, "I release this limiting belief into the fire. In the light that its burning creates, I replace it with the affirmation: ____." The affirmation you create needs to be positive and worded as if it is already true. Each time we release or let go of something, it is important to replace it as quickly as possible with something positive. As they say, "nature abhors a vacuum," and so we want to be the ones deciding how to fill that vacuum rather than taking the chance that those long-held patterns of what we just released will come back to fill the space again. And I recommend that you write all of your affirmations down as well. Keep them in a journal or somewhere easy to work with so that you can repeat them on a daily basis until they have become a natural and integrated part of your new belief system. Begin to notice how different you feel over time.

I will give you another exercise to do to demonstrate the power of both positive and negative thoughts. You need to have a partner for this process, and it can be done in a group setting as well.

Step 1.   To establish the "control," extend your strongest arm out to your side parallel to the floor. As your partner then pushes down on your arm, you resist as hard as you can.

Step 2.   Close your eyes and spend 30 to 60 seconds or so thinking all the most positive and loving thoughts you can about yourself. Lay it on thick! Then have your partner test your strength again in the same way as the first time.

Step 3.   Close your eyes again and spend about 30 seconds silently repeating to yourself the various negative things you say about yourself when your mind is in a self-criticizing mode. Then have your partner test your arm strength again.

Step 4.   I would highly recommend finishing the process by repeating Step 2
again, so that you end the experience on a positive note.

To demonstrate the power of group mind, for Step 2 and 4, have the group focus positive, loving thoughts on you while you keep your own mind blank—or, if you can't, at least moving in a positive self-talk direction.   And for Step 3, have the group focus critical, petty thoughts toward you, but only for about 10 seconds, as this is not a very pleasant experience.   Be sure to have them finish with Step 4—directing positive, loving thoughts toward you again.   And have your partner test your strength at each step just as in the first exercise.

Most people experience significantly increased strength during Step 2 and 4, and significantly decreased strength during Step 3.   Although Step 3 is unpleasant, the fact is that this kind of self-judgment goes on a great deal of the time.   Do an honest inventory of your own internal dialogue and assess how much of your internal dialogue is negative self-talk, and how much of it focuses negative and critical thoughts towards another person—or even groups of others. Perhaps you are one of the growing numbers of people who are taking more conscious responsibility for your thoughts and the percentage of time spent in negative ones is minimal.   If not, you can be!

For those who seek the blessed peace of non-thinking, there are many methods for arriving there.   As I mentioned in the chapter on the current rooms of the Casa, one way to calm your thoughts is by placing your full attention on the movement of your breath in and out of your body.   Should you find your attention beginning to stray into thinking, gently bring it back again and again. Some people use a mantra to calm their thoughts—a mantra being the repetition of a single phrase—typically a positive and spiritual message—over and over. Some like to gaze at a candle flame and make it the sole focus of their attention. And still others enjoy putting on an audio tape of a guided meditation to help them focus.

People who have difficulty sitting for long periods of time may prefer more active forms of meditation.   Yoga and tai chi are excellent, but there are even simpler methods.   One is to take a walk or go jogging, and to place all of your focus on feeling the rhythmic movement of your arms and legs.   You can also still the mind by bringing all of your senses into play no matter what you are doing: notice how your environment looks, smells, tastes, sounds and feels in as much detail as possible.   It might be easier at the beginning to focus on one sense at a time, and eventually bring more and more into play simultaneously, as if you were listening to a symphony of many instruments being played at the same time.

No matter whether through a sedentary or more physically active form of concentration, as you arrive at internal silence, you open yourself up to the miraculous nature of being in the moment, in direct perception of life—your own and all that is around you—as it is happening.

For many people this is a most transcendent experience. Eckart Tolle, in his book *The Power of Now,* describes his personal revelation of realizing that within himself there was a silent observer always witnessing his thinking process, a consciousness that was separate from the thoughts—and ultimately, the reality—of who he was. Up to that moment he had been quite miserable for a long time. Here is his experience leading up to the moment of revelation shortly after his twenty-ninth birthday:

"'I cannot live with myself any longer.' This was the thought that kept repeating itself in my mind. Then suddenly I became aware of what a peculiar thought it was. 'Am I one or two? If I cannot live with myself, there must be two of me: the 'I' and the 'self' that 'I' cannot live with. Maybe,' I thought, 'only one of them is real.'"

At that, his mind completely stopped, and he was catalyzed into an intense transcendent and transformative experience that completely changed his life. He discovered that the saying, "I think, therefore I am" is not truth, but rather the bragging of the mind, and that the silent observer within us all is who we really are: a spirit created from love that is temporarily inhabiting this body and perceiving this world through the body's senses. I believe that Tolle's experience is what Jesus was referring to with his term, "innocent perception."

What Tolle learned is what mystics have learned throughout the ages, and what each of us can learn as well. When we are in the state of the observer or silent witness, we step out of judgment, fear, and isolation—out of the entire mythology of pain that we have created for ourselves based on our past and the thoughts that we have created about and from it. We find that we have been the host of an illusory entity that has been called the ego, ego-mind, internal dialogue, the inner demon, etc. This entity, as we all know, can be a true tyrant if we allow it to rampage uncontrolled. It can drive us to despair and even acts of violence against ourselves or others, including suicide. The one thing it is unable to do is to be fully in the present. There, it is powerless to exist. And it is only in the present that we can be at peace, in the full joy of our divinity.

True meditation brings us into the now, which is why people so frequently feel states of ecstasy arising from meditation. We are home. We are connected with our Source. We are who we are.

Some people feel they cannot meditate, whatever their concept of that is. But we can all become the silent witness, observing the ongoing prattle of the inner dialogue that generally tries to make us miserable one way or another by repeating its endless mantras of pain, its endless accusations of our unworthiness. Once we focus our awareness - the light of our consciousness—on these repeating messages, we begin to transmute the pain entity. A truly good psychotherapist can help patients arrive at this magic of transmutation by listening to their patients' litanies of self-hate and criticism without judgment, simply by shining their own attention and compassion on the patient. This is a form of love, and helps the patient to begin to emulate it. Tolle quotes St. Paul on this issue: "Everything is shown up by being exposed to the light, and whatever is exposed to the light itself becomes light."

Therefore, true healing involves this willingness to witness the false pain entity within, to hear its words without identifying with them, to know that the pain entity is like a child wailing in the dark who simply needs us to turn on the light in order to reassure him that there is no need to fear: our love is here and fully present. Over time, if we can simply witness the noise of the pain entity without getting engaged with it ourselves, it will slowly dissolve into the light of our consciousness.

I have spent a great deal of time describing the various aspects and functions of the mind, primarily because most of us spend so much time thinking. We need to know something about the mind's nature in order to be able to have choices about how we want to use it and relate to it.

And what, you may ask, does all of this information have to do with miracles? Well, if our belief systems and thinking processes create much of what we experience as reality, then a belief system that is open to the miraculous nature of life is going to allow more room for the perception—and experience—of miracles. For example, those people who come to the Casa de Dom Inacio with such an open belief system are able to avail themselves more consistently to the healing powers of the entities and to their own internal healer.

And miracles of healing—or other forms of miracles—can take place anywhere. Joao de Deus says "I have never healed anyone. It is God who heals." And if God is everywhere, then miracles can take place here. Now. Always.

***

I would like to end this chapter with a brief story about the power of belief and faith that was shared by Deepak Chopra in his book *Unconditional Living*:

"'Baba,' my grandfather exclaimed to the [yogi] saint [after seeing numerous double scars covering the yogi's exposed arms and legs and seeing a large cobra nearby], 'you are living with snakes all around you.'

"'Snakes?' the yogi said. 'I've never seen one here.'

"'But you are covered with bites,' my grandfather protested.

"The yogi gazed at him with penetrating sweetness. 'Perhaps you see snakes here, but I see only God, and believe me, sir, he does not bite.'"

Chapter 14: The Role of Emotions

"...[from our research, we are led to think] that the chemicals that are running our body and our brain are the same chemicals that are involved in emotion. And that says to me that we'd better seriously entertain theories about the role of emotions and emotional suppression in disease, and that we'd better pay more attention to emotions with respect to health."
Candace Pert, Ph.D., Researcher in Brain Biochemistry,
Peptides and Mind/Body Connections

Just as we are finding more and more evidence of the body/mind connection, over recent years we are seeing the role of the emotions in our overall health. From science to the personal growth field and the many related therapies and approaches to health, more and more people are realizing the powerful effect of emotions on our physical bodies and well being.

In my own personal life as well as in my work as a psychotherapist and healing practitioner, I have witnessed the power of emotions. Like many people in our Western culture, I was not encouraged to express intense emotion as I was growing up. I interpreted this lack of support for doing so as a taboo against even *feeling* anger or sorrow or intense joy. I feared that "losing control" emotionally in my home environment would make me even more vulnerable to what I perceived as my parents' criticisms and efforts to control me. As a child I had already developed problems of self-esteem, and after a certain point rebelled against letting my parents have an additional "edge" by seeing me at my most vulnerable. So I began to do what many people do: "stuff" my emotions.

By the time I was eight or so, when I did allow myself to cry, it was almost always in private. This at least gave me some release, but since it took place in isolation, I received little in the way of comfort from my solitary tears. Thankfully, I have since gained much more acceptance of my own emotions and find it easier to express them now than in the past, either in private or in public.

I learned several things from my many years of stuffing my emotions. Over time the pattern of doing so resulted in intermittent bouts of depression. True depression is not really an emotion. It is more the lack of being able to feel emotions. Life seems empty, bleak, pointless, hopeless and one-dimensional when one is depressed. This is why there can be a danger of suicide when people are suffering long-term depression. In addition, when we are depressed, not only are we not feeling fully, but we are often less responsive to our outer environment, a fact that can carry its own dangers.

To heal from depression, we need to know that it is safe for us to feel again, whatever the emotions may be. Most people suffering depression usually need some kind of support from others in order to be able to experience that safety, whether it be a counselor or a good friend or family member. Whoever that support person is, he or she needs to be comfortable herself with the whole range of human emotions in order to be able to create an environment in which the person suffering from depression can also learn to do so.

Some people think that certain emotions are "good for us" while others are "bad for us" and need to be suppressed. There is evidence that this not the case, but rather, what is more important is how *long* we sustain ourselves in various emotional states. Here is a brief discussion between Bill Moyers and Margaret Kemeny, psychologist and researcher in immunology (including in the relationship between psychology and the AIDS virus) on this issue and the effect of emotions on our immune system:

Moyers: "So the emotion of fear [for example] that is an instant and temporary response to danger could have a positive impact on your immune system. But if you sustain yourself in that state over too much time, it can actually have a negative impact on the immune system."

Kemeny: "Exactly. It seems that emotions are important and have their adaptiveness when they are short-term, when you experience them for a number of minutes, or maybe hours. But when you get into situations that provoke emotions over the long term, then you run the risk of ending up with physiological responses that are no longer adaptive."

Kemeny also commented that it is beginning to look like natural killer-cell activity increases with both "positive" and "negative" emotional states, and that even negative feelings, if not sustained for too long, can strengthen natural killer-cell activity.

I found this last comment very interesting in that I related it to something an acupuncturist once told me. I had unknowingly ingested a somewhat toxic substance and my body was feeling a bit poisoned. So I made an appointment to see my acupuncturist and he gave me a treatment. What most surprised me that day was when he told me that my body's response to dealing with a toxin could actually be a very positive thing. He felt that, according to the system he had been trained in—Chinese medicine—my immune system had mobilized to ward off any potential effects from the toxins, and in doing so, was strengthened. So rather than be alarmed by my situation, his attitude was quite positive.

The Chinese theory resonates with that of homeopathy, in the sense that homeopathic remedies contain minute doses of the very thing one is trying to "get rid of," and if given the appropriate dose, the patient's body or emotions will then be even more stimulated to fight off the problematic poison or illness.

So again, it seems our health problems, in regard to emotions, don't necessarily result from "negative" feelings, but rather from either stuffing them or sustaining them long term. From the perspective of Chinese medicine, even an overly long state of intense joy can be disruptive to our overall health. All is balance.

Because I am somewhat intrigued with the issue of emotions and their correlation with immune activity, and because this may be an important issue for you, the reader, as well, I'm going to share some more findings on the subject.

Dr. David Felton, M.D., says that according to scientific research, "...every time we have a thought or feeling, hormones are released that somehow send a message to the immune system...a constant traffic of information goes back and forth between the brain and the immune system."

Candace Pert, who I quoted earlier, commented that she never gets a cold when she goes skiing—an activity that she loves—despite the harsh weather and possible exposure to others with colds during that time. She feels our emotional state affects whether or not we'll get sick from the same loading dose from a virus due to the kinds of biochemical agents released from various emotional states and fluctuations. Her emotions are obviously in a very happy and positive state when she goes skiing.

Conversely, I have noticed that some people will often get sick when faced with something that they are dreading doing, while others will "accidentally" be injured just prior to a dreaded event. Both situations are an "acceptable" excuse for not doing what they didn't want to do anyway. And still others will become ill or injure themselves to fulfill other needs that they don't feel they can ask for directly, such as the need for nurturing, love and attention.

We are amazingly powerful beings in this sense. Our emotions—just like our minds—can bring dis-ease or health into our lives. Knowing that, we might want to become more conscious of what we are doing with our emotions. I like to think of our emotional body as a river that, in order to stay clean and fresh, needs to be able to keep flowing. It's okay if some leaves or other debris drop in the river now and then, or even frequently, as long as the river can flow unobstructed. But if we erect a dam and interfere with the natural flow, then any debris entering the river will begin to decompose, and over time, the river will become increasingly sluggish and stagnant and unable to provide pure water for those who need to drink of its life-sustaining liquid.

In that same way, damming up our emotions can make us ill on various levels. I'm not saying we need to vent every feeling with—or on!—another person. We can express some of our feelings in private through weeping, wailing, gnashing of teeth, pounding on pillows, etc. We can also let them flow through painting, writing, playing music, dancing and other creative forms of expression. Mostly, we need to accept our feelings for what they are—natural and transient parts of ourselves but not the totality of who we are. Remember the "silent witness" I mentioned in the previous chapter, the deeper self who observes the fleeting processes of the mind, emotions and body but is not bound by them.

And the more that we can find healthy ways to accept, express and release our emotions, the more we can accept the feelings of others without judgment. I remember once, when I was in my early twenties, I had an experience that was truly mind-expanding. I was sitting in my house in a rather contemplative mood, and suddenly I found myself thinking about all of the most horrendous criminals and acts of violence that had taken place throughout human history. And I realized that within me was the potential for every possible kind of good and evil myself. I knew I had experienced rage, hatred, jealousy, greed, selfishness, bigotry—fear of the unknown "Other"—and all the rest of what we call "negative" emotions that can give rise to destructive actions. I also knew I had experienced compassion, generosity, selflessness, love, and all of the rest of what we call "positive" emotions that can give rise to constructive and creative actions. In that moment, I suspended all judgment of my fellow human beings. This is not to say that I support hurtful actions, but rather that I could not place myself above or below anyone else, knowing our common humanity. The "aha!" I received was not to judge emotions, but rather, to learn to let them flow in healthy ways and to choose what kinds of actions I wanted to take in the world with as much awareness, responsibility and love that I could muster moment to moment.

I have also found that frequently when we judge others, the underlying feeling behind this action is some form of internal pain. Frequently when we become judgmental, it is because we are feeling vulnerable or helpless, and rather than experience this, we try to compensate by externalizing the feeling. For example, if we judge someone for cutting close in front of us in traffic, often the primary emotion is fear: that person's action could have harmed us. But rather than acknowledge the fear and helplessness, we get angry at the other driver and judge them for their "stupid" or "inconsiderate" actions. So part of the journey of personal healing is to become more self-aware, more in touch with our underlying emotions, and then to take responsibility for them and release them appropriately without judgment.

Patti Conklin has an interesting perspective on the kind of experience I described two paragraphs above as "mind-expanding." We were talking one day about the tunnel of light that many people have seen during near-death experiences. Her feeling is that going through the tunnel is not really an out-of-body experience, but rather, a journey through the inner landscape of the heart and to the light that is at the end of that tunnel and that is the true essence of the heart. Her feeling on the matter is that in order to reach that light—preferably while we still have plenty of life left to live rather than waiting until we are at the end of life—we have to be willing to make the journey through the tunnel of the heart. As we journey, we need to look at, and ultimately embrace with love and compassion, every single "unacceptable" emotion within us.

Some people call this journey the dark night of the soul, as it is often difficult to see the light when we are facing the shadows in the tunnel. These shadows seem to be monsters and demons, and our first impulse may be to run from them. But just as the frog was transformed into a prince by a kiss, so can our internal monsters be transformed into wonderful teachers by embracing them with love. After doing so with each one of them, we arrive at the heart-light at the end of the tunnel, and are once more reconnected with the experience of God, of love.

Because many of us carry unexpressed, unreleased emotional pain from our past like so much excess baggage that weighs down our heart, body and spirit, it can be a great relief to periodically take some time to release as much of it as possible. We don't necessarily have to take on everything in the "tunnel" in one fell swoop. We can do it in manageable chunks. In *The Return of Spirit*, I described a process that can help us do so called "cutting the cords." This process has been helpful to many people who are carrying stagnant emotional energies that are connected with various people in their past—especially family members and past sexual partners or perpetrators of sexual abuse. I invite you to use the process for your healing.

There are many other processes that can help us release the past. One friend of mine does the following each day in her morning shower: while standing under the water, she states out loud that she is releasing all negativity from the past and is receiving healing. Some people write what they wish to release on paper and then burn it in a fire. Symbolic rituals have real power. You can create your own releasing processes or borrow those created by others.

One such process that I have borrowed is from Patti Conklin. She generously wrote it out on her web site and I have adapted it slightly in my own way. The purpose of the exercise is to release all negativity—including emotional—from our past and from the cellular and DNA level of our bodies, including tendencies toward physical dis-ease that we may have inherited from our parents.

Here are the basics.

Close your eyes and see and feel yourself walking slowly down a marble staircase. When you get to the bottom, you will see a long corridor stretched out in front of you. On either side of the corridor are doors. Each door represents a year of your life (and I included one door for the nine months when I was in my mother's womb), and the door that represents the earliest year is the one closest to you.

Go to that first door and open it. Once you do, you can begin to clean it out until it is empty. Use any cleaning "implements" you wish! It is not necessary to remember what happened during that year. Simply clean out what is in there, (which might look like a pile of dirt or rubbish or just about anything) and then close the door behind you, knowing you have cleansed and released all negativity from that time of your life. Depending on your level of energy, you may do more than one room in any given session. When you are done, climb back up the marble stairway and return to your present surroundings. When you are ready to do another session, simply go back and pick up at the room where you left off the last time. Eventually you will have cleared yourself of any harmful or stagnant energies from the past. Hopefully from that day forward, you will release pain as it occurs, but in case you don't, at the end of that year do another housecleaning of anything you may have stored up during that time.

I have added a bit to this process myself. When I first began the process, I would methodically shovel junk into a cart and haul it out of the particular room I was cleaning out. This was pretty time-consuming. So then I created a huge "Rug Doctor"-type cleaning machine with a long tube that just sucked everything up. But some of the junk was in big pieces, so I then developed a crushing machine that I'd send in first to pulverize everything, and then sucked the pulverized stuff into the other machine. Then, after a few more sessions, I decided that all of that pulverized matter could be put to good use. So I added another tube to the back of the sucking machine. This tube led out of the room, down the corridor and outdoors to a garden, where the pulverized stuff was put to use as compost for new growth—of lots and lots of flowers and other beautiful plants. And finally, when a room was completely clean, I added a blessing to the process by leaving a handful of sweet scented rose petals in the middle of the floor. This was not only a blessing, but a kind of thank-you for all that I learned during that year of my life, whether from pain or from happier experiences. Only when that is done do I close the door and walk away to the next room.

This addition (of using the pulverized junk as compost and blessing the room at the end) was symbolic to me of the fact that good and beauty and blessings can come from all of our life's experiences, even those that may seem emotionally, mentally or physically traumatic at the time. For all are part of the soul's journey and learning.

Author and medical intuitive Caroline Myss gives another encouraging perspective for doing exercises like the one I described above. She comments that healing does not always mean "...that the physical body recovers from an illness. Healing can also mean that one's spirit has released long-held fears and negative thoughts toward oneself or others."

Deepak Chopra comments, "...many people...prefer to struggle against their pain, fighting off grief, depression and fear...Struggle only slows down the process and makes it more painful. Complete healing depends on your ability to stop struggling."

We human beings have a tendency to cling to the known, even when the known is painful. We cling to relationships that may no longer be serving us because at least they are familiar. We cling to jobs that no longer satisfy us for the security that they bring. We cling to loved ones whose purpose on earth has been fulfilled and who are preparing to leave their bodies behind. We cling to our habits. We cling to our past pain and all of the behaviors that have sprung up around it because to let go of it will mean change.

Letting go of our past, of objects and people that we are attached to, is a form of mourning. And it is very healthy to mourn and then to move forward into a new phase of our lives. In her book *Love Without End,* Glenda Green describes one of the conversations Jesus had with her on the subject.

"Mourning is the free flowing of tears as acceptance and releasing are experienced. In that state, the heart can perceive a continuity of life even though certain attachments have been lost. **In letting go of that which cannot be retained, one heals.** It is through releasing that one is blessed. Grieving is clinging to that which has been lost—**mourning is the act of letting go.** No one feels blessed at the onset of grief. Never would I suggest such a thing. Yet, in the releasing of grief through purging, relinquishing, and the flowing of tears, healing can occur at last."

Many people who go to the Casa de Dom Inacio go through this process of mourning. Often people begin to weep as soon as they step foot inside the current room for the first time, or during their invisible operations or elsewhere during their time in Abadiania, like at the sacred waterfall. I believe the entities assist us in getting in touch with old, blocked emotions, and with their help and the incredible Love that is so manifest there, we let go, bit by bit, and enter more fully into the healing process.

Our emotions are part of the human experience. Wherever we are in our lives, may we let the river flow by releasing the past and by living more and more in the moment with a heart of compassion for ourselves and for others. We can all experience the many miracles of healing that will occur by doing so.

Chapter 15: The Role of Community

We humans are, by nature, tribal beings. In ancient times, our physical survival depended on banding together for protection from animals that could threaten our lives or from other tribes competing for food in the same territory.

Community was important for the sharing of the many tasks of survival as well, such as caring for the young and elderly, hunting and gathering food, and making the various implements key to comfort as well as to life itself. And the sharing of knowledge took place within the tribe as well, handed down from the elders to the younger generation, or from the tribal shaman or spear-maker or weaver to his or her apprentice.

If a mother was ill or had just delivered a new baby, the other women of the tribe would take up her responsibilities till she was once again able to handle them. If a husband died or was injured, often his brother or brothers would continue to help provide for his wife and children. There was usually someone nearby who you could go to for counsel, company or comfort. And whether you liked everyone or not wasn't as critical as the continuation and well being of the tribe as a whole.

In today's Western culture, we have gained much in the way of knowledge and technology in regards to survival and creature comfort needs. But many of us have lost this sense of place, of belonging to and being rooted in a solid and ongoing community. Many people move a number of times during their lives, not only within a city or state, but often to other states and even other countries. Not only that, but the extended and nuclear family, once a part of life that was taken for granted, is no longer such a secure thing. When a person or couple or family moves far away, they don't expect their sisters and brothers, nieces and nephews, parents and grandparents, to uproot themselves and join them in their new location. And the divorce rate being what it is, often the nuclear family is disrupted as well.

As a result of all of this mobility and flux—which has both its upside and downside—an increasing number of people feel the loss of a sense of community. Added to this loss is the loss of many people's sense of connection to nature. "Where do I belong, where is my tribe, my community, my place?" is a deep cry of many Western souls at this time.

When I go to Abadiania with my groups or on my own, as I mentioned in an earlier chapter, I sense that one of the greatest benefits to people in their healing process is the sense of loving community that they find there. There is the community of dedicated staff people at the Casa itself and the care that they give the hundreds of people that arrive each day, but it is even more than that.

Whether it be with the other group participants, the other people staying at one's *pousada,* or those people one encounters who are attending sessions at the Casa, a given individual might make several or many deep connections during his stay in Abadiania. Everyone knows that they are there for a limited period of time, be it days, weeks or months, and the time they spend with others during that period is lived in shared community.

Many people who come to Abadiania for healing have serious and sometimes life-threatening illnesses or injuries. But unlike in the U.S., for example, where we too often tend to shy away from people in such situations and leave them even more isolated in their pain and difficulties, in Abadiania such things are discussed openly and with a great deal of love and support. Many times people almost forget their own problems in trying to help someone else. Many share information on health issues that might be helpful to others needing it. People offer massages, hugs, a listening ear, or simply the comfort of their company. Personal stories are shared with little inhibition, and people are more easily able to talk about death without the taboo of denial so often found in our Western culture.

Even though this is a temporary situation for those visiting Abadiania, it gives us a taste of what is possible and of what might be lacking in our daily lives. I know that the experience of community is one of the things many of my group participants often miss most when they return home. And people going through intense health challenges need the support of community even more than at other times of their lives.

There was a couple—who I shall call Philip and Elise—that I met during their first stay in Abadiania, and whom I have met several times since as our visits there often tend to coincide. Philip had decided to seek treatment for cancer at the Casa, and Elise, his partner of many years, was there to offer him support.

The entity told Philip he would help him in his healing. As it turned out, both Philip and Elise went through many layers of healing during their time at the Casa, including deep emotional healing. During the time between trips to Abadiania, Elise gave Philip what I feel was an incredible gift that was ongoing for about a year during his most difficult time. She pulled together a support group of various kinds of healers and friends who she sensed would be most helpful to Philip. This group met regularly and was an ongoing part of Philip's healing process in addition to the inner work he did on his own and to the work of the entities.

I was in Abadiania at the same time as Elise and Philip when they returned for their third or fourth stay a year after their first time at the Casa. I was sitting in the current room a few feet away from Joao "in entity" when Philip passed by to inquire about his own progress. The entity looked him over and said, "It is finished. You are healed. You can leave whenever you wish."

At the end of the session, I translated for them what I had heard the entity say, as Philip wasn't sure if his translator had told him verbatim everything that the entity had said. We laughed and wept and celebrated, and later there was a great celebration dinner among the locals and foreigners in Abadiania who knew this couple and knew both their difficulties of the prior year and the wonderful news they had received that day. "This is how life should be," I thought at the end of the evening.

I believe this community of support can be created everywhere with some effort on each of our parts. It is important to the well being of most people—with the exception, perhaps, of natural hermit types. Studies have been made of women with breast cancer, for example, who joined support groups. The results showed that those women with the same kind of illness did better psychologically and physically than those women who had no such support.

Our elderly are another example of a population that very much needs to continue to partake in community life and who benefit by doing so. In other societies and other times, the elders were respected as valued resources of wisdom and life experience for the younger generations. Too often in Western culture they are shunned, isolated, made to feel useless. This too can be changed with some loving effort.

We all need love, and we all need to feel loved and valued. We need company during our difficulties and to share in our triumphs. We need the tribe—and its collective healing power—as we always have.

I will close this chapter with a relevant quote from Dean Ornish.

"A number of studies have shown that people who feel isolated have three to five times the mortality rate, not only from cardiovascular disease, but from all causes, when compared to people who don't feel isolated. What is also interesting is that this mortality rate is usually independent of their blood cholesterol level, their blood pressure, and even whether or not they smoke."

Chapter 16: Spiritual Healing and Miracles

"...there are no structures that cannot be superseded and rearranged by love. Otherwise, how could there be miracles? How could there be freedom for the soul?"
                              Glenda Green, *Love Without End*

I feel that the most profound and yet simplest learning I have experienced from my many months at the Casa de Dom Inacio is that love is the source of all true healing. On the human level, it is love of self, or self-acceptance. But that true self-love connects us to the greater Love of our Creator, the Source itself.

One day when I was at the Casa, I accompanied one of the women in my group past the entity to help translate for her. She had a serious illness and was going to be leaving for the U.S. the next day after having spent two weeks in sessions at the Casa. She asked the entity what she could do when she returned home to help continue and support her healing process. The entity answered her with one word: "Love."

If I—and all of us—could fully understand that message, there would be no need for me to write this book, nor would we need to travel to the Casa or go see any doctors or other healers. In fact, humanity might—hopefully soon—arrive at this point of understanding, after which there may not be any more illness. Until we arrive at this place of constantly and unconditionally loving, however, there are a variety of ways by which we can progress toward true healing and a life lived in love. We have already looked at the role of the mind, emotions and community. This chapter will explore the role of spirit and energy in healing, and what it is that makes us more available to what we call miracles.

Let's first look at ourselves from the perspective of being an energy body. Everything in the universe is a manifestation of energy, each form vibrating at its own frequency. The slower the vibration, the more dense the matter, while the faster the vibration, the lighter.

In the human energy system, energy flows naturally in various patterns and pathways that have been studied and mapped out in depth through Chinese medicine and other ancient traditions. When we block the natural flow of energy through suppressing or sustaining for too long various emotions and negative thought patterns, we can disrupt our health. We also weaken the flow of energy in the same ways and lower our overall vibratory level, thus becoming more susceptible to ill health.

Some people reading this may not think they know what I'm referring to when I talk about raising or lowering vibration. But I know we have all felt it. When we are burdening ourselves with too much negative thinking and feelings of helplessness or hopelessness, we feel dense, heavy. When we release stagnant emotions—or are simply in a place of love or joy—we feel much lighter. These are shifts of vibration, not just of moods.

Caroline Myss has written, "Power is essential for healing and for maintaining health." She notes that when people feel powerless, especially as a result of holding negative mental attitudes, they not only suffer from low self-esteem, but can also deplete their body of energy and weaken their overall health.

Myss's thoughts are relevant to the subject of raising or lowering vibration. So part of our personal responsibility toward our own well-being is to exchange attitudes of powerlessness for empowering attitudes; to help our emotional body stay light and uncluttered through awareness and releasing of the past; and to keep ourselves even stronger by regularly doing some kind of energy-gathering. I have described a number of energy-gathering practices in both *The Return of Spirit* and *A Season of Eagles,* but I will give you one example now.

Simply sit or stand in a comfortable, relaxed manner with both feet flat on the floor—or earth, if you are doing this outdoors. Breathe through your nose if at all possible. As you inhale, see or feel yourself pulling energy up from the earth, bringing it up through your feet and all the way to the top of your head. As you exhale, send the energy into your belly, just below the navel, and begin to fill your belly with this energy as if your belly was a bowl just made to store power—which in fact it is. If it helps, you can imagine the earth's energy as a flow of liquid light in whatever color you prefer, and as you direct it into your belly, see the bowl slowly filling with this liquid. With each breath the bowl is increasingly full until finally—usually after eight breaths or so—it is completely full. Then rest and feel your newly gathered reserves of available power.

In Glenda Green's book, *Love Without End,* Jesus suggests to her yet another energy-gathering exercise. "…watch the sun in the morning and the evening, because watching the sun can actually set your physical, etheric and spiritual hearts into a harmonic resonance which will attract what you need and process what you have more perfectly. Doing this will improve your experience of the day, as well as your energy, your nutrition, and your sleep…"

He also suggests the following: "Always receive with love, for it is love which instructs the food on how to nourish your body. Bless the food and thank the givers and preparers of it. Your love will be attuned to the energy frequency your heart has set for your body and will properly instruct your body on how to use the nutrients. For better nutrition, strengthen your heart. A strong heart sets the body at a higher frequency, and establishes a lower resistance mode of energy utilization which is not only more efficient, but is also more able to process and manufacture vitamins and minerals."

This and other energy-gathering practices can not only raise our vibration and fill us with more power for health, healing and anything else we choose to use it for, but can increase our sense of being more pro-active in our own life rather than being "victims of circumstance." But simply doing energy-gathering practices alone will not prevent us from losing energy if the rest of the time we are sustaining beliefs that we are worthless, are abusing ourselves in other ways and allowing ourselves to be abused, or are hanging onto emotional energies that need to be released. Health and healing—and life itself—are all very holistic, in that we need to approach them from more than one angle until we each arrive at the place of total self-love and constant Divine union with the highest Love—with God. Then there is only that love and wholeness.

Until we arrive at that point, we can continue to peel the layers of the onion that rob us of power and health.

Sometimes people with health challenges will try a number of different kinds of therapies and find they are making little or no progress. In that case, it's important to look at the possibility that either on some level they need this illness as their teacher and have not yet gotten the teaching, or that they may be actually blocking their own healing. The reasons for doing the latter will vary from person to person, but they generally fall under several categories.

One is that on some level, becoming healthy threatens us. It might simply be that old "fear of the unknown" rearing its head again. Although being ill isn't pleasant, if we've been ill for some time, it is at least familiar, while being healthy has become less familiar and thus, to a certain extent, unknown. So we need to look and see if that is the case in our own lives, and then begin to release this fear and establish positive goals for what we would like to do once we have our health again.

Another category is that there may be something in the past—probably on the emotional level—that we are hanging onto that needs to be released before we can come into balance again. Ask your intuition, your heart and your body to speak to you and let you know if this is the case, and if so, what it is that you need to release. If you are unable to find the answer on your own, have someone help you—either a good counselor, an intuitive friend, etc. Once you've identified what it is that needs to be released, look at what kind of reality you've built up around this emotional pain.

For example, say someone close to you did something in the past that caused you great pain. You felt betrayed or hurt or angry or all of the above. And rather than let go of those feelings, you've nursed a grudge for years, perhaps even building a network of other people who support you in being angry at the person who you feel was the cause of your pain. The people in this social circle feel sorry for you, angry at the "jerk," help you feel justified in sustaining your anger and hurt, etc.

This party of one—you and yourself—or party of many have constructed a chunk of "reality," and if you let go of it, release and forgive, this would shift your relationship to yourself and to others. But release and forgive we must, if we are to experience true healing.

Yet a third category of how we can block our healing has to do with the balance of power in our relationships. Perhaps it is only when we are in ill health that we feel we can get the attention and nurturing from others that we need. (This pattern, by the way, is often learned when we are very young and within our family of origin). Perhaps illness is a way through which we subtly or overtly control others. Can you learn to be more straightforward with what you feel, want and need, and accept that in a given moment the other person may or may not respond in the way you want?

Or perhaps the shift in the balance of power that you fear the most is between you and you. If you could release your illness—which is an act of power in itself—how powerful might you be in other ways in your life? Can you adjust to seeing yourself as a powerful person? Does that feel like a burden or a joy? Does it frighten you, and if so, how?

Women in many cultures are partly frightened of being as powerful as we can be because of our social conditioning. In fact, many women get jittery just hearing the word power, understanding it only in the paradigm of "power over others," or abuse of power. Many women are afraid they will not be able to find a man who can accept them being as wonderfully powerful as they can be. Others are afraid their friends will reject them out of envy or fear if they truly manifest their total self. Sadly, this has often been true, but what is the greater cost: having to find new friends and possibly being alone for a while till we do, or making ourselves weak and sick by denying the power and gifts God has given us? Out of fear, so many women often mask and subvert their own power, and it twists around inside of them and creates illness or comes out as subtle manipulation of others.

I believe our culture is changing and that there is more respect for the feminine and for women generally than there was even thirty years ago. There is still more room for growth in this area. But each one of us needs to start with ourselves and not wait for some time in the indeterminate future for it to be "safe" to be who we are.

This is true for all of us. Men too can have fears about their own power and about the balance of power in their relationships. It is likely that men have more fear about the power of their own feminine, intuitive nature than of being powerful in other ways, again, due to the centuries of social conditioning within Western culture. One might call this softer kind of power "heart" power, and I feel it is possible that men in our culture are more prone to heart attacks due to their fear of expressing the power of the heart. But step by step, we can all change for the better whatever needs to be changed within ourselves, thus also touching the collective in a positive way and supporting others along their path of healing and growth.

We are each an energy body. We can block or raise or lower our overall energy or vibrational frequency. The higher and more powerful our energy level, the more healthy we can be. There is an infinite amount of available energy. All that's necessary is that we hunt and gather it.

A particular kind of power is something that we call "will," and each one of us has it within us. I see will as an aspect of our spiritual being, and it is something that, when mobilized, can stun us with its amazing potential.

In an interview with Bill Moyers, Dr. David Felton said, "...those of us who have dealt with patients know that a patient's will to live makes a difference...Yet we don't understand how that works."

The role of will *is* mysterious. I wrote a great deal about it in *A Season of Eagles*, going as far as to call will a spiritual organ of sorts, something that we can strengthen and use in our spiritual development. I'm not sure if Dr. Felton is using the term in the same sense. However, there is something of the human spirit—a kind of driving force—that can rise up in the face of great adversity and transcend the boundaries of belief and limitation, and we often call that force "will."

Probably most of us have either experienced or heard stories of others who—by all that we know of science and medicine—lived far longer and/or functioned far better than their particular illness or injury would have predicted. We say that it was the person's will to live, or to walk or to talk again, that mobilized and drew the person forward despite all odds.

I sense that this force of will is partly tied to a person's goal-making mechanisms. If a person has powerful goals that they are determined to fulfill at some future point, it seems these goals mobilize a great deal of raw energy. The goal is like a beacon ahead of us, calling to us, showing us the way, and the energy that is called in by its light then draws us forward along the path that leads to it.

I think most people can relate to this. If we have something that we really want to accomplish and are enthused about and motivated toward it, we feel very energized as we take the various steps needed to arrive there. Conversely, if we are going through a period in which we have either lost sight of our goals or haven't created any new and exciting ones, our energy begins to drop. I believe this is what happens to those people who have retired who have not set any goals for their time after retirement, or to women going through the "empty nest syndrome" who didn't set any goals for themselves for after their children have grown and left home. The same thing can be true for any of us when we've completed a major project and don't yet have a new one formulated. Because of the lack of goals in all of these cases, our energy has no driving focus, and so it begins to dissipate. The more it does so and the longer we are without goals, the more vulnerable we are to illness. Our will is dormant.

Therefore, as we enter a healing process, it may be very important for us to look at what it is we would really like to do if we were well enough to do it. Or even before we are completely well physically, what smaller things are possible for us at this time that we might we like to accomplish this hour or today or this week that we would feel good about and that would serve to mobilize our will into action?

People who are in a state of depression are in a state of repressed will. They have suppressed their emotions to the point where they have difficulty getting excited about doing anything. Their energy level then drops so that they have less energy to contemplate goals, their depression deepens, and a vicious cycle can set in. In order to break the cycle, some action that will raise the person's energy is called for.

Sometimes simply engaging in a regular exercise program can help considerably in lifting depression. Vigorous movement—even brisk walking—raises our energy level and releases those wonderful endorphins that make us feel better. Setting small, manageable goals that can be accomplished each day also raises the energy level and can then be expanded on as the person's energy increases. Of course, sometimes the depression is so severe that a person needs medication to break the cycle. Serious, long-term depression should always be taken seriously and the help of a trusted medical practitioner enlisted. God can work through psychiatrists and appropriate drugs as well as through trance medium healers!

Sometimes we say, "oh, so-and-so has lost the will to live," or conversely, "so-and-so seems to have found the will to live again." I believe that both of these situations are spiritual events, not simply psychological ones. There are times when, after a great trauma, a person can actually begin letting go of his life force and will, abandoning all goals for any kind of future. Often this happens in the case of a profound loss, such as the death of a loved one or of some critical aspect of physical functioning (like the loss of sight, of a limb, of the ability to walk, etc.), or of one's business, finances, or something else we have been deeply attached to.

In such a case, it's as if our energy and sense of identity have been so bound up with the object of our loss that we feel an important part of our soul is gone and we give up on ever feeling whole again. We literally abandon our will to live, and people are quite capable of leaving their mortal form behind through this abandonment of will.

As I mentioned in the chapter on the role of the mind, a death curse or hex can have a similar result in regards to the will. In our Western culture, a death curse can take the form of a medical diagnosis—correct or incorrect—of a terminal illness. Some people respond to such a diagnosis by losing their will to live. Even if they have been feeling fine up to the moment of the diagnosis, upon being told, for example, that they have cancer, some people abandon both hope and the will to live so fast that within days they are a shadow of their former selves. Others respond to the same diagnosis with a fighting spirit and the will to do everything in their power to survive as long as possible. I say this without judgment, because each soul's journey is unique and what we each need to learn from a situation is a part of our own path. I am simply observing the function of will and how it can mobilize energy, or how, by abandoning it, we can lose energy quickly.

I do feel that most powerful healers, whether they be medical doctors, psychotherapists or shamans, seem to have the ability to help mobilize a patient's will to heal. Perhaps it the healer's faith in his or her own methodology—or in the patient's inner healing power and will—or in God, or some combination of all of the above, that enables them to transfer sufficient energy and optimism to cause the patient's will to respond with purpose and vitality.

Albert Schweitzer once said, "The witch doctor succeeds for the same reason all the rest of us succeed. Each patient carries his own doctor inside him. We are at our best when we give the doctor who resides within each patient a chance to go to work." He too noted the importance of individual will in tandem with a network of support and a trusted physician or other healing practitioner. It seems our will is an active aspect of our own spirit, and I believe that at the most profound level, it is our spirit and its connection with the greater Spirit that does the healing work.

The entities of the Casa de Dom Inacio have commented that all healing is, at the core, spiritual healing. I have observed that for many people, dealing with a serious illness is often the catalyst for their conscious spiritual awakening, and this awakening is a part of their healing, no matter what the outcome of their physical illness. Dr. Michael Lerner feels that, "...in the West, with our less contemplative tradition, it is often only when we become ill that we begin this journey of inner exploration that we might not have undertaken under any other circumstances."

I—and many others—call this set of circumstances the "wounded healer" syndrome. Embarking on the inner journey is a strong part of our healing, and many people who have taken the journey because of pain or illness on some level. They have then faced the internal demons, reconciled and released them, and have come out the other side not only in better health themselves, but able to transmit this healing power in service to others. Lerner again comments that "...this is what it is to be ill: to wrestle through the long night, injured, and if you prevail until the sun rises, to receive a blessing."

Traditionally, many who were called to the shamanic path went through this kind of intense, wounded healer journey. Often shamans became such after surviving a serious illness or near-death experience. Others, as part of their apprenticeship or training with an older, experienced shaman, would be put through intense ordeals in order to mobilize their power and healing gifts. Some were given strong psychotropic plants that brought to light all of the fears and other inner demons of the psyche that needed healing. These rejected parts of self would often appear as true monsters that the shaman apprentice would then have to face and overcome. Sometimes in these visions, the shaman apprentice would literally be dismembered—taken apart bone by bone—by some terrifying spirit, and then reassembled by that same spirit but with new power and abilities. The spirit, once seen as a monster, was then recognized as the ally and benefactor it truly was. Other times the apprentices would have to go on extended fasts or face other intense physical challenges that required them to draw on inner and spiritual resources that they had been unaware of until that point.

There is a Taoist proverb that says, "When you have a disease, do not try to cure it. Find your center, and you will be healed." This is the challenge of the shaman's path and life's challenge for all of us. It is the spiritual path.

The wounded healer journey is the journey of each one of us. If we are alive in a human form, we have all survived challenges—including birth itself—and learned from the experience, drawing on inner resources and emerging with new insights, power, and hopefully compassion for our fellow human beings, all of whom face their own challenges. We are not all shamans, but each of us is a potential healer of self, and thus has the ability to catalyze the inner healing resources of others.

One of the most spiritual ways through which healing energy can be transmitted from one person to another is by touch.

In the mid-'80s, a neonatal study was conducted at the University of Miami medical school, with infants born prematurely and confined to incubators for an extended period of time. The nurses who were caring for them were instructed to touch one group of these infants three times daily in a nurturing way for a while, and the other group of infants did not receive this attention. Those infants who were touched three times daily gained 47% more weight, were more alert and started acting like normally delivered babies significantly sooner than those who weren't.

We actually transmit spiritual energy through loving touch. In Glenda Green's book, Jesus calls this energy that is transmitted the "adamantine particles." He says that the latter are "...the fundamental building blocks of physical existence...particularized energy potentials which activate, unify and give form to infinity...The sharing of adamantine particles is the breath of life...In the presence of love a natural rebalance occurs. This is how the laying on of hands can help to restore health to another. Such is the power of healing touch or even a simple hug."

We all know the comfort derived from being touched in a nurturing, loving way, whether by family, friends, lovers, or by a massage therapist. We feel something mysterious being transmitted to us that is beyond the simple mechanics of warm skin on skin. When the person touching us consciously puts a lot of love into the touch, or has learned to open themselves as a medium of loving energies even beyond their own, the power and degree of "adamantine particles" and universal love transmitted can be truly magnificent and catalyze profound healing. This transmission of energy is what Joao de Deus or other kinds of spiritual healing practitioners are able to do.

I have some other thoughts about why the work of Joao and other trance medium healers of his style effect spiritual healing. Let me first put their work in a historical context.

Joao may be one—if not the most—powerful of his kind today, but there have been other such healers in recent history. I mentioned the famous Brazilian medium Ze Arrigo earlier, who, like Joao, was also was a medium for spiritual entities. Since Arrigo's death, there were several other well-known mediums like him in Brazil. And there are the many less known Brazilian mediums of Spiritism and Umbanda, some of whom I have mentioned briefly in this book. I also know of a healing medium who is English, and a number of Europeans have sought treatment from him. He too does some paranormal physical operations with the help of his entities. And before him, there was yet another English medium named George Chapman who became well known at around the same time Ze Arrigo was doing his work.

Chapman was from Liverpool, and he turned to the metaphysical world of Spiritualism in 1945 shortly after the death of his baby girl. During one of his first visits to a Spiritualist center, he entered a trance state while hypnotized, and received messages from a series of spirits including that of Dr. William Land, the famous British ophthalmologist and surgeon who died in 1945. Chapman took to mediumship and began to practice what he described as "etheric surgery."

During the course of his work, he claimed to carry out everything from cataract removal to open heart surgery. Chapman believed that he and the entity

Lang were able to do this kind of work because they treated the etheric body, a field of energy that is said to exist in correspondence with the physical body.

Someone describing his work observed, "…[Chapman] manipulates invisible surgical tools…[he] snaps his fingers during 'surgery,' claiming that the gesture alerts his spirit aides about which instrument he requires…Chapman said that the purpose of Dr. Lang's spirit return 'is not solely to cure sick people. *It is to touch the soul and to give us a new, convincing insight and understanding of the spiritual reality which surrounds us.*'" [author's italics]

I believe that last statement is part of the core healing work of the entities that assist us through Joao and other mediums, and the main point I wanted to make in sharing the somewhat historical perspective. Part of my own spiritual healing as a result of my early visits to the Casa de Dom Inacio was a deepening of faith in the eternal nature of each human spirit. This perspective, based on the experiences I had at the Casa, was deeply comforting. Prior to going to the Casa for the first time, I thought that when we left this world, we simply merged into the Light and lost any sense of individuality or consciousness. Even though I figured such a merging might be blissful, who was it exactly that was going to experience the bliss if the individual consciousness was gone?

Since experiencing the entities of the Casa and their work, I sense that an essence of the individual person continues—albeit without a physical body— when it moves on to the spirit world. I believe that the comfort many other people and I have received from knowing—or at least strongly sensing—this reality allows us to face the idea of some day leaving this body with less fear. Our unique spirit will not be annihilated but rather will continue on, perhaps even choosing to help and guide those who are still on Earth, as do the entities of the Casa.

In *Love Without End*, Jesus spoke about the issue of the continuation of individual identity and some of its challenges. I found his words fascinating, and they felt very relevant to some of my own experiences.

"There is the original birth trauma, which most people are still working through. There was a time before which you were, but there will never be a time after which you are not. There was a time when you were one and complete within the Source of Love. Love, however, decided to give you immortality **as yourself** and to grant you an identity of your own. It was a great and glorious gift that you were given, full of promise, opportunity, and responsibility. But the children of God, having no point of reference other than the simplicity of a common light, experienced it as shock and interpreted the gift of life as separation. Many deeply wounded themselves by viewing it as rejection. That was a tragic misconception, and many of the problems and pains that have been suffered by humanity are the result of this birth trauma."

Many people I know—myself included—have at some time in their lives felt that when they came into this world, they had been ejected from the Garden of Eden and that their union with Divine Love had ended at birth. We experienced this life—as Jesus stated above—as a form of separation and rejection, and often longed to return to that time of total union.

To be able to look at the path of the individual spirit—whether here or on some other plane—as a gift from God can be of profound healing to the human heart. We are not here on Earth as a form of punishment or rejection from our Divine Parent, but rather as a way to have a multitude of individual experiences and learning, while at the same time knowing that we can always turn to the Love that is our Source. We have never been cut off from that Love. We simply turn our attention away from it at times.

So it seems that part of the journey of spiritual healing is to understand this and to begin to see through new eyes, through eyes that are able to perceive this Love everywhere: in all of Nature, in our fellow human beings, and most importantly, within ourselves. Then our hearts can open to a true sense of gratitude for the opportunity that we have been given, and the illusion of separation from God can be dispelled in the light of a higher truth.

Healing is so much more than restoring health to the physical body, although certainly that can be a component of it.

Well-known writer and conference speaker Dr. Rachel Naomi Remen has gone through serious health challenges throughout much of her lifetime. In an interview with Bill Moyers, she says:

> Remen: "Seeking physical healing is important, but it may not be the ultimately important thing, at least not for me."
>
> Moyers: "What is?"
>
> Remen: "Being alive, which is not a matter of length, but of moment to moment. Being alive is being aware...to grow in wisdom and learn to love better."

For Caroline Myss, healing entails "...deciding to focus more on the positive than on the negative and to live in a manner spiritually congruent with what we know is the truth."

For Deepak Chopra, "...when healing is deep enough, it solves much worse problems than physical illness. The search for meaning is brought to an end, and nature's immense ability to purify and restore balance asserts itself once more."

Sometimes, in their search for healing from a serious illness, people will try many kinds of approaches in order to regain their physical health. Although at times, as I commented in the chapter dealing with the role of emotions, we can block our own healing in various ways, it may be that in some situations—and eventually for all of us—our healing may include preparation to leave this earthly existence.

Such preparations include the deepest forms of letting go, and therefore are often challenging to our mind, which loves to hold on to structure and to the known. Frequently such letting go brings the person to a spiritual healing and a profound sense of peace and joy. Occasionally, the letting go process catalyzes a physical healing as well. Again, in Glenda Green's book, Jesus comments on both processes.

"Do not ever underestimate the power of the heart to bring forth a higher intelligence, a higher awareness and greater solution to existence than you would ever have anticipated. This is why so many times people will experience a miracle of healing in the face of death; because in the face of death, they go ahead and let the structures die. They think, 'I only have six weeks to live,' and then let go of external demands. The mind loses all importance, and loved ones become more dear than ever. All of a sudden the heart-fire burns brightly, whether through grief, joy, contentment or resignation. Only then, through the fire of the heart is a miracle possible. Most people facing death go ahead and die to the world of structure, and then at last they really live. That is what I meant when I said you must die first in order to live. Because when you live in the heart, you live immortally, you live eternally."

To live in the heart, connected with the love we have erroneously sought outside of ourselves throughout our personal journey, is spiritual healing. And we don't need to wait until we are seriously ill and facing death in order to do so. What we call death can in a sense be the friendliest of reminders. Never knowing which day is to be our last here on Earth, we can live each day from the heart, in gratitude and celebration of all that is available to us in the way of growth and experience. If we believe that we won't leave this world until our soul's purpose for this life has been fulfilled, then we can open ourselves fully to life and trust that all is following Divine order.

A friend of mine sent me an email recently, saying that we do not need to create illness in our body in order to have permission to die. She said that all we need to do, when it is our time, is to release ourselves from our body. For many people, adopting this attitude would be a true paradigm shifter. Most of us assume that we will die "from" an illness or injury. Maybe that method for dying is a learning experience that some souls call in for their own growth or for that of loved ones who need to learn something from it. But it is quite possible that gently releasing ourselves from our body, without suffering, is yet another decision our soul can make once its purpose is complete. I welcome that possibility into my personal paradigm collection!

In the quote several paragraphs earlier, Jesus spoke about the need to die to the world of structure in order to truly live: to live from the heart, from love.

Love knows no limits and is not dependent on structures of any kind. It travels far beyond the structures of our thinking, our ego, our beliefs and judgments, our ideas of space and linear time. I have seen love manifest miracles of healing again and again at the Casa de Dom Inacio, and in the lives of people who have never heard of the Casa as well. It is obvious in the cases I have witnessed and been told of that love does not always follow what science and medicine might predict in terms of miracles of physical healing. The ways in which we think the structures of the human body—and of illness and injuries to it—should respond are simply flattened or ignored by love when it wants to show us that there is more to the story.

Again, from Jesus in *Love Without End*: "Miracles come to those who appreciate the miraculous nature of life and surrender to the experience of it. The Creator will dazzle you every now and then, but **only to get your attention.** Never will He dazzle you in order to separate you from the miraculous potential of reality. This is because miracles bring **fulfillment to reality**—not a diminishment of it...God is waiting to greet you with a miracle, if you would only receive the Presence that is with you and before you. Man is blocking the path to miracles primarily with two obsessions. **One is dependency upon structure. The other is trying to recreate existence to match his every illusion.**"

I always smile—somewhat abashedly—when I read those last two sentences. They point out my own tendencies quite clearly—tendencies that I am aware of but have not yet transcended! One part of my being is quite fond of structure, although I do love my freedom and the ability to be wildly creative or fly into the unknown on my way to encounter yet more of the Great Mystery. And I plead guilty to having tried repeatedly to pound the round pegs of reality into the square holes of my various illusions. Those efforts usually bring me pain on some level, although occasionally they have resulted in me laughing at myself and at the futility of my efforts. Laughter is good medicine, and helps us let go of our obsession with life being the way we think it should be.

And so we walk and leap and stumble and twirl and laugh and weep our way along the journey of life. We come into this world and perceive miracles everywhere. We then grow up and demand them of God to prove His existence, for by that time we have developed strange filters of limiting beliefs over the eyes of our heart and can no longer see God so clearly. And then at some point we begin the spiritual journey, much of which is about peeling off those filters so that we can arrive once again at the open heart-space we occupied as infants, but with the awareness of the time-traveler enhancing our perceptions.

In the stillness of the inner chamber of the heart, the miracle of love blossoms. In that Garden, it is always dawn, always the place of new beginnings and potential, always a place of miracles. I go there now, to bask in the light and sweetness and peace.

Perhaps I will meet you in the Garden too.

References

Chopra, Deepak, *Unconditional Life*, Bantam Books, New York 1991.

Fuller, John G., *Arrigo: Surgeon of the Rusty Knife,* Pocket Books, New York 1974.

Green, Glenda, *Love Without End,* Hartwings Publishing, Fort Worth 1999. *

Kardec, Allen, *The Book on Mediums,* Samuel Wiser, York Beach 1970.

Moyers, Bill, *Healing and the Mind,* Doubleday, New York 1993.

Myss, Caroline, *The Anatomy of Spirit*, Harmony Books, New York 1996.

Pellegrino-Estrich, *The Miracle Man,* Triad, Australia 1997.

Powers of Healing, Time-Life Books, 1989.

RavenWing, Josie, *A Season of Eagles,* Writer's Showcase/Writer's Digest, New York 2000.

RavenWing, Josie, *The Return of Spirit,* Health Communications, Inc., Deerfield Beach 1996.

*To learn more about Glenda and her experiences and paintings, visit her web site at www.lovewithoutend.com or call 1-888-453-6324

Josie RavenWing

About the Author

Josie RavenWing, B.A. in dance movement therapy and M.A. in clinical and humanistic psychology, had her first visionary experience when she was about 10 months old, and this set her on a lifelong journey of spiritual exploration and discovery.

In the early 1970s, she began her work in the field of human development as an innovative pioneer of dance therapy and holistic healing. She also started exploring shamanistic traditions, which she has incorporated into her work since that time. At Antioch University in Seattle, she developed and taught courses in the first Holistic Health graduate program in the U.S. During that same period, her growing concern about women's issues and self-esteem inspired her to organize one of Seattle's first women's support groups and later led her to create a variety of workshops and retreats to meet women's needs for spiritual exploration and growth.

RavenWing continued to expand her work. Throughout several decades as a psychotherapist, she has integrated Western theory with spiritual, shamanistic and hands-on healing practices of many cultures. Described as a "practical visionary" by author Joan Borysenko, she applies her grounded, ongoing synthesis in counseling work with individuals and as an accomplished workshop leader. She has lectured at college campuses and national conferences, and offered her seminars and workshops throughout the United States and abroad since the mid-80s. She has also been widely interviewed by the media, including radio and television, and has had a number of articles published in various newspapers and magazines.

More recently, Josie has spent a great deal of time within the spiritual healing cultures of Brazil. Her own effectiveness as a healing facilitator has been enhanced greatly by her exposure to and involvement in Brazilian healing practices, which she has creatively incorporated into her work.

RavenWing's creativity also expresses itself in her song writing, poetry, ceremonial leadership and spiritual dance choreography. In addition to this book, she has written two others: *The Return of Spirit: A Woman's Call to Spiritual Action* and *A Season of Eagles*.

Josie presently divides much of her time between the U.S. and Brazil—where she continues to learn and to take groups for healing and spiritual work. To contact her about her "Brazil Healing Journeys," her spiritual journeys to Peru, and other retreats and workshops she offers, to schedule individual healing sessions, to find out how to host her workshops in your own community, or to order her books, music tapes, Brazilian healing crystals and other products, you can email her at jravenwing@aol.com. For additional information on her work, please visit her web site at www.healingjourneys.net.

Printed in the United States
31960LVS00005B/160-177